ELEMENTARY EDUCATION AND CHILD RIGHTS

ELEMENTARY EDUCATION AND CHILD RIGHTS

Some Reflections

Edited by

C. Naseema

V. K. Jibin

SHIPRA

ISBN: 978-81-7541-708-3

First Published in India in 2013

Elementary Education and Child Rights: Some Reflections

Published by:
SHIPRA PUBLICATIONS
H.O.: LG 18-19, Pankaj Central Market, Patparganj,
Delhi-110092, Tel: 91-11-2223 5152, 2223 6152
Br.Off.: 4617/18, Ansari Road, Darya Ganj,
New Delhi-110002, Tel: 9650028065, 9810522367
E-mail: info@shiprapublications.com
www.shiprapublications.com

Preface

In the last few decades there has been growing support for giving children a full- fledged position in society. Education consists of a form of learning that is necessary for the development of children's personality and identity, as well as their physical and intellectual capabilities. Education permits, notably, the transmission of common principles to new generations and the conservation and perpetuation of social values. It also contributes in flourishing the individuality through the enhancement of social and professional integration.

In developing and developed countries alike, children do not have access to basic education because of inequalities that originate in sex, health and cultural identity. Children's rights in education need to be seen as inclusive and comprehensive, so it is important that these be addressed in the context of a basic legislative framework, namely the Convention on the Rights of the Child. By adopting this framework we are able to address fundamental questions about expectations and demands on the various factors in the school culture, particularly teachers and students.

New understandings of childhood and changing perceptions of children have led to children's right to enjoy here and now being widely advocated. Thus children area recognized as individuals entitled to human dignity. Respect for children as human beings means that they are no longer perceived as mere objects of protection but as subjects and bearers of human rights like all human beings. This new perception applies to the child as an individual as well as to children as a social category. This raises implications for both psychologists and sociologists of education.

This conceptual switch in the construction of the child is not easy to implement and practice in daily life. Since it is not customary to treat children from a human rights standpoint, it requires a complete revision of approach. The UN Convention on the Rights of the Child (CRC) strongly promotes this human rights approach. The CRC is a Convention, which means that State Parties ratifying it accept the legal obligation to implement the provisions of the Convention.

The CRC contains 54 articles of which 41 are substantive articles defining the rights of the child and the obligations on State Parties ratifying the convention. Since the CRC is a Convention and so legally binding, children have the right to legal protection of their rights.

The Convention on the Rights of the Child has done a great deal to change attitudes towards children. More and more people regard it as self-evident that children are entitled to respect for person and integrity. One of the basic ideas of the Convention is that children and adults have the same human dignity. Among other things, children are entitled to express their opinions freely and to be listened to the values permeating the Convention.

Many people in Sweden work professionally with children, with the result that the community has a large fund of knowledge concerning children's needs and development. Great efforts are being made to offer children the best possible formative conditions, both within the family and in the community at large. Association with the activities of Child Rights in Sweden and other countries and experiences from India motivated the Editors to collect articles on child rights and elementary education from India and other countries. The present book is the fulfillment of such an attempt. The book covers important aspects of Child Rights, CRC, Education as a child right, experiences of eminent personalities from India and other countries regarding child rights and education and an overview of Child Rights in different countries.

The major contribution of the book is the illustration of experiences of eminent personalities from the field of Child Rights and Education. The editors express their indebtedness with gratitude to the contributions, Prof. C.P. S. Chauhan, Prof. K.P. Pandey, Prof. R. G. Kothari, Dr. Jignesh B. Patel, Prof. K.S. Misra , Dr. Magre Sunita Vithalrao and Prof. P.N. Muthiah from India and Dr. Anthony Mugagga Muwagga, Dr. Per Wickenberg, Dr. Ulf Leo, Grace Kafulatira Mulima and Dr. Ngasbun Egar from other countries, for presenting their experiences in child rights and education.

We hope that the book may be a major contribution to the researchers working in the field of child rights and education. The book should be especially useful to students, teachers, prospective teachers, teacher educators and to the teacher training courses. It may also be beneficial to different organizations working for child rights and policy makers while framing activities in child rights and curricula in school level.

C.Naseema
V.K.Jibin

Contents

I

Child Rights and Education

1

Introduction

> "Children are human beings, therefore they are entitled to all human rights".
>
> —UN Convention on the Rights of the Child

In the last few decades there has been growing support for giving children a fully-fledged position in society, but questions often are raised as to the usefulness and/or necessity of a separate convention on the rights of the child. The consequence of all this is that today, on account of the processes of deconstruction and reconstruction, we find ourselves in a rather confused situation of transition. On the one hand our old child-image is as forceful and dominant as ever, while on the other children are regarded as entitled to human rights.

A Short History

Around the turn of the twentieth century, a considerable degree of interest in child protection was already evident, including on the part of legislators. Almost everywhere in the industrialized world so-called 'child-protection' and 'compulsory education' laws were passed. The book "The Century of the Child", published in 1903 by Ellen Key, a Swedish feminist, was a sounding success and widely read, even outside the narrow circle of reform-educationalists. This international attention to children was also expressed in new rules. In 1902 the Hague Conference on Private International Law considered" the interest of the child" as an important criterion in the convention on guardianship of minors. In 1919 the ILO

(International Labour Organization) adopted a convention which set a minimum age for employing children in industry. Despite the fact that these rules apply internationally, it is the Geneva Declaration (1924) which is regarded as the first international (human) rights instrument dealing with the rights of children.

It is quite clear that the new Convention (1989) was strongly influenced both by the changes in child-image, which occurred at the end of the twentieth century.

Geneva Declaration (1924)

The Geneva Declaration is clearly a defensive instrument by virtue of its origin. The First World War had left millions of children in deplorable circumstances. In 1920 Eglantyne Jebb, president of 'the Save the Children Fund' and the 'International Red Cross Committee' decided to set up the *Save the Children International Union*. This International organization soon had numerous national sections dealing with the plight of children.

The important thing is that the five fundamental aims of the organization were put in a five-points-programme called the "Declaration of the Rights of the Child".

1. The child must be given the means needed for its normal development, both materially and spiritually.
2. The child that is hungry should be fed; the child that is sick should he helped; the erring child should be reclaimed; and the orphan and the homeless child should be sheltered and succored.
3. The child must be the first to receive relief in times of distress.
4. The child must be put in a position to earn a livelihood and must be protected against every form of exploitation.
5. The child must be brought up in the consciousness that its best qualities are to be used in the service of its fellowmen.

In simple terms (there is in fact no reference to rights as such) the Declaration points out adult's obligations to children. The child was protected as a person with his/her own rights, but remained dependent on adults to assert the rights included in the Declaration.

Although in content it also takes a defensive line on the consequences of the First World War (Physical neglect, malnutrition, interrupted education, economic exploitation), the Declaration does go further. It stresses social and economic needs (rights), over and above traditional civil and political rights.

In 1924, the Declaration was adopted and solemnly proclaimed in the General Assembly of the League of Nations. Since then it has been known as the Geneva Declaration. Ten years later, in 1934, the Declaration was reconfirmed by the League of Nations' General Assembly and the states 'promised' to enact its principles in their own legislation.

For the first time ever, because of the Declaration, children's rights became a concept in public international law, The Declaration was to become the cornerstone of all future international legislative initiatives regarding children's rights.

Features of Children's Rights

Child Image: Shift from Legal Object to Legal Subject

The Geneva Convention still regards children merely as objects of the law. The UN Declaration departs from this viewpoint and takes the first step towards recognition of children as legal subjects (people with their own rights): "The child shall enjoy all the rights set forth in this declaration". On the text we see a shift of emphasis from welfare and protection of the child to the protection of the *rights* of the child. The vocabulary no longer sounds native, and has become more legal in nature.

Although the Declaration regards the child as a *legal subject*, it does not recognize his/her *competence* to exercise his/her rights independently. The Declaration deals almost exclusively with *protective rights*, the leitmotif being the *best interests of the child*; the child as separate entity in other words. During preparation of the Declaration, the desirability of this separate declaration was a subject of discussion. There was already the Universal Declaration of Human Rights after all. Was there any real need for a specific declaration for children? It was however the general feeling that the Universal Declaration needed to be "Complemented" by a series of specific declarations. The Declaration of the Rights of the Child was meant to be just such a specific declaration, because of children's special needs.

Normative Value

First of all, we have to note the fact that individuals in general (and therefore also children), for the protection of their rights in international law depend upon the implementation of international rules in their national legal system. Furthermore, a declaration is merely a moral code, with no binding effect.

Looked at in this light, the fact that the 1959 Declaration was unanimously approved is a strong argument in favour of its normative value. In fact, this unanimity reflects a consensus reached both on formulation of the principles and on their interpretation,

However, the two 1966 Covenants, which aimed to make Universal Human Rights a binding, are extremely important in this context. Both Covenants refer to the status of the child, and indeed devote several passages to it. It is also worthy to not that during preparation for the International Covenant on Civil and Political Rights there was a fierce debate on the need for a separate and therefore specific article on the rights of the child. The main impetus to starting work on the Convention on the Rights of the Child came not only from this fundamental debate on the question of the need for separate children's rights, and on the normative effect of the Declaration but also from the confusion engendered by the increasing number of international human rights instruments, each containing scattered references to the status of children.

In conclusion, we can say that the normative effect of the 1959 Declaration was limited. It was more important as a guideline for our relationship with children and as a frame of reference (rather than a legal standard) for evaluating this relationship. It was first and foremost a weapon in the struggle to improve the position of young people in society, both for voluntary organizations and the authorities.

Genesis of the Convention on the Rights of the Child (1950-1989)

For the realization of human rights treaties, the most important bodies are the General Assembly and the Economic and Social Council (ECOSOC). All members of the UN have a seat in the General Assembly, the UN's central organ, which formally adopts international treaties, to be signed and ratified by the members. For substantive matters a two thirds majority of members present is required, less important decisions being taken by simple majority. Every member state has one vote.

The Economic and Social Council (ECOSOC) deals with economic, cultural and humanitarian co-operation and is also responsible for human rights issues. ECOSOC makes recommendations on these matters and drafts treaties to be put to the General Assembly. It can also call international conferences on matters within its purview.

It is also part of ECOSOC's mandate to co-ordinate the activities of the specialized agencies. These area organizations which came about as the result of treaties and, legally speaking, are autonomous. The ILO and UNESCO are examples of such organizations. The main objective of UNESCO (United Nations Educational, Scientific, and Cultural Organisation) is to contribute to world peace and security by promoting co-operation between nations through education, science, culture and communication, Both organizations report to ECOSOC and are UN financed.

UNICEF was one of the organizations which contributed to the Convention on the Rights of the Child, even though the Convention was drafted by ECOSOC's Commission on Human Rights. The actual drafting work was carried out by a working party of the Commission on Human Rights.

On 8th March 1989, at its 45th session, The UN Commission on Human Rights decided to submit the draft convention on the Rights of the Child to the General Assembly, via ECOSOC. On 20th November 1989, the Convention was adopted without dissenting vote by the General Assembly, in its resolution 44/25.

Rights Guaranteed by the Convention

The rights guaranteed by the Convention are covered by Articles 1 to 41. Indeed, the intention of bringing them all together *in one comprehensive instrument* was precisely to indicate that they words, none of these rights can stand alone. Respect for human dignity moreover requires this. The comprehensiveness of the Convention on the Rights of the Child is underlined especially by the fact that both first-generation and second-generation human rights have been brought together here. This is unique in the history of human rights. This emphasizes the indivisibility and the non-hierarchy of these rights. In short, looked at from various angles, the Convention on the Rights of the Child can be said to be all-embracing or comprehensive.

General Provisions

First of all, in Article I we find the definition of the child: "For the purposes of the present Convention a child means every human being below the age of 18 years". This text also contains the extremely complex and delicate procedure, for reconciling opposing views on protection of the child before birth. It is debatable, of course, whether an international convention, involving 159 countries, is a suitable instrument for attempting to agree on an issue which still causes division within many countries.

Inconceivable big exception on the 18 years as the general age-level, is to be find in Article 38, on the involvement of children in armed conflicts and their recruitment into the armed forces. Here the age level is determined on 15 years! Already during the drafting process of the Convention the debate on this issue was very heated. The protocol raises the age from 15 to 18 for the involvement of children in armed conflicts, unfortunately however not for the recruitment into the army.

We must also mention Article 3, which states that the best interests of the child must be the primary consideration in all decisions concerning the child, and that the state must provide appropriate assistance if parents, or others legally responsible, fail in their duties.

In this context, Articles 5 and 18 are also extremely important. Article 5 stipulates that states undertake to respect the right and responsibility of parents to provide direction and guidance in the exercise by the child of the rights recognized in the Convention. In addition, Article 18 states that both parents are jointly responsible for the upbringing and development of the child. The state undertakes to under appropriate assistance where necessary.

Possible Sub-Divisions of Rights of the Child

A) Traditional Subdivision of Human Rights

The rights of the child, recognized by the Convention, can be sub-divided in five headings in line with the traditional classification of human rights:

1) *Civil Rights*: In general, these correspond to the rights recognized by the first 18 Articles of the Universal Declaration of Human Rights (1948). Examples are the right to a name and to acquire a nationality (Article 7) and the right to an identity (Article 8); the right to life (Article 6) and the principle of non-discrimination (Article 2). But there are also the so-called "integrity rights", such as the ban on torture (Article 37), the right to protection from physical violence (Articles19 and 34), from arbitrary arrest (Articles 37 and 40), the right to privacy (Article 16),
2) *Political Rights:* These cover freedom of opinion (Article 12), freedom of expression (Article 13), freedom of association (Article 15), freedom of opinion, religion and conscience (Article 14), freedom of access to information (Article 17). Note should be taken that in the Universal Declaration the heading Political Rights also covers the right to vote and the right to stand for election.
3) *Economic Rights*: Article 4 states in general terms that states parties shall take all appropriate legislative, administrative and other measures regarding economic, social and cultural rights. More specifically this involves, among other things, the right to be protected from exploitation (articles 32 and 36).

4) *Social Rights*: Again Article 4. This heading also covers the right to education (Article 28 and 29), Health care (Article 24), and social security (Article 26).
5) *Cultural Rights:* In addition to Article 4 once again, in this context we need to mention Article 31, recognizing the right to rest and leisure, to engage in play and to participate fully in cultural and artistic life.

The rights recognized by the Convention clearly coincide with traditional human rights.

B) Sub-Division according to Objectives

The Convention has three main objectives:

i. *Right of Self-determination*: A number of universal human rights are now explicitly recognized and therefore confirmed as applying to children. This was uncontroversial in the case of certain rights, such as the right to protection from torture. Others were much contested (see above on debate during preparation of the Convention)
ii. *Right to Protection*: The Convention contains a number of provisions addressing the special needs of children and especially of their vulnerability, e.g. conditions of employment for children (Article 32): A number of these provisions impose more stringent requirements in the case of children than general human rights instruments.
iii. *Specific Rights*: There are rights which apply specifically or even exclusively to children: the right not to be separated from their parents ((Articles 9, 10, and 11), and provisions regarding adoption (Article 21). The best example under this heading is Article 31, recognizing the right to engage in play.

The Convention also aims to afford protection for specific categories of children: refugees (Article 22), handicapped children (Article 23), minorities (Article 30) and children caught up in armed conflicts.

The Three Ps Sub-Division

It is possible to subdivide in other ways, e.g. one commonly used the 3 Ps.

- *Provision:* rights providing access to certain goods and services;

the right to food and health care (Article 6 and 24), the right to education (Article 28 and 29), the right to enjoy social security (Article 26),

- *Protection*: the right to be protected from certain activities; the right to be protected against maltreatment and neglect (Article 19), the right to be protected from all forms of exploitation (Article 32 up to and including a 36);
- *Participation*: the right to act in certain circumstances and the right to be involved in decision-making (Articles 12 upto and including 17).

Especially Article 12 is a key Article. It recognizes the right of the child to express an opinion, and to have that opinion taken into account in any matter or procedure affecting the child. Thus the Convention recognizes the child as having an opinion and no longer as having a "not-yet" opinion.

Each subdivision throws a different light on the Convention. The first demonstrates that children have very few political rights. The three P's approach shows that the lion's share of their rights are to social services and protection. If one looks at the Convention from the point of view of its objectives, the right to self-determination is placed at the forefront.

The international community itself can also attempt to reinforce some of the weaker Articles. This can be done for instance by designing *optional protocols.*

Already on 25 May, 2000 the General Assembly of the UN adopted two optional protocols to the Convention on the Rights of the Child. *The optional protocol on the sale of children, child prostitution and child pornography* provides a higher legal protection than enshrined in the Articles 34, 35 and 36 of the Convention. *The optional protocol on involvement of children in armed conflicts* is raising the age from 15 (as it is now stated in Article 38) to 18 as the minimum age to involve children in armed conflicts. (*For detailed CRC, see Appendix I*)

Elementary Education—An Essential Right

Education also consists of a form of learning that is necessary for the development of one's personality and identity, as well as his physical and intellectual capabilities. Education permits, notably, the transmission of common principles to new generations, and the conservation and perpetuation of social values. It also contributes to the flourishing of individuality through the enhancement of social and professional integration. Education has as its ultimate objective the improvement of a person's quality of life. It offers to underprivileged adults and children a chance to escape from poverty. It is thus an essential tool for the economic, social and cultural development of all populations around the world.

Education is an essential right, which permits each person to receive instruction and to blossom socially. The right to an education is vital for the economic, social and cultural development of all societies. Education entails that its subjects acquire a variety of knowledge. It begins with the acquisition of elementary knowledge—that is to say, literacy—on the part of the youngest members of society. This is an essential stage which will permit the child to pursue his/her education by integrating secondary and post-secondary instruction.

Recent studies on child labour and poverty have suggested that when poor families reach a certain economic threshold where families are able to provide for their basic needs, parents return their children to school. This has been found to be true, once the threshold has been breached, even if the potential economic value of the children's work has increased since their return to school. But without capacity, there is no development. A study conducted by the UNESCO International Institute for Educational Planning indicates that stronger capacities in educational planning and management may have an important spill-over effect on the system as a whole.

The rapid changes in cognitive, social, and moral growth of an elementary school student makes the elementary classroom an ideal setting for shaping individual attitudes and behaviours. The elementary classroom may provide the best opportunity to set in place moral and ethical characteristics and understandings that have the potential to improve society. Children in the elementary schools are still malleable, and this emphasis on character education is seen as an important factor. The right to education is enshrined both in international human rights law as well as international humanitarian law

Education must be Accessible to All Children

Education is a human right which ought to be accessible to everyone, without any discrimination. All children must be able to go to school, and thereby benefit from the same opportunities to build a future. Additionally, educational instruction must be equally gratuitous so that children from disadvantaged environments will be able to enjoy their right to an education. Beyond the question of accessibility, the right to education also supposes that the objectives of learning will be attained.

This means that all children have the right to benefit from a quality education adapted to their needs.

It is the responsibility of countries to guarantee each child's right to an education. They must focus their efforts on primary instruction so as to make schools accessible and free for all children and thus enable them to learn to read and write. Today, education remains an inaccessible right for millions of children around the world. More than 72 million children of primary education age are not in school and 759 million adults are illiterate and do not have the awareness necessary to improve both their living conditions and those of their children.

Factors Affecting the Right to Education

i) Marginalisation and Poverty: For many children who still do not have access to education, it is notably because of persisting inequality and marginalization. In developing and developed countries alike, children do not have access to basic education because of inequalities that originate in sex, health and cultural identity (ethnic origin, language, religion). These children find themselves on the margins of the education system and do not benefit from learning that is vital to their intellectual and social development.

Factors linked to poverty such as unemployment, illness and the illiteracy of parents, multiply the risk of non-schooling and the drop-out rate of a child. Undeniably, many children from disadvantaged backgrounds are forced to abandon their education due to health problems related to malnutrition or in order to work and provide support for the family.

ii) Financial Deficit of Developing Countries: Universal primary education is a major issue and a sizeable problem for many countries. Many emerging countries do not appropriate the financial resources necessary to create schools, provide schooling materials, nor recruit and train teachers. Funds pledged by the international community are generally not sufficient enough to allow countries to establish an education system for all children.

Equally, a lack of financial resources has an effect on the quality of teaching. Teachers do not benefit from basic teacher training and schools, of which there are not enough, have oversized classes. This overflow leads to classes where many different educational levels are forced together which does not allow each individual child to benefit from an education adapted to their needs and abilities. As a result, the drop-out rate and education failure remains high.

iii) *Gender Inequality*: Today, it is girls who have the least access to education. They make up more than 54 per cent of the non-schooled population in the world. This problem occurs most frequently in Arab States, in central Asia and in Southern and Western Asia and is principally explained by the cultural and traditional privileged treatment given to males. Girls are destined to work in the family home, whereas boys are entitled to receive an education.

In sub-Saharan Africa, over 12 million girls are at risk of never receiving an education. In Yemen, it is more than 80 per cent of girls who will never have the opportunity to go to school. Even more alarming, certain countries such as Afghanistan or Somalia make no effort to reduce the gap between girls and boys with regard to education. Although many developing countries may congratulate themselves on dramatically reducing inequality between girls and boys in education, a lot of effort is still needed in order to achieve universal primary education.

Right to Education Worldwide

As a result of poverty and marginalization, more than 72 million children around the world remain unschooled. Sub-Saharan Africa is the most affected area with over 32 million children of primary school age remaining uneducated. Central and Eastern Asia, as well as the Pacific, are also severely affected by this problem with more than 27 million uneducated children.

Additionally, these regions must also solve continuing problems of educational poverty. Essentially this concerns Sub-Saharan Africa where more than half of children receive an education for less than 4 years. In certain countries, such as Somalia and Burkina Faso, more than 50 per cent of children receive an education for a period less than 2 years. The lack of schooling and poor education have negative effects on the population and country. The children leave school without having acquired the basics, which greatly impedes the social and economic development of these countries.

Changing Constructs of the Child and Child Rights

Children's rights in education need to be seen as inclusive and comprehensive so it is important that they be addressed in the context of a basic legislative framework, namely the convention on the Rights of the child. By adopting this framework we are able to address fundamental questions about expectations and demands on the various actors in the school culture, particularly teachers and students.

For very important historical reasons children tend to be seen as future performers in a yet-to-be-created splendid Enlightened Society. This social construct of childhood, which defines it as a stage of preparation for adult life, had and continues to have enormous consequences for children and for those who relate to them. By defining childhood as a preparation or transition period, children are place in a state of limbo. They are obliged to wait and are required to prepare themselves as future performers. In reçent decades this adult-centric construct of the child has been questioned.

New understandings of childhood and changing perceptions of children have led to children's right to enjoy their rights in the here and now being widely advocated. Thus children area recognized as individuals entitled to human dignity. Respect for children as human beings means that they are no longer perceived as mere objects of protection but as subjects, bearers of human rights like all human beings. This new perception applies to the child as an individual as well as to children as a social category. This raises implications for both psychologists and sociologists of education.

This conceptual switch in the construct of the child is not easy to implement and practice in daily life. It requires a complete revision of approach, since we are not used to treating children from a human rights standpoint. The UN Convention on the Rights of the Child (CRC) strongly promotes this human rights approach.

Universal Ratification of CRC

The preamble of the CRC, which does not present binding principles, nevertheless outlines the terms of reference within which we should interpret the various binding Articles which follow. The preamble stresses that the CRC is an integral part of the human rights project.

The Convention itself contains both civil and political and social, economic and cultural rights. It effectively reminds us that these rights are, in fact, inseparable. All rights are equally important and interdependent. No right can stand on its own. This would be in contravention of the spirit of the CRC.

This requires governments, lawyers and other experts to take a novel approach since they are used to reading and interpreting Conventions Article by Article. In other words the CRC demands a comprehensive and interactive interpretation, thus setting a standard for future human rights instruments and for the human rights project as a whole. The process of transforming children's rights standards into reality may act as a catalyst for future democratic development.

For heuristic reasons only and keeping in mind the indivisibility of rights, it is useful to divide the CRC into categories or subdivisions. So, for example, it is helpful to consider the 3 Ps: Provision, Protection and Participation rights (Helio *et al.,* 1993)

Protection rights exist because of children's vulnerability and dependence. Children have the right including the right to life, survival and development (Article 6), and the right to protection from abuse, neglect and exploitation (Article 19). The basic idea behind protection rights is that children have the right to be protected, to be shielded from individual and structural harmful acts and practices. The right of access to provisions include information (Article 17), social security (Article 26), the highest level of health (Article 24), and education (Article 29).

The most revolutionary part of the CRC is found among the Articles addressing participation rights. These recognize the right of children to make certain choices for themselves and present them in dialogue with others. Such rights include the right to express an opinion, freedom of thought, conscience and religion, freedom of association, protection of privacy (Articles 12-16). These participation rights recognize children as meaning-makers and acknowledge their citizenship.

The CRC is a Convention, which means that State Parties ratifying it accept the legal obligation to implement the provisions of the Convention. At the domestic level, State Parties that adopt the Constitutional provision of the so-called 'self-executing force' are found via their courts to apply this strong provision to the CRC. Hesitations in this regard can cause weakening of the CRC since amending laws is not always a guarantee that they are strengthened. Countries that have a dualistic system have to transpose the CRC into nation laws.

At the international level there is a Committee on the Rights of the Child (Article 43) which monitors all State Parties' compliance via a system of initial and periodic reports (Article 44) from these States. State Parties are required to make their reports and the observations of the Committee widely available to the public in their countries (Article 44.6). This provision in its turn is a consequence of Article 42, which obliges State Parties to make the rights contained in the CRC widely known to both adults and children.

The over-riding importance of this binding duty, both to report and inform, clearly strengthens the legal power of the convention. The implementation of the Convention is thus a sustainable process.

In itself, and as part of the international human rights project, the CRC has quite a long history. On 20th November 1989, after ten years of preparation, the General Assembly of the UN adopted without a dissenting vote, the convention on the rights of the child. The CRC contains 54 Articles of which 41 are substantive Articles defining the rights of the child and the obligations on State Parties ratifying the convention. Unlike the two former instruments which address children's rights, the CRC is a convention and is thus legally binding.

Legal Protection of Children's Rights

The CRC irrevocably closed the era of children's protection and opened a new era of the legal protection of the *rights* of children. In other words, in legal terms, it underlined the evolution of the child as a legal *object* into the child as a legal *subject.*

The legal protection of rights implies more than just judicial procedures. It has to comply with simple but basic requirements. To mention some:

- You must *have* rights
- You must be *informed* about your rights
- You must be able to *exercise* your rights
- If necessary you must be able to *enforce* your rights
- There must be a community of interest to *advocate* your rights (Verhellen, 1995)

Each of these requirements is interdependent. If one of them is not met or is inadequately met, legal protection is seriously jeopardized. Just as the construct of the child is undergoing processes of deconstruction and reconstruction, so such requirements are not self-evident in discussions of legal protection of children's rights.

Children's Rights Within the School (Verhellen, 2000)

Children spend a considerable part of their existence at school. School, as an instrument of socialization, is expected to reflect developments in society. The global social development of new constructs of the child creates new need. Education has to take these new developments into account or, at the very least., to be aware of them. In ideal circumstances, education can even provide the stimulus to such developments. Developments in the concept of human rights go a long way towards explaining why the law is now a hot topic in education. Surveys, an increasing number of court rulings, show that in many countries pupils are going to court to resolve disputes arising at school. This is a remarkable development, given that in the past education, traditionally based on the absolute power of teachers, remained untouched by the law. A century ago, it would have been unthinkable for a pupil to appeal against the decision of a head teacher.

Although, because of the nature of the rights it confers, the CRC in many cases imposes obligations on State Parties, it also grants a number of general human rights to children. This new impetus to children's self-determination cannot but produce new, important tasks for education. Describing the relationship between education and the rights of the child is not easy. It is a relationship with many facets and problems, not always immediately obvious. When a State ratifies the CRC, the implementation carries serious consequences for the school system. Though ratification three important tasks are imposed on schools: namely, the right to education; right in education; and right through education (Verhellen, 1993). These tasks have implications for the school culture or ethos.

The Right to Education

In various national and international legal instruments, the right to education is recognized as a universal fundamental right in society. The right to education is covered by Article 26 of the Universal Declaration on Human Rights (1948), which, however, is not binding. It was later repeatedly confirmed in binding international legal instruments. Article 13 of the International Covenant on Economic, Social and Culture Rights, adopted by the UN in 1966, imposes an obligation on State Parties to recognize the 'right of every person to education.' In its Article s 4 and 5, the UNESCO Convention (1960) develops this right still further and deals more particularly with the principle of non-discrimination in education. Article 2 of the first Additional Protocal (1952) to the European Convention of Human Rights also reaffirms this right by stating: 'No person shall be denied the right to education'.

The CRC obviously also reconfirms this right. Article 28 provides the means of enforcing it. The principle of non-discrimination, the right of free access to education, and the introduction of compulsory primary education are examples of subjects covered by this right to education. Article 29 contains detailed provisions concerning the aims and values involved: the development of the child's personality to its fullest potential; the preparation of the child for a responsible role in society; the development of respect for nature; mutual understanding the friendship among all peoples; and especially the development of respect for human rights and fundamental freedoms. Both Article s therefore impose the obligation on States Parties to implement the convention directly through their education policy. A first sight, most Western industrialized countries do seem to live up to the obligation imposed by the above mentioned international instruments.

First of all, much doubt has been expressed about the concept of 'every person', which can be regarded either as a negative reference to the principle of non-discrimination, or as a positive reference to the democratization role which education can play. Various studies have demonstrated the existence of inequality of educational opportunity for certain categories of people. Access to education may be free, but that is not the end of it. Free access means there are no school fees, but it does not mean there are no other (sometimes quite substantial) expenses for all kinds of compulsory or optional activities. These extra costs may well indirectly cause problems for certain people in asserting their right to education. Recent surveys have demonstrated that democratization in education is stagnating. The proportion of children from the so-called lower social classes in higher education and at university us extremely now.

Phenomena such as dropping out, truancy, unsuitable curricula, all have to do with the content and formal quality of education. This is directly connected to the real aim of education, which may be regarded as in many ways in conflict with Article 29 of the convention-i.e., with the development of the child's personality, talents and mental and physical abilities to their fullest potential. Expelling children subject to compulsory schooling (see Blair, this volume) or refusing to enroll them is also a focus of highly topical debate. These are incidents which occur regularly and have far-reaching consequences for children, who cannot fight these decisions. The growing number of court cases involving students and the education authorities clearly demonstrates that the former have had little protection until now (Verhellen, 2000)

Rights in Education

The right to education as a fundamental human rights has to be guaranteed directly. However, the rights enshrined in the CRC must be implemented by the school system in indirect ways. In other words, one of the first tasks for State Parties is to clarify children's legal position in education and to prevent breaches of children's rights. For example, attention needs to be given to such issues as disciplinary rules and procedures.

In its Articles 12 to 16 the CRC contains important fundamental freedoms: the right to express an opinion; freedom of expression; freedom of thought, conscience and religion; freedom of association; protection of privacy. This clearly implies the introduction of rights to self-determination which much also be implemented in the daily school culture. It implies human rights in education. Far too little thinking has been done on this matter. Effectively little attention has been given to ensuring that children are guaranteed respect in schools. To illustrate this statement consider Article 12.2 (CRC)

For this purpose, the child shall in particular be provided the opportunity to be heard in ay judicial and administrative proceedings affecting the child. This is a clear reference to the need for participation in daily school life.

Rights Through Education

The UNESCO-Convention (1960-Article 5) and the International Covenant on Economic, Social and Cultural Rights (1966-Article 13) clearly indicate that State Parties must aim at promoting respect for human rights through education. This is also in line with the spirit of the UN charter and the Universal Declaration of Human Rights (Article 26.2), in that familiarity with human rights is the best protection against infringements.

The Council of Europe Committee of Ministers has also adopted a recommendation (Recommendation R (85)7) in which it urges Member State to give firm encouragement to education in human rights and its promotion. It asks Member States to draw its recommendation to the attention of everybody involved in education. The recommendation contains a large number of detailed suggestions to this end. The Parliamentary Assembly of the Council of Europe later reaffirmed the need for human rights educating by adopting its recommendation 1346 (26 September 1997). Such initiatives are re-affirmed by the UN Decade for Human Rights Education 1995-2004.

A permanent, large scale information campaign on the Convention and its content is obviously essential if it is to be implemented effectively.

It is equally obvious that education has a major responsibility in this respect. Spending an occasional hour or two on the subject of children's rights in schools could clearly fall short of the obligations State parties have taken upon themselves. Essentially, there has to be a shift in fundamental attitudes on respect for children's rights. Theoretical teaching on the values of human rights and democracy serves little purpose if these values are not also put into practice.

Apart from this shift in attitudes, we will need changes in existing school curricula. Respect for human rights can be taught not only in history lessons but through practically every subject. Teacher training will have to be adapted to this new task. There might also be specific training for (regional) press and information officers and the setting up of a specific information system. Finally, all kinds of educational aids could be designed, for example, texts, audio-visual aids, educational games and exhibitions.

But some governments, some schools, some teachers, some parents and some children are addressing children's rights. Although such initiatives are somewhat piecemeal, they are characterized by high levels of commitment.

Application of CRC in Education

Although only a few countries have an explicit regulation against corporal punishment, all but two (the USA and Somalia) have ratified the UN Convention on the Rights of the child, Article 19 where Article 19 states:

> "States parties shall take all appropriate legislative, administrative, social and educational measures to protect the child from all forms of corporal and mental violence…."

The UN Committee set up to monitor compliance with the Convention has taken the provision of Article 19 to imply a prohibition of corporal punishment.

The Convention on the Rights of the Child has done a great deal to change attitudes towards children. More and more people regard it as self–evident that children are entitled to respect for their person and integrity. One of the basic ideas of the Convention is that children and adults have the same human dignity. Among other things, children are entitled to express their opinions freely and to be listened to Corporal punishment of children is not in correspondence with the values permeating the Convention. An authoritarian upbringing which includes corporal punishment and degrading treatment is out of harmony both with the Article of the Convention on the protection of children from all forms of mental and physical violence and with the Article s concerning the best interests of the child and the right of the child to be listened to.

Sweden-An Example

Sweden was the first country the world to outlaw corporal punishment, and various survey have shown this measure to be strongly supported by the Swedish population. In many countries, forces are at work to change attitudes to corporal punishment and to introduce similar legislation, and so people are interested to know how Sweden went about things. Why are attitudes to corporal punishment so negative in Sweden? Some explanations can be discerned:

There is a tradition in Sweden of resolving conflicts by discussion and agreement. This applies, for example, in working life.

A great deal of progress has been made with regard to the equality of women and men. Women occupy a relatively strong position both at work and in the family. As result, their way of rearing children, which most often implies less authoritarian methods, has had a powerful impact. A stronger position for women also means a stronger position for children.

Sweden is a relatively child-centred society. Many people work professionally with children, with the result that the community has a large fund of knowledge concerning children's needs and development. Great efforts are being made to offer children the best possible formative conditions, both within the family and in the community at large.

The legislation has been successfully modified to indicate that questions of custody and access, for example, shall be decided according to the best interests of the child. Many changes have also been aimed at strengthening the role of fathers. Joint custody, for example is the general rule today, even if parents are not married, and fathers have been given more scope for taking parental leave. Greater opportunities for men to take care of very young children probably lead to stronger emotional bonds between fathers and their children, which in turn presumably leads to less reliance on corporal punishment.

The negative attitude to corporal punishment in Sweden, then, is rooted in a variety of favourable historical and structural factors. Of course, not all the problems have been solved. There are still children in Sweden who are being maltreated and neglected. But they have made a good deal of progress towards children being treated with respect for their physical and mental integrity and regarded as full members of the community.

Modern Sweden makes strong demands on the individual. It is a matter of community interest that children should grow up into independently minded, socially competent, mentally strong individuals with powers of initiative. Such qualities are not promoted by a form of upbringing which suppresses and humiliates children. Thus, from both a human and a societal perspective, there are good reasons for campaigning against corporal punishment and other humiliating treatment of children.

"If you aren't allowed to hit your children., what are you to do instead?" One Swedish study shows that parents have a whole arsenal of methods for bringing up their children. How different educational methods are perceived by and affect the child depend much on the parent-child relationship the researcher concludes. The relationship between parents and children, combined with the extent to which the child understands the parent's methods of upbringing as legitimate, decide the child's social and personal development.

The essential thing is not only to develop new methods of child rearing but also to transform attitudes towards children and the relationship between adults and children. Above all, children have to be granted with a fundamental human right-the right of being spared physical violence.

Conclusion

If children were regarded as human beings, and it was therefore regarded as normal for human rights to apply to them, there would be no problems. In principle all human rights conventions would also apply to children. A separate convention on children's rights would be superfluous, because children could refer to existing instruments to assert their rights. However this is not the case.

If children's competence were generally recognized, it would be sufficient to add "age" as a non-discrimination criterion to existing human rights instruments. Article 14 of the ECHR, covering non-discrimination, offers ample possibilities to do so: the text contains a reference to "other status", which could also be read as meaning "children". Were the European Court for Human Rights to interpret or use Article 14 in this way, the controversy over human rights and children would be considerably closer to being resolved. So far, however, this has not happened.

New universal and regional children's rights instruments are still being drafted while, simultaneously, both in law and in the courts, children's rights are gradually being integrated into existing human rights.

The Convention on the Rights of the Child does not state explicitly that human rights apply to children. However, for the first time in history, it does grant a number of fundamental human rights to children (Articles 12 to 16). This recognition of fundamental human rights for children is an important new element in the debate on children's right to self-determination.

The debate on the distinction between human rights and children's rights is clearly still in its infancy. The Convention is not the final word, but only the beginnings of solution, though at the same time it is an important strategic factor giving new impetus to the debate.

Generally, it is assumed human rights "in principle" also apply to children, but there is no agreement on the principle of children's legal competence.

The chapter follows gives an idea of realities existing in the field of elementary education and Child Rights.

References

Child Rights, Classroom and School Management-Lunds Universitet. Handbook for Training Programme.

Verhellen, E. (2006). Convention on the Rights of the Child. Philadelphia: Garant

II

Experiences from the Field

2

Elementary Education in India: Some Emerging Issues

C.P.S. Chauhan

India is the largest democracy of the world with a population of about 1210 million people, which is nearly17.5 per cent of World's total 7000 million (PRB, 2011). This means that every 6th person on the Earth is an Indian. Our ever-growing millions stay is in the background of many of our socioeconomic problems because the limited resources available are very thinly distributed over huge human population. Many of the so called developed countries do not suffer from this disadvantage. The population of some of our states like UP which equals the total population of Brazil is more than that of many developed countries. Similarly, Maharashtra equals Mexico and Bihar is larger than Germany in terms of population. Only on 2.4 per cent of the total global land area and about 5.5 per cent of the total world's income we maintain a major portion of humanity. The poorest 5 per cent of Americans are richer than the richest 5 per cent of Indians.

With 51 births every minute, 18.1 million are added every year to our exploding population. We are essentially the land of youth and children since the median age of our people is 25 years, and over 65 per cent are below the age of 35 years (Census of India, 2011). About 30 per cent of our population-about 363 million, consists of children in the age group 0-14 years of which about 206 million (17 per cent of the total population) are of the elementary school age-group. Poverty, illiteracy and high fertility rate are some of the reasons for rapid growth of our population. About 72 per cent people live in 638,000 villages where agriculture is the main source of earning livelihood. As per the latest published data, over 30 per cent of the people of India live below poverty line. The World Bank report says that India is home to 22 per cent of world's poor.

It is said that India has the largest illiterate population in the World. According to the most recent published reports, our literacy rate is 74 per cent-about 82 per cent for male and over 65 per cent for female sub-populations. Of course, some of the states like Kerala (92 per cent) and Mizoram (89.4 per cent) have achieved high literacy rates. Thus, we are counted among World's most populous, poorest and most illiterate societies. Under the backdrop of this scenario, we will assess the progress of our elementary education system.

Significance of Elementary Education

One important characteristic of democracy is that it requires an educated and enlightened society for its effective functioning. The government of India realizes that faster pace of socioeconomic development, using modern means of production, transportation and communication, cannot be achieved unless common masses are able to benefit from scientific and technological advancement for which the prerequisite condition is that a common man should be enlightened enough to take advantage of new discoveries and inventions. In order to achieve this goal at least two conditions are to be met. First, elementary education of a reasonably good quality must be provided for all children in the age-group 6–14 years. Second, the entire society must be made functionally literate for which programmes of liquidation of illiteracy among adults should be taken up on a priority basis. These two areas of development–compulsory elementary education and full adult literacy, constitute the essence of Education for All (EFA). After achieving independence in 1947, provisions for 'education of the masses' were introduced in the Constitution of India which was enforced on January 26, 1950. The erstwhile Article 45 of the Constitution provided for free and compulsory education for all children in the age-group of 6-14 years, which corresponds to the elementary education of eight years' duration from class I to class VIII. The government of India has been making continuous efforts to achieve the goal of ensuring free and compulsory education for all eligible children since independence. But, the goal has remained elusive even after more than 60 years of sustained efforts, though considerable progress has been made. The purpose of this article is to highlight some of the major problems and issues related to access, quality, equity and relevance of elementary education which require immediate attention

Expansion of Schooling Facilities

Before 1947, educational opportunities in India at school and college levels were limited and available only to children coming of well-to-do families. Therefore, the first priority of the government was to expand educational opportunities so as to make them available and accessible to all sections of the society. Therefore, a constitutional provision was made (Article 45) which entrusted the government with the responsibility of providing, within a period of ten years from the commencement of the Constitution, for free and compulsory education for all children until they completed the age of fourteen years. Thus, the goal of universal of elementary education (UEE) was to be achieved by 1960. In view of it, the major emphasis, during the first three five-year plans (1951–1965), was laid on expansion of elementary education by establishing new schools and increasing enrollment of children. The Education Commission (1964-66) appointed by the government reviewed the entire education system and found that the target of providing free and compulsory elementary education was still far away. During the period of 15 years from 1950-51 to 1965-66, the number of elementary schools increased from about 223,000 to about 467,000 with corresponding increase in enrollment from 22.3 million to 61.0 million (Chauhan, 2004). Only about 55 per cent of children aged 6-14 years were attending schools including some over- and under-age children. There were wide disparities based on gender, caste and rural-urban location. While gross enrollment ratio (GER) for boys was about 70, it was only 38 for girls. There was a heavy dropout rate of about 78 per cent-over 74 per cent for boys and about 84 per cent for girls. The growth rate of enrollment of children had been more than that of the number of schools made available. The overall literacy rate improved marginally from about 16.7 per cent in 1951 to 24 per cent according to 1961 Census. The literacy rates for SC and ST communities were 10.35 and 8.5 per cent with wide male-female disparities.

The Commission, therefore, suggested that the target date for achieving UEE might be shifted to 1985-86 and that the goal should be pursued vigorously. Consequently, based on the recommendations of the Commission, government of India launched the NPE-1968 which, in addition to many other useful programmes, proposed to launch strenuous efforts for early fulfillment of the constitutional promise under Article 45. However, the next two decades witnessed some political uncertainty in the country and the progress towards UEE remained slow. In the year 1986, the government of India launched another National Policy on Education under which several new proposals were made for expansion of facilities, improvement of quality, reaching the unreached and ensuring requisite amount of learning. Towards the end of the last decade of 20th century, a massive programme called *Sarva Shiksha Abhiyan* (SSA) on elementary education was launched with increased financial inputs and mobilization of human resources. The SSA targeted that all children aged 11 years would have acquired primary education of 5 years by 2007. Similarly, it was targeted that all children aged 14 years would have acquired elementary education of 8 years from class I to Class VIII by the year 2010.

According to the recent reports of the Government (GOI, 2011), there are about 1,200,000 elementary schools including 823,000 primary schools spread over the length and breadth of the country. The number of teachers working in all elementary schools is about 4.4 million including 2.5 million at primary stage only. About 88 per cent of all teachers are trained and about 40 per cent are women. These schools have enrolled 195 million children including about 136 million at primary school stage. Girls constitute about 47 per cent of the total enrollment. The Scheduled Caste and Scheduled Tribe children are about 18.5 per cent and 10.5 per cent respectively. These figures are slightly higher than the share of these communities in the total population of the country. The overall scenario indicates that nearly 94.5 per cent children of the relevant age-group are enrolled in schools and 5.5 per cent are still out of school. Thus, total number of out of school children aged 6-14 years is about 11 million at present.

The overall progress appears to be fairly satisfactory as far as enrollment of children is concerned. But, average pupil-teacher ratio is 44. The overall number of teachers per school is 3.7 and it is only 3 at primary stage (GOI, 2011). This shows that there is acute shortage of teachers. Not even 4 teachers are available to teach 8 classes in an elementary school. The situation in rural schools is worse. Even there are schools without teachers, without building, and without requisite minimum instructional material. In urban areas, condition is better with 7 teachers posted per school. Moreover, there is shortage of classrooms, urinal facilities, laboratory material, books, ICT facilities and playgrounds. Above all, there is heavy dropout rate with 29 per cent and 42 per cent children leaving school before completing class V and class VIII respectively. The dropout rates are still higher among girls (44 per cent) and children of SC (51 per cent) and ST (59 per cent) groups. The situation is worse in rural areas. This shows that during the period of last six decades, only quantitative development of school education, in terms of number of schools and enrollment, has taken place, and there has been little attention on the development of quality.

Degrading Quality

The analysis presented in the previous section shows that there has been tremendous quantitative expansion of schooling facilities during the post-independence period. But, such a large-scale quantitative expansion has had adverse impact on the quality of education imparted in the schools. Of course, it is very difficult to define the quality of education imparted in a school operationally, because there are many different *in-put*, *process* and *output* variables that might be taken into consideration while measuring quality of education. For instance, quality of children admitted and infrastructure facilities, including teachers, may form input variables; the curriculum, instructional approaches, use of ICT, and administrative and managerial efficiency may form process variables; and level of children's learning achievement may be an effective index of output variables. It is widely accepted that children's academic achievement after a course of instruction is the most dependable measure of the quality of education imparted in an educational institution. But, unfortunately no comprehensive national level survey aimed at assessing minimum levels of learning of children has been published by any government body except a baseline survey conducted by the NCERT several years ago. This survey has shown that mathematical and linguistic skills of children declined with their rise on the educational ladder.

One of the most authentic surveys of quality of education in elementary schools in India is 'Annual Status of Education Report (ASER)' published every year by *Pratham,* a Mumbai based NGO. According to ASER-2011 published in January 2012, it has been found that 96.7 per cent of children aged 6-14 years in rural India are enrolled in schools. This finding may be very satisfying to our policy-maker. But, it is only one face of the coin. The survey has also reported that reading levels of elementary school children have declined over the years in many states of India, especially in the north. It was found that about 52 per cent rural children (as against 46 per cent in 2010) of class V were unable to read a class II level text, though in a few states some improvement was reported in 2011 over 2010 results. Similar trends were found in case of Class III children reading class I level text. Likewise, learning levels in basic arithmetic skills also showed a decline. At the national level, over 70 per cent children of Class III and 39 per cent of Class V could not solve a 2-digit subtraction problem with borrowing. Of course, a few states showed some improvement over the previous years. The ASER-2010 reported that 40 per cent of class VIII children could not read simple sentences; 20 per cent of those who could read did not understand their meaning. There are several other similar results of this survey which must open our eyes. These data on reading and arithmetic skills bring to light the hard fact that most of elementary school children are two to three classes/years behind the level of learning expected of their age or class. This means that the level of learning of a class V child is at the most equivalent to that of a class III child. It appears that 'right to education' does not give children a 'right to learn'.

These evidences are sufficient to inform the people of the country as to how our public-funded education system is functioning. Who should be held responsible? More than 80 per cent of the total school budget is accounted for by teachers' salaries despite the fact that many primary schools are running at the mercy of less qualified, ill-trained and ill-paid para-teachers. There is a large-scale teacher-absenteeism. A World Bank survey published a few years ago (World Bank, 2004) reported that 25 per cent Indian primary school teachers remain absent from their schools at a given point of time which results in the wastage of 22.5 per cent of the total funds available for primary education. Moreover, 50 per cent of those who present themselves in schools on duty do not perform actual teaching that day. The incidence of teacher-absenteeism is more in government schools than in private ones. Interestingly, only one out of every 3000 headmasters initiates some kind of action against absenting teachers. The major causes of this kind of situation are: security of service, weak legal structure, rampant corruption in education system, and increased political interference. The incidence of absence varies from 15 per cent in Maharashtra to 42 per cent in Jharkhand.

Dwindling Public Faith

A continuous fall in the level of performance of children has shaken the faith of parents in the school system created, funded, and managed by the government. This has in turn resulted in two major unexpected phenomena: (i) Mushrooming growth of private schools (ii) Roaring business of personalized private tuition. According to reports published by NUEPA (2011), the number of private elementary schools in the country has increased from only 10 per cent in 1999-2000 to about 28 per cent in recent years. The enrollment in private schools has increased from 18.7 per cent in 2006 to 25.6 per cent in 2011. In some states like Kerala and Manipur, about 60 per cent children of elementary school age are enrolled in private schools. In some other states the private school enrollment is reported to be as high as 30-50 per cent. What is more worrying is the fact that middle-class parents are withdrawing their children from government schools and putting them in the private schools under the popular belief that private schools impart better education. Some research studies have also justified this belief.

Research studies have shown that private schooling is more cost-effective as compared to public-funded schooling. The unit-cost in private schools is 41 per cent of the unit-cost in government schools and 55 per cent of that in aided schools. The average salary of a teacher in private schools is 42 per cent of that in government schools and 43 per cent of that in aided schools. The overall earning of a government school teacher is 3 times that of a teacher in a recognized and 7 times that of a teacher in an unrecognized private school. Another important research finding is that increase in salaries in private schools results in improved student-performance, while in the government school such a strategy has no impact. Thus, cost-effectiveness and efficiency in terms of better school performance of children are the factors promoting greater public acceptability of private schools over government schools.

But, education in private schools is costlier for parents and guardian than in government schools. Some private schools rated as the best ones are beyond the reach of even middle class parents, not to talk of the poor ones. Over the years, availability of educational and employment opportunities are becoming increasingly competitive due to increasing demand, especially, among the middle and lower socioeconomic strata of the society. In a quest of better future for their children and to ensure better school performance, parents are compelled to hire private tutors for their children. Private tuition is a 70 million US dollar business in India and has developed into a parallel 'hidden schooling'. In educationally developed states like Kerala and Maharashtra, about 75 per cent children of classes IX-X and over 50 per cent children of classes XI-XII go for private tuitions (ASER-2011). In the states, like Bihar and Orissa, where private schooling has not developed much, parents have to send their children for private tuitions at high prices. Incidence of tuition is higher in Eastern states than in other states where, in both government and private schools, between 20 to 25 per cent of all children attend paid tuition classes outside school.

One ill-effect of private tuition is that school teachers do not work hard with their students during the regular school hours and spend their time and energy in private tuitions before and after school timings. Reacting to this situation, children also do not attend schools regularly. It is heard that there are schools in Kota (Rajasthan) which enroll students only to fulfill the regular attendance requirement of boards of examinations. The students enrolled in them do not attend regular classes and attend only tuition classes. At the All India level, children's attendance in rural elementary schools is about 71 per cent and is on the decline. In some states the attendance is as low as 50–60 per cent. These facts explain the large-scale teacher-absenteeism. The overall situation in some states has reached such a stage that many government schools are facing closure. This situation is alarming. If some measures are not taken to improve the quality of education imparted in government schools, people may completely loose their faith in government supported schooling system and bank entirely on private schools.

Rethinking Priorities

The exponential growth of high fee-charging private schools, even in rural areas, during a short period of one decade, and increasing enthusiasm of parents to send their children to such schools despite high fees, give us a clear message that people want quality education even if it is available for a price. People do not mind paying reasonable amount of fees if it results in a better education of their children. This situation has come about partly due to improved socioeconomic condition of the people (as compared to 1947) and partly due to poor parents' awareness about the value of education in the contemporary age of technology and competition. Now, the time has come when we should rethink our constitutional provisions and concept of free education. Instead of talking of free and compulsory education, we should now talk of 'affordable and compulsory good-quality education'. We may charge some reasonable amount of fees in order to provide for education of reasonably good quality, but we must not impart inferior education under the guise of free education.

This kind of idea is bound to give rise to a serious debate, especially in the context of children of people below the poverty line, but we may think of giving such children full fee-waivers and required academic and financial support. The author is of the opinion that our government should give a serious thought to this idea. These days, even drinking water is not available free. How can we provide for free quality education? If someone installs charitable drinking water facilities on the roadside, hardly anybody come to drink water there, rather, people prefer to purchase a packaged and sealed water-bottle. So, let us read the psychology of the people.

Right from the time of independence, we have laid increased emphasis on expansion of schooling facilities in terms of number of schools and enrollment. Subsequently, we have succeeded in creating quantitatively a very large school education system. We have succeeded in bringing more than 80 per cent of all children in the relevant age-group to school, and to some extent have controlled dropout rate. But, we have not been able to ensure that children enrolled and retained at school must learn.

We must understand that enrollment and retention do not ensure learning. This is evident from the findings of the annual surveys conducted and published by *Pratham* (ASER-2011). Many schemes, such as 'non-detention policy' have been used to ensure children's retention at schools for 8 years, but no scheme has so far been launched to ensure requisite learning at each grade level. The National Policy on Education–1986 had suggested an idea of Minimum Levels of Learning (MLL) to be implemented at each class level, but what happened to it is unknown. The net result is that class-VIII and class-V children of our schools cannot subtract and divide 2-3 digit numbers and cannot read class-II text. The annual survey reports published by NUEPA have revealed time and again that many schools have no buildings, no teachers, no play-grounds, no urinal facilities and no instructional material. Our schools suffer from a 50 per cent shortage of teachers on an all India basis. We are working with ill-qualified, ill-trained and ill-paid para-teachers.

Since 2004, the government of India has been charging the tax-payers 3 per cent surcharge on income tax in the name of education-cess. But, expenditure on education, as a percentage of GDP, has been hovering around 3.5 and has never touched the magic figure of 4, even after 45 years of the Education Commission's recommendation of spending 6 per cent of the GDP on education. Despite all the tall talks, education as a sector of economy has received the last priority. Of course, huge amounts are being allocated to and spent on schemes like 'Mid-day Meal', which provide good opportunities to NGOs and the bureaucracy to siphon out money. We must rethink our priorities objectively and decide whether providing for mid-day meal is more important than posting requisite number of teachers in the schools. The author does not undermine the need and importance of mid-day meal for children, but feels that priorities have to be sorted out in view of the limited financial resources.

We have been talking for a long time about creating ICT facilities in schools. The published data of the government suggest that more than 85 per cent elementary schools in the country do not have computer facilities. Wherever such facilities are available, these are poorly maintained and utilized. In fact, the level of ICT used by a country depends on the stage of its socioeconomic development. If ICT facilities created do not match with the level of development, these are not properly utilized and become a huge financial burden on the society. A large majority of teachers at all levels does not know how to use computer and Internet services for improving their classroom teaching behaviour. It is, therefore, not surprising that a sizeable number of teachers in our schools and colleges does not have even personal E-mail addresses. How can we expect from such teachers that they would use ICT in their classrooms? There is an urgent need to organize large-scale training programmes for school and college teachers in the use of ICT in the classroom. The Government of India must spend money on these programmes by placing them on the priority list. Of course, some schools popularly called public schools, have excellent multimedia facilities, but serve only a microscopically small portion of the population. These schools are the main source of socioeconomic disparities in the society. The dual schooling system created by the ruling elite has given birth to two societies–a dominant minority of *haves* and an oppressed majority of *have-nots* (India and Bharat).

Education Commission (1964-66) had given the concept of neighborhood school wherein it was proposed that all children residing within a certain demarcated geographical area, irrespective of their social origin or status, would be enrolled in the same school, which would be located within a walking distance from the home of every child. Had this proposal of the Commission been implemented many social barriers would have tumbled down. The children of all castes, races, religions and socioeconomic groups would have received opportunities to play, study, and work together. The social segregation, which is the main cause of many conflicts and strives, would have been minimized. All social groups, irrespective of caste, religion, language, and region would have learnt to live in complete harmony. But, our political class did not want this situation to come about. The idea of neighborhood school, as conceived of by Education Commission, was never taken seriously by the politicians and the bureaucracy because it was not in the interest of the privileged classes.

It is good that the Government of India has passed the Right of Children to Free and Compulsory Education Act-2009, which is popularly known as 'RTE Act–2009'. This Act states, "Every child of the age of six to fourteen years shall have a right to free and compulsory education in a *neighborhood school* till completion of elementary education." But, it does not define the 'neighborhood school' which it refers to. Obviously, it refers to the school available in the vicinity of child's residence, whatever the quality of education imparted by it. The concept of neighborhood school, as envisioned by the Education Commission stands distorted against the interests of the poor and the deprived. This means that a rural and disadvantaged child has a right to education in a school which does not have adequate facilities in terms of building, number of teachers and instructional material while a child living in a cosmopolitan city has a right to be enrolled in a good quality school available in the vicinity. If a fundamental right divides people into privileged and deprived, it is not a right at all; it is simply a political tool to maintain the status-quo and hegemony of the dominant minority. Unless the quality of education imparted in all elementary schools in the country is comparable, R*TE* Act has no meaning.

There are many other issues related to the Act which need to be thoroughly examined and debated. The Act ensures compulsory enrollment, attendance and completion of eight years of retention in the school, but does not ensure that the child concerned must acquire requisite knowledge and skills appropriate for each age/grade level. Thus, along with access, attendance, and retention in school for 8 years, it has to be ensured that no child is promoted to the next higher class until he acquires minimum knowledge and develops essential skills expected of the child at the given class-level. It means to say that no child studying in class I should be promoted to class II until he acquires minimum level of learning expected of a child at class I level.

The foregoing discussion emphasizes that from now onwards we should be more concerned with the quality-aspects of elementary education than with quantitative development as we have already provided satisfactory level of availability of elementary schooling facilities for about 97 per cent eligible children within easy reach.

References

Annual Status of Education Report (ASER)–2011, *Pratham*, a Mumbai based NGO, January, 2012.

Chauhan C.P.S (2004), *Modern Indian Education–Policies, Progress and Problems*, Kanishka Publishers and Distributors, New Delhi;

Government of India, Census 2011, Registrar General and Census Commissioner, Ministry of Home Affairs, New Delhi, 2011.

Government of India (2011), Annual Report, Department of Secondary and Higher Education, MHRD, New Delhi.

Mehta, A.C. (2011), Elementary Education in India-Analytical Report (2009-10), National University of Educational Planning and Administration and Ministry of Human Resource Development, New Delhi.

Population Reference Bureau (PRB), The World Population at 7 Million, World Population Data Sheet-2011, Washington DC.

World Bank (2004), *World Development Report 2004*. Making services work for the poor. World Bank, Washington D.C.

3

Action Research Strategy for Teacher Educators in Elementary Education

K.P. Pandey

In the context of the massive implementation of Sarva Shiksha Abhiyan (SSA) by Government of India, there is a growing realization now for pressing into service the various capacity building measures. Action research is one such highly dynamic and situation specific strategy which has great promise and potential for augmenting competencies required by teachers at the level of elementary school education scenario. The present paper deals with the background and conceptual clarification in respect of action research before it is inducted into the training programmes of teachers with an eye on promoting quality concern in school education.

It may be mentioned at the very outset that the last six-seven decades paradigms of research have shown a visible shift from the traditional hypothetico-deductive patterns to empirio-inductive-qualitative moulds. Action research form belongs to the latter category as its prime concern is to improve both the practices and the practitioners. In this write up an attempt has been made to orient the young teacher educators with a view to empowering them to undertake qualitative researches with focus on depiction of educational reality as it obtains and as it should move in the context of global to local priorities.

The contention of the advocates of action research is that teachers, supervisors and administrators would make better decisions and engage in more effective practices if they, too, were able and willing to conduct research as a basis for these decisions and practices. The process by which practitioners attempt to study their problems scientifically in order to guide, correct, and evaluate their decisions and actions is known as 'action research'.

Stephen M. Corey, one of the proponents of action research observed in 1953 as follows:

> "I have lost much of the faith I once had in the consequences of asking only the professional educational investigator to study the schools and to recommend what they should do. Incorporating these recommendations into the behaviour patterns of practitioners involves some problems that so far have been insoluble. This leads to my third belief: Most of the study of what should be kept in the schools and what should go and what should be added must be done in hundreds of thousands of classrooms and thousands of communities. The studies must be undertaken by those who may have to change the way they do things as a result of the studies. Our schools cannot keep up with the life they are supposed to sustain and improve unless teachers, pupils, supervisors, administrators, and school patrons continuously examine what they are doing. Singly and in groups, they must use their imaginations creatively and constructively to identify the practices that must be changed to meet the needs and demands of modem life, courageously tryout those practices that give better promise, and methodically and systematically gather evidence to test their worth.
>
> This is the process I call action research. I hold no especial brief for the name, but it has some currency and is sufficiently descriptive. What I will talk about is research that is undertaken by educational practitioners because they believe that by so doing they can make better decisions and engage in better actions."

The Background

According to Corey the expression action research has originated from at least two somewhat independent sources. One is the activities and writing of Collier during the period (1933-45) when he was Commissioner of Indian Affairs and who was convinced that since the findings of research must be carried into effect by the administrator and the layman, and must be criticized by them through their experience, the administrator and the layman must themselves participate creatively in the research, impelled as it is from their own area of need.

The second source is Lewin and his associates, many of whom have attempted to study human relations scientifically and to improve the quality or' human relations as a consequence of their enquiries. In the field of education, most of the practices of the evaluation staff of the Eight Year Study were close to action research. As early as 1949, Wrightstone used the term 'research action' in describing one of the functions of curriculum bureaus. Stephen M. Corey (1953) popularised the term by his excellent book entitled "Action Research to Improve School Practices". The action research form has now been utilized in a variety of educational, social and management related situations with a focus on remedying or improving the decision making and decision implementing processes.

The Goal of Enquiry

Louis Cohen and Lawrence Manion (1980) observe that 'action research is a small-scale intervention in the functioning of the real world and a close examination of the effects of such intervention. Its usage may range at one extreme from a teacher trying out a novel way of teaching social studies with his class to a sophisticated study of organizational change in industry using a large research team and backed by Government sponsors.

The goal of enquiry in action research is not to arrive at generalizations. It is rather to obtain a solution to an immediate issue and to better the actions and decisions pertaining to a complex reality frame. It is pertinent to quote in this connection from John W. Best (1970) who avers as follows:

> "Action research is focused on the immediate application, not on the development of theory, nor upon general application. It has placed its emphasis on a problem, here and now, in a local setting. Its findings are to be evaluated in terms of local applicability, not in terms of universal validity. Its purpose is to improve school practices and at the same time, to improve the practices. The purpose of action research is to combine the research function with teacher growth in such qualities as objectivity, skill i~ research processes, habits of thinking, ability to work harmoniously with others, and professional spirit."

Cohen and Manion have identified the following five purposes of action research in relation to school and class room:

(1) It is a means of remedying problems diagnosed in specific situations, or of improving in some way a given set of circumstances;

(2) It is a means of in-service training, thereby equipping the teacher with new skills and methods, sharpening his analytical powers and heightening his self-awareness;
(3) It is a means of injecting additional or innovatory approaches to teaching and learning into an ongoing system which normally inhibits innovation and change;
(4) It is a means of improving the normally poor communications between the practising teacher and the academic researcher, and of remedying the failure of traditional research to give clear prescriptions; and
(5) Although lacking the rigour of true scientific research, it is a means of providing a preferable alternative to the more subjective, impressionistic approach to problem-solving in the classroom.

Exemplification

The examples of action research from classroom, school and other educational context may be multiplied. In such a research form the practitioners—either the teacher, the headmaster or the principal individually or in groups may become researchers. The following examples, as given by Cohen and Manion, while by no means exhaustive, give some idea of the contexts in which the action research strategy may be employed. They are not mutually exhaustive so there may be considerable overlap between some of them. There is the kind,

(1) which acts as a spur to action, its objective being to get something done more expeditiously than would be the case with alternative means;
(2) which addresses itself to personal functioning, human relations and moral and is thus concerned with people's job efficiency, their motivations, relationships and general well-being;
(3) which focuses on job analysis and aims at improving professional functioning and efficiency;
(4) which is concerned with organisational change in so far as it results in improved functioning in business or industry;
(5) which is concerned with planning and policy-making, generally in the field of social administration;
(6) which is concerned with innovation and change and the ways in which these may be implemented in ongoing system;
(7) which concentrates on problem-solving virtually in any context in which a specific problem needs solving; and

(8) which provides the opportunity to develop theoretical knowledge, the emphasis here being more on the research element of the method.

It may be observed that equally diverse are the situations in which these different kinds of intervention may be used-almost any setting, in fact, where a problem involving people, task and procedures cries out for solution, or where some change of feature results in a more desirable outcome. Notable: instances of the use of action research may be found in such starkly contrasting worlds as insurance, prisons, social administration, ships, hospitals, community projects, education, industry, coal-mining and business management.

Critical Features

The characteristic features of the action research strategy as given by Corey (1953), Best (191\0) and Cohen and Manion (1980) may be summarised as follows:

1. Action research is 'situational' as it is concerned with diagnosing a problem in a specific context and attempting to solve it in that context. In other words, it is essentially an on-the-spot procedure designed to deal with a concrete problem located in an immediate situation.
2. The context of action research is informal and flexible. It deals with the ongoing reality context and hence it bas a highly dynamic frame of reference.
3. The goal of action research is to bring about an improvement in a given situation by bettering the actions and decisions.
4. The problem of an action research is derived from the grass root level of reality and it is by its very nature as concrete as the local situation itself.
5. The hypothesis in action research is in the form of a proposed action and the anticipated result or consequence. It is, therefore, designated by a special term 'action hypothesis: It is usually in the form of a conditional if-then' proposition.
6. The design of an action research is quite adaptive. It allows for flexibility and variation in its implementation. Since the very context of action research is dynamic, it is impossible to have a rigid approach in the execution of its design.
7. In the action research, formulation of a generalization is not the

goal. At the most generalizations, if any, have a relevance to the future situations and hence they are known as vertical rather than lateral generalizations as in the case of fundamental and applied research.

8. Action research is usually, though not inevitably collaborative which means that teams of investigators and practitioners work together on a project. It is also said to be participatory in the sense that members of the team themselves take part directly or indirectly in Implementing the research.
9. The action research is self-evaluative which implies that modifications and effects are continuously evaluated within the ongoing situation, the ultimate objective being to improve practice in some way or other.
10. The reporting of action research outcomes is not done in a formal manner. It is instead, in the shape of a communication which has a ring of informality. The action researcher may transmit his findings to his colleagues even orally.
11. The use of action research is quite direct and immediate. It has a dual purpose: to improve, remedy or ameliorate the situation, to enhance the professional expertise of the practitioner and to increase his grip over the functional knowledge of the phenomena he deals with. According to Blum (1959) the use of action research in the social sciences can be resolved into two stages: a diagnostic stage in which the problems are analysed and the hypotheses developed and a therapeutic stage in which the hypotheses are tested by a consciously directed change experiment, preferably in a social life situation.

The Rationale of Action Research

The logic of action research is quite simple. It is aimed at minimising the gap between theory (knowledge) and practice. One of the reasons why fundamental or applied researches do not influence educational practice is the fact that they are not adopted by the practitioners but by the professional students of education, the university professors and staff members of research bureaus or other agencies. In the action research the practitioner is the researcher. He is both the producer and the consumer of research findings. Therefore, the improvement that accrues through research to both the practitioner and his situation is direct and immediate.

The rationale underlying action research strategy may be summed up in the words of Stephen M. Corey thus:

> "Learning that changes behaviour substantially is most likely to result when a person himself tries to improve a situation that makes a difference to him. He then does his best to obtain and interpret some evidence describing the consequences of his presumably more adequate practice. When he defines the problem, hypothesizes actions that may help him cope with it, engages in these actions, studies the consequences, and generalizes from them, he will more frequently internalize the experience than when all this is done for him by somebody else, and he leads about it".

The Action Research Method

In the action research the emphasis is laid on the direct participation of the practitioner, on collection of evidence, on the action hypothesis and upon the collaborative or cooperative approach. The significant elements of the action research process may be shown in the following five steps as suggested by Corey:

1. The identification of a problem area about which an individual or a group is sufficiently concerned to want to take some action.
2. The selection of a specific problem and the formulation of a hypothesis or reduction that implies a goal and a procedure for teaching it. This specific goal must be viewed in relation to the total situation.
3. The careful recording of actions taken and the accumulation of evidence to determine the degree to which the goal has been achieved.
4. The inference from this evidence of generalizations regarding the relation between the actions and the desired goal.
5. The continuous retesting of these generalizations in action situations.

It may be interesting to note that the action research strategy is acquired best by trying it. In this connection, it will be pertinent to reflect on the following observation of a team of action researchers:

> "We feel that the only way we can become more competent in classroom research is to do classroom research, even though we may lack many needed skills and insights:'

When is the Application of Action Research as a Strategy Appropriate?

When is the use of action research fitting and appropriate? Cohen and Manion (1980) provide the following answer to this question.

> "Action research is appropriate whenever specific knowledge is required for a specific problem in a specific situation; or when a new approach is to be grafted on to an existing system. More than this, however, suitable mechanisms must he available for monitoring progress and for translating feedback into the ongoing system. This means that. other things being equal, the action research method may be applied to any classroom or school situation where these conditions apply."

Some of the specific areas in school life where action research may be regarded as appropriate may be indicated as follow:

(1) *Teaching methods*—perhaps replacing a traditional method by a discovery method;

(2) *Learning strategies*—adopting an integrated approach to learning in preference to a single subject style of teaching and learning;

(3) *Evaluative procedures*—improving one's methods of continuous assessment;

(4) *The realm of attitudes and values*—possibly encouraging more positive attitudes to work, for instance, or modifying pupils' value systems with regard to some aspect of life;

(5) *The personal in-service development of teachers*—improving teaching skills, developing new methods of learning, increasing powers of analysis, or heightening self-awareness, for example;

(6) *Management and control*—the gradual introduction of the techniques of behaviour modification; and

(7) *Administration*— increasing the efficiency or some aspect of the administrative side of school life.

Action Research for School Teachers

The use of action research for modifying teacher behaviour is specially advised. It improves the teacher's perception, diagnosis and action with reference to the classroom interactional setting. The handling of cognitive, social, managerial and linguistic skills by the teacher and his understanding or insight into the dynamics of classroom situation may also be considerably improved as a result of participation in action research projects.

Limitation

The action research strategy is sometimes assailed as representing nothing more than a common sense approach to solving a problem. It is also criticized because of its fluid and informal frame of reference where application of scientific method may be hazardous if not totally erroneous. Another serious limitation attached to the strategy of action research is that it does not yield generalizations of wide applicability. Also, as Corey observes, 'making action research cooperative introduces all complications involved in group work.'

To Conclude

Action research strategy is highly dynamic and practitioner friendly. It requires constant visioning and re-engineering of the systems and approaches with an intent to assure quick and prompt delivery of desired results. The 21st century world, with its ever widening challenges and tasks, needs to further capture and capitalise, assimilate and sophisticate and regulate and refine this strategy in all sectors of life where humans and human institutions are involved.

References

1. Best, John W., *Research in Education*, Prentice Hall, Ine. 1970.
2. Cohen, Louis and Manion Lawrence: *Research Methods in Education*, Croom Helm, London, 1980.
3. Corey, Stephen M., *Action Research to Improve School Practices*, Bureau of Publications, Teachers College, Columbia University, New York, 1953.
4. Kerlinger, Fred N., *Foundations of Behavioural Research*, Surjeet Publications, Delhi, 1973.
5. Varma, M., *An Introduction to Educational and Psychological Research*, Asia Publishing House, 1965.
6. Pandey, K.P., *Fundamentals of Educational Research*, Vishvidyalaya Prakashan, Varanasi, 2010.
7. Pandey, K.P. and Bharadwaj, Amita, *Sikshha Mein Kriyatmaka Anusandhan*, Vinod Pustak Mandir, Agra, 2008.

4

In-Service Teacher Education Programme and Its Effectiveness at Elementary Level

R.G. Kothari and *Jignesh B. Patel*

It is said that the quality of a nation depends upon the quality of its citizens. The quality of its citizens depends not exclusively but in critical measures upon the quality of their education. The quality of their education depends, more than any other single factor, upon the quality of their teachers.

The entire educational system of our country is in the process of change. Everybody all know that no educational reform can be successful unless the quality of teacher is improved, but in turn the quality of teacher depends to a large extent on the quality of teacher education. Education Commission (1964-66) says, "Of all different factors which influence the quality of education and its contribution to national development, the quality, competence and character of teachers are undoubtedly the most significant. Nothing is more important than securing a sufficient supply of high quality of recruits to the training profession, providing them with the best possible professional preparation and creating satisfactory conditions of work in which they can be fully effective".

Education prepares the future generation to take their due place in the society; a teacher plays a pivotal role in this process. A Teacher happens to be the key person to initiate and support change for educational improvements. With the increasing complexity of problems, expectations from teachers are also increasing. To enable a teacher to create thirst for knowledge amongst his pupils, he must continue to learn and grow professionally. Thus, education of teachers at all levels is highly significant. In order to enable the teachers to act as catalyst in the process of developing the future citizens, the Teachers needs to be provided training not only pre-service but most importantly the in-service also. In this paper the authors tried to examine the relevance of teacher education with the quality at schools. Major emphasis is on in-service teacher education at elementary level.

During the last two decades the school curriculum in India has undergone a series of changes. After National Policy on Education (NPE, 1986), school curriculum has undergone a big change in terms of educational concerns and priorities. NPE (1986) stated that 'the implementation of various parameters of the New Policy must be reviewed every five years'. National Council of Educational Research and Training (NCERT, 1988) developed in response to the NPE (1986) which stressed on ten core elements in the curricula. These ten core elements were (1) The history of India's freedom movement (2) The constitutional obligations (3) The content essential to nurture national identity (4) India's common cultural heritage (5) Egalitarianism, democracy and secularism (6) Equality of sexes (7) Protection of environment (8) Removal of social barriers (9) observance of small family norms (10) inculcation of scientific temper. These were identified to strengthen national identity and promote national integration and social cohesion by activating values as enshrined in the constitution of India through school curriculum. Syllabus at school level was revised and new textbooks have been designed accordingly and now it is left to the institutes of teacher education to respond to these core curricula and ultimately to improve the quality of school education. A meaningful school curriculum has to be responsive to the society, reflecting the needs and aspirations of its learners. In the new millennium, some of the country's important societal concerns have remained unchanged because these could not be addressed adequately in the past. At the same time, many new concerns have emerged in response to the fast changes in the social scenario of the country as well as the world. The curriculum has to lead to a kind of education that would fight against inequity and respond to the social, cultural, emotional, and economic needs of the learners. The National Curriculum Framework for School Education, 2000 has pointed out eighteen curriculum concerns as: (1) Education for a cohesive society (2) Strengthening National Identity and Preserving cultural heritage (3) Integrating Indigenous knowledge and India's contribution to mankind (4) Responding the Impact of Globalization (5) Meeting the Challenges of Information and Communication Technology (6) Linking Education with life-skills (7) Education for value development (8) Universalisation of Elementary Education (9) Alternative and open schooling (10) Integrating diverse curricular concerns (11) Relating education to world of work

(12) Reducing the curriculum load (13) the child as a constructor of knowledge (14) Interface between cognition, emotion and action (15) culture specific pedagogies (16) Development of Aesthetic sensibilities (17) Continuous and Comprehensive Evaluation (18) Empowering Teachers for curriculum development. Stereotyped instructional approaches are not conducive to realize the goals stated above. To make teachers aware of this menace, teacher education has to come forward with thorough preparation. Teachers prepare men and education is an effective instrument of man making process. The teachers learn this through his education. A weak programme of teacher education is a national calamity. Dave (1999) emphasized five performance areas for effective teacher education. They are as follows: (i) performance in classroom (ii) school level performance (iii) performance in out of school activities (iv) performance related to parental contact and co-operation (v) performance related to community contact and co-operation. National Council of Teacher Education (NCTE, 2008) also emphasized on these performance area for practical training. In terms of forgoing stipulation of required performance areas NCTE (2008) suggested to give due emphasis to community based field work and community based social work. Thus the professional education of teachers must relate to pedagogy and the way the instructional materials can be put to a judicious use. This envisages a teacher training which may suggest a way of working with young learners, to help them seek and find answers to problems to their immediate concern.

The role of the teachers becomes important in this scientific era. The teachers must be knowledgeable about the new innovations and technological advancement. Teaching is considered as an art, a science and a skill. Thus, content mastery as well as expertise over skill and performance is essential qualities of a teacher. For producing competent and committed teachers, there are teachers education programmes in which training is imparted to the teachers and he/she gets mastery over skills, content and performance. But one important thing is only getting training once in a life is not enough for any teacher. Therefore in-service training programmes along with the pre-service training programme are needed for the teachers. It has been confirmed through various researches and studies that in-service training programmes positively improves the quality of education imparted by the teacher. Kothari (2011) Gupta (1998), Rao (2003) concluded in their studies that in-service training programmes were useful to perform more effectively and makes a difference in teachers' behaviour and most of teacher desired to have continuing education in school subjects to get mastery over them. It was also found in the above studies that these training programmes were finally beneficial for school students also.

In-service education aims at the continuous professional growth of the teacher so as to develop in him a positive attitude towards improving his own performance as a teacher. In the present days the horizon of knowledge is expanding at a tremendous pace and today's knowledge becomes outdated tomorrow. If the teachers fail to keep up with the latest knowledge, will be giving yesterday's knowledge to tomorrow's citizens. Therefore, if a teacher is to keep oneself updated with the best and latest information and innovations in their subjects and teaching methods, teachers have to learn throughout their professional life. The in-service education and training programmes attempts precisely for the same. Regarding teacher training, NPE (1986) states, "Teacher education is a continuous process, and its pre-service and in-service components are inseparable". Thus, in-service education of teacher at all levels is very important. Realizing the importance of such training to teachers and other related personnel, the Government of India has taken positive steps in this regard by establishing District Institutes of Education and Training (DIETs), Colleges of Teacher Education (CTEs) and Institutes of Advanced Studies in Education (IASEs).

Establishing an institute is not enough for achieving the requisite results, but constant review of its performance in various areas and taking corrective actions to achieve the desired goal is of prime importance. DIETs are engaged in various kinds of in-service programme like Special Orientation Programme for Teachers (SOPT), Minimum Levels of Learning's (MLLs), District Primary Education Programme (DPEP), Tarang Ulhasmai Abhyas Programme, Sarva Shiksha Abhiyan (SSA), and Principal Orientation Programme for Principals.

According to Report to the People on Education, 2010-11 (MHRD, 2012) To improve teacher presence in schools, around 11.13 lakh teachers have been recruited till September, 2010 and significant progress has been made in many states like Andhra Pradesh, Goa, Madhya Pradesh, Gujarat, Rajasthan, Chhattisgarh, Haryana etc. SSA provides for annual in-service training up to 20 days to all teachers to upgrade their skills and 39.48 lakh teachers have been approved for in-service training in 2010-11 under SSA. All the training programmes cover pedagogical issues aimed at improving teaching-learning transactions at classroom level and also focus on major areas including guiding principles of NCF 2005. The revised SSA norms provide for strengthening of academic support to BRCs and CRCs through availability of subject specific resource persons for teacher training, resource persons for inclusive education and MIS coordinators.

Along with this numbers of reforms have been made in teacher education as well. The NCTE prepared the National Curriculum Framework of Teacher Education (2009) in the light of the NCF, 2005 and the principles laid down in the Right of Children to Free and Compulsory Education (RTE) Act, 2009. The Framework has highlighted the specific objectives, broad areas of study in terms of theoretical and practical learning, and curricular transaction and assessment strategies for the various initial teacher education programmes as well as in-service teacher training programmes. Implementation of 'The Right of Children to Free and Compulsory Education Act, 2009' would also lead to qualitative improvements in teacher education and school system. The provisions have been made for enforcing standards for training of teachers; essential minimum qualifications; existing teachers not possessing prescribed qualifications to acquire the same within a period of 5 years; maintaining the specified Pupil-Teacher Ratio in each school and vacancy of a teacher shall not exceed 10 per cent of the sanctioned strength in a school established, owned, controlled or substantially financed by the Government. The NCTE in August, 2010 laid down the minimum qualifications for a person to be eligible for appointment as a teacher in classes I to VIII. In addition to the academic and professional qualifications, every person, in order to be eligible for appointment as a teacher, has to pass a Teacher Eligibility Test (TET) conducted by the appropriate Government. The Government is in the process of revising the Centrally Sponsored Scheme of Teacher Education to meet the qualitative and quantitative challenges in teacher education, especially in the light of the RTE Act.

The present era is changing into new era very rapidly. Telecommunication, computer and other kinds of information technology have turned the whole world into a global village. Information about each and every event taking place in any part of country reaches other parts of that country and the rest of the world in a short time. Scientific and technological influences have brought about many significant changes in the society as well as in the world. Today, one must also think in terms of changes in values, perception, political interference in educational planning, changes in educational needs, cultural changes, and changes in teachers' role expectation by the society. All these changes require more and more knowledge to be imparted effectively to more and more people in less and less time. The sole responsibility lies on the shoulders of teachers. It is only teachers who can mould the character of society according to the societal needs of the day.

In the view of the above, the teachers must have desired theoretical knowledge, skill orientation, linguistic ability, pedagogical skills, management skill, accountability, impressive personality etc. For this, teachers have to be trained and their preparation depends on the teacher education curriculum.

Teacher education means programme of education, research or training for human resources, equipping them to teach at pre-primary, secondary, senior secondary stages of school education, non-formal/adult education and correspondence education through distance mode. The educational objectives focused on students' behaviour to be developed through specific learning experiences. The curricula for teacher education were designed by NCTE to observe these changing objectives (Mangla, 2001). These teachers go into the field and apply the given knowledge in their real professional life. Moreover, there are changes in society, its values, norms, etc. The Field of technology is expanding day by day, secondly; a teacher can not be a computer. Once a certain amount of knowledge is fed, it will remain there in the mind of computer till it is diminished. But after a period of time, a teacher forgets whatever was taught to him during his training period.

It has been fairly established that education is a life-long process. Life-long learning should be the motto of every teacher. If a teacher stops learning, he degenerates into a bad teacher. This realization is at variance with the belief that education is a formal activity being conducted in the four walls of classroom, and also against the belief considering the end of education with the termination of schooling. Education is very broad and comprehensive activity commencing from the moment the child comes in to the world and terminating with his death (from cradle to grave). It is therefore, a force which exerts continuous influence on the growth of individuals.

Hence, there is a need for some sort of provision which may make the teachers up to date with respect to the knowledge of their subjects of teaching, methods and techniques and innovative ideas in each sphere of their academic lives. For this reason, the idea of in-service education has emerged.

In-service education may be defined as continuing education of teachers and other educators which commences after initial, professional education is over, and which leads to the improvement of professional competence of educators all throughout their career. The term in-service education is commonly used to denote planned efforts to promote the professional growth and development of teachers. In-service education includes all those courses and activities in which a serving teacher may participate for the purpose of extending his professional knowledge, interest or skill. Teacher education institutions can extend their services outside their premises either through the visits of their staff for consultations, lectures, or conducting courses, or through lending of books and equipment. Such services are also called as 'Extension Service', because these are extended beyond the physical limits of an institution and aim at promoting the professional growth of teachers by adding to their repertoire of skill and knowledge. If the teachers are to keep themselves up to date with the best and latest in their subjects and teaching methods, teachers have to learn throughout their professional lives.

The whole process of formal education begins with primary education, so it forms an important part of the entire educational system. Primary education extends from standard I to VII, generally covering the age group of 6 to 14 years. The education that child receives at this stage forms the foundation of physical, mental, emotional, intellectual and social development. Primary education is very essential for the all round development of an individual as well as that of a nation. So if one wants to ensure better quality of education and the progress of nation, one must strengthen its basis or foundation and for that primary education should be given highest priority and prime importance.

Recognizing the importance of primary education, the constitution of India has stipulated free and compulsory primary education for all citizens of the country without any kind of discrimination on the basis of caste, creed, sex, religion, etc. The Government of India (GOI) is committed to the goal of Universalization of Elementary Level (UEE) and continuous, determined efforts have been made in that direction right from 1947, when the country attained her independence. The Education Commission (1964-66) has given a directive to state, to provide free and compulsory education for all children up to the age of 14 years. Infect, this was to be achieved by 1960, but due to certain reasons, adequate progress in primary education could not be made possible and the constitutional directive remained unfulfilled.

Operation Black Board (OBB) came up as a follow up of the NPE (1986) with a purpose to ensure provision of minimum essential equipments and facilities to schools. MLLs was another outcome of NPE 1986. Realizing that efforts made so far to emphasize enrollment resulted in poor quality of education, a committee was appointed by the Ministry of Human Resource Development (MHRD) in 1990 and this committee laid down the minimum levels of learning for primary stage. Here MLLs refer to the competencies that a child is supposed to achieve at the end of a particular stage. The revised NPE (1992) gave a new scheme for achieving UEE with financial support from international agencies i.e. the DPEP, launched in 1993.

Thus, it can be clearly envisaged that number of commissions and committees appointed since independence, aimed at the attainment of UEE but the objectives of UEE was not achieved and final result was postponed every time. In spite of the constitutional directives and stringent measures taken during the last four decades, it has not been possible to achieve the target of UEE.

There has been a steady growth in primary education, especially in enrolment and retention. But the quality of primary education remains a major concern before the nation, especially the teacher education programmes. In order to empower primary education at the district level, the NPE (1986) envisaged the establishment of DIET. Accordingly, the MHRD resolved to start 453 DIETs in our country. As per the DIET Guidelines (1989) twenty five DIETs were established in the State of Gujarat.

Professional or pre-service training of teachers is a prerequisite in all parts of the country. Most of these institutions suffer from inadequate resources—human, physical and academic to provide good professional education. In many universities curricula are not made up to date and teaching practices are perfunctory to a great extent (Sharma, 2004). In view of the emerging roles of teachers under NPE (1986), it has been envisaged that both pre-service and in-service courses for teachers should be developed and organized at the DIET level. These teachers also include the personnel working in non-formal and adult education programmes. According to Programme of Action (POA, 1992) the programmes of an Elementary institution would includes:

1) Pre-service and in-service education of teachers for the formal school system.
2) Induction level and continuing education of non-formal and adult education instructors and supervisors.
3) Training and orientation of heads of institutions in institutional planning and management and micro-level planning.
4) Orientation of community leaders, functionaries of voluntary

organizations and other influencing school level education.

5) Academic support to school complexes and District Boards of Education.
6) Action Research and experimentation work.
7) Serving as evaluation centre for primary and upper primary schools as well as non-formal and adult education programmes.
8) Provision of services of resources and learning centers for teachers and instructors.
9) Consultancy and advice, for example, to District Boards of Education (DEB).

Steps have already been taken for identifying and setting up of the DIETs and recruiting suitable personnel as Heads and Staff Members of these institutions. These personnel would be trained and reoriented in cooperation with NCERT, State Council of Educational Research and Training (SCERT), National Institute of Educational Planning and Administration (NIEPA), University Departments of Education and Advanced Teachers Training Colleges. The AE/NFE resource units would be an integral part of DIETs for which additional staff would be appointed with the Central Government assistance. Facilities of latest technologies would be provided at DIETs, and the faculty members would be encouraged to develop learning resources and media programmes and should also improvise their own instructional materials.

The Colleges of Teacher Education would continue to prepare teachers for secondary schools, and the Universities in cooperation with NCTE would exercise responsibility for their academic matters, e.g. conduct of examinations, award of degrees and ensuring the quality of secondary teacher education institutions. These institutions would also be entrusted with continuing education programmes for secondary teachers. Some colleges of Teacher Education would be developed as comprehensive institutions for organizing programmes for primary teacher education and possibly, four year integrated courses after higher secondary stage, in addition to usual Bachelors of Education (B.Ed.), Master of Education (M.Ed.) Courses. These comprehensive institutions would also be provided with facilities and staff for undertaking research and for supplementing the efforts of SCERTs. Good colleges and Departments of Education would be given autonomous status in order to promote innovations and experimentation. The IASEs and CTEs would also work more intensively in the areas of in-service and pre-service training, research, publication of materials, etc.

The SCERTs would be required to play a very crucial role of planning, sponsoring, implementing, monitoring and evaluating the in-service education programmes for all levels of teachers, instructors, supervisors and so on. The needs for in-service education of these personnel would arise from change of national goals, revision of school curricula, new inputs in teaching-learning system, improving background of teachers, etc. The SCERTs would also prepare suitable materials for in-service education of teachers, undertake orientation of key-persons monitoring and evaluation of programmes.

Since all in-service education programmes cannot be organized in face to-face modality, especially in view of the numbers involved, distance in-service education should be provided with the help of broadcasting agencies SCERTs would be equipped with necessary resources for production of learning materials other than print. Minimum essential equipment to record audio and video programmes would be provided to each SCERT. The comprehensive colleges of education, IASEs, CTEs and DIETs would also be provided production facilities in a phased manner. Experiences especially those of voluntary organizations should be drawn upon in designing courses, developing materials and modalities for in-service education.

The POA (1986) has also visualized that a separate cadre would be created for appointment of personnel in SCERTs, Teacher Training Colleges and DIETs. These selected persons would be given various incentives, better service conditions and continuing education. There would also be interchange of teaching and teacher education personnel. The NCTE has to be strengthened to meet the emerging challenges and be conferred autonomous as well as statutory status. The curricula for teacher education programmes should be revised in the light of the new policy thrusts and with emphasis on integration of education and culture, work experience, physical education and sports, unity and integration of India, planning, management, educational technology, etc. are emerging areas of importance bearing impact on curriculum development, innovations, research and experimentation. Besides, need-based printed materials, modern media and methods would be utilized to an increasing extent for improving competence of the personnel.

Emergence of DIET

Various commissions and committees appointed after independence have taken initiative in restoring the Indian education; its indigenous character and universal converge. The Education Commissions (1964-66) strongly pleaded for internal transformation of education of the nation, qualitative improvements in education so that the standards achieved were adequate and kept continually rising and became internationally comparable in a few sectors and the expansions of educational facilities on the basis of manpower needs with accent on equalization of educational opportunities.

The NPE (1986) emphasized that the existing system of teacher education will have to be overhauled. A novel educational institution has been conceived and defined in the NPE (1986). To establish such an institution called DIET is the result of the determination for the improvement of teacher education at elementary level.

As per DIET Guidelines (1989) DIET's were established with the following objectives:

1. To provide highly enriched training to elementary school teachers and non-formal and adult education functionaries.
2. To provide training to the grassroots and personnel of the education system.
3. To provide facilities of qualitative improvement for the professional growth even of the lowest personnel.
4. To provide facilities for the education of the deprived children, adults and other neglected members of the society.
5. To develop educational curriculum, methodology and technology in keeping with the latest advancements.
6. To make available the fruits of development to the lowest level worker without being hampered by distance and expenses within the district.

DIETs will create a feeling of belongingness among the lowest workers of the field, i.e. the elementary teacher. DIETs will create among these people the sense of being cared for and looked after. DIETs will also generate a climate of 'ever welcome' for every worker, who will feel assured that he can consult and receive guidance and solve his problems, which are generally neglected by high officials for whom they are small and routine.

The new structure of DIET envisaged in the NPE (1986) has been a new landmark in the educational system based on the theme of decentralization of education. It shall have far reaching effect on the qualitative and quantitative improvement of the elementary education in the country. Considering the importance of this new concept the investigator felt it fit to discuss the various aspect of the DIET, such as characteristics, mission and role, programmes and activities, functions, linkage.

The NPE (1986) and the subsequent POA (1986) signified a new landmark in the educational development in India. The teacher has been paid the highest compliment. The teacher is the principal means for implementing educational programmes and of the organization of education. New roles have been expected from the teachers, like the statement "child centered and activity based process of learning should be adopted at the primary stage, has its implication that the teachers instead of acting as a disseminators of information would act more as mediator of learning. The emphasis is shifted from teaching to learning. Similarly, the concepts of equality of opportunity to all, not only in access, but also in the conditions for success," this brings another important role for teacher. There are other aspects also wherein teaching is now to provide prestigious leadership roles in policy implementation.

The new dimension of teacher's role arising out of policy thrusts necessitates in-service education for teachers so that proposed reforms are understood by teachers and properly implemented. An education system has to be geared to the changing demands of the society. No system of education, however comprehensive in content and terms can meet these changing demands, unless the teacher, who is the driving force behind it, is fully equipped with academic and professional competency. Therefore, efforts must be made to reorient the system of teacher education from time to time. Considering these, NPE 1986 recommended opening of institutions at district level known as DIET, to provide the necessary support for the professional development of elementary teachers.

The functions of DIET, as spelt out in the POA (1986) are as follows:

1. Training and orientation of the following target groups:
   - Elementary school teachers (both pre-service and in-service education).
   - Head master, Heads of school Complexes and officers of Educational Department, Instructors and supervisor of Non-formal and Adult Education.
   - Members of DBE and Village Education Committees (VECs), Community leaders youth and other volunteers who wish to work as education activists.
2. Academic and resource support to the elementary and adult education systems in the district in other ways e.g. by (i) extension activities and interaction with the field,

(ii) provision of service of a resources and learning centre for teachers and instructors, (iii) development of locally relevant materials, teaching aids, evaluation tools etc., and (iv) serving as an evaluation centre for elementary schools and programmes of NFE/AE.

3 Action research and experimentation to deal with specific problems of the district in achieving the objectives in the areas of elementary and adult education.

DIET at a Glance

To carry out the functions, following academic branches have been recommended by the DIET guidelines from MHRD (1989).

1) Pre-service Teacher Education (PSTE) branch
2) Work Experience (WE) branch
3) District Resource Unit (DRU) for adult Education and Non-formal Education.
4) In-service programme, Field interaction and Innovation Co-ordination (IFIC) branch
5) Curriculum, Material Development and Evaluation (CMDE) branch
6) Educational Technology (ET) branch
7) Planning and Management (PM) branch

As mentioned above, each branch has specific functions in its own field so as to achieve the basic objectives. Here Investigator has concentrated on fourth branch i.e. IFIC Branch. The IFIC branch is working in three fields i.e. In-service programme, Field interaction and Innovation Co-ordination. Here investigator has concentrated on in-service programme.

Establishing an institute is not enough for achieving the requisite results, but constant review of its performance in various areas, and taking corrective actions to achieve the desired goal is of prime importance. Review of related literature showed that more number of studies have been carried out in in-service teacher education but very few at primary level. Studies at primary level focused on the different aspects such as infrastructure of DIETs, human resource, effectiveness of programmes and functions of DIET as spelt out in the guideline. Therefore, it is important that studies are conducted from time to time mainly to assess the achievements of DIETs in various related fields.

One such study was conducted by authors about DIETs of Gujarat State with reference to in-service teacher education. The objectives of the present study were (i) To analyze the in-service training programmes in terms of its objective, its relevance to the emerging educational contexts, its content, its mode of presentation. (ii) To study the infrastructure facilities available for implementation of various in-service training programmes at DIETs. (iii) To study the problems and expectations of primary teachers, resource persons and teacher educators of DIETs regarding in-service training programmes. (iv) To study the process of selection of resource persons and the theme of the in-service training programmes.

For the present study authors used survey method and used multistage sampling method. To collect data questionnaires were prepared for Teachers, Resource Persons and Teacher Educators of DIETS. An opinionnaire and interview schedule were prepared for the teachers, observation schedule was prepared for checking quality of training programmes, checklist was also prepared to check the infrastructure facility available at different DIETs. For preparing tools, authors identified major areas to be covered and then items were prepared on each area. Tools were also sent to experts for validation. Data were collected with the help of above tools with the permission of higher authority, i.e. Gujarat Council of Education Research and Training (GCERT). The data collected by questionnaire and checklist were analyzed with the help of frequencies and percentages. Some of the data of questionnaire were also analyzed through content analysis techniques. The data collected by opinionnaire were computed with the help of frequencies, percentages and Chi-square. The data collected by observation schedule and interview were analyzed through content analysis techniques.

Major Outcomes

The findings obtained from this study regarding the objectives of in-service training programmes report that objectives of the in-service training programmes have been clearly mentioned in invitation letter and teachers have clarity about the objectives and according to objectives teachers prepared themselves in advance for attending in-service training programmes. Teachers also added that time allotted for in-service training programmes was adequate and duration was also enough for the attainment of objectives of the programmes. Similar findings regarding objectives were reported by Indian and foreign studies. [Blunck (1993), Chadwick (1999), Richmond (2002), Stewart (2000), Baker (2001), Castenda

(2002), Butala (1987), Ramana (1997), Gupta (1998), Rao (2003), Shajoin (1996), Yadav (1999), Swaminathan (2002)]

The findings with respect to the in-service training programmes and its relevance to the emerging educational contexts showed that lecturers of DIETs made efforts to organize in-service training programmes, which were related to the theme of emerging educational contexts and majority of lecturers used ICT in training programmes and gave importance to life skill and other emerging contexts. Teachers also responded that in-service training programmes were able to cope with emerging trends of education. Gupta (1998) found that knowledge of teachers in emerging educational concerns of primary education improved significantly. This result was also supported by Chadwick (1999) indicating that integration of arts can be a powerful teaching tool for teachers and an interesting way for students to learn. Ray (2001) also indicated that information and communication technology works significantly and teachers reported a change in teaching while they used technology. This shows that in-service training programmes were organized with different themes and importance was given to emerging educational context, so that teachers became aware of emerging trends in education. While contradictory results were found by Butala (1987), which indicated that very few training colleges focused on areas like educational technology, management and modern trends in education.

The findings obtained from the study about the content of in-service training programmes showed that no definite conclusion could be derived regarding the improvement in the content of in-service training programmes, while resource persons opined that they discussed about the difficult points of content matter and it was observed that modules regarding the content were given in in-service training programmes, which were informative, content was nicely presented and well organized. Butala (1987) arrived at a similar type of finding which reported that major achievement of in-service training programmes was update in the teacher and content area. In the present study, teachers also responded that new concepts were well explained in in-service training programmes. Shajoin (1996) supported this view, which showed that teachers felt that the programme had helped them to acquire the necessary knowledge regarding the content. Yadav (1999) arrived at a similar type of findings, which reported that teachers expressed their views that they had clarity about the objectives up to extent; course content met the training needs comprehensible to some extent. This shows that in-service training programmes were organized with different content matter and modules were given related to content matter and course content met the training needs.

Views regarding the mode of presentation in in-service training programmes showed that resource persons and teachers felt that there was a scope for the discussion and fruitful discussion took place and opportunities were given to teachers for presenting their questions. Along with this, in response to question regarding teaching method, teachers opined that lecture method was mostly used, followed by lecture cum discussion method, while project method and demonstration method were used sometimes. It was also observed in observation of training programmes that mostly lecture method was used for teaching but it was also fact that resource persons present their ideas very nicely even though they used lecture method. This result was supported by Yadav (1999) indicated the lecture method was mostly used in in-service training programmes (i.e. 98.4 per cent), this was followed by lecture cum discussion method (47.4 per cent). These findings further strengthen the findings of Butala (1987), which stated that the main modes employed in the in-service training programmes were lectures, seminars and workshops. But this result was contradictory with result obtained by opinionnaire of teachers, questionnaire for lectures and observation of training programmes. In opinionnaire, teachers responded that resource persons and lecturers of DIETs used different method of teaching. It was also observed that lecturers of DIETs and resource persons used content related teaching aids, i.e. Teaching Learning Material, Overhead Projector, charts etc. This finding was supported by Butala (1987). But it was seen in the observation that lecturers and resource persons was used teaching aids but they were not using ICT based or modern teaching aids. i.e. computer, video clips, virtual tours, power point presentation, animation etc. In connection with this finding Kishore (1998) found that primary teachers prefer mostly the learning by doing method for in-service training programmes.

With respect to infrastructure facilities available in DIETs, it has been observed that most of facilities were available in DIETs; while women's hostel and land area of the institute campus and building were less than suggested in DIET guideline. This result was supported by DIET (1992), which indicated that residential facilities were not sufficient. From this result, it can be observed that, this study carried out in 1992 about Vadodara DIET and in the present study where one of the sample was Vadodara DIET, even after ten to fourteen years, position remain the same regarding the residential facilities in Vadodara DIET. The findings, further strengthen those findings of NIEPA (1992), Lobo (1996) and Gafoor *et al.* (1998), which stated that building, hostels and other civil works needed immediate attention. About the library facilities, it was observed that library facilities were not up to the mark, books were less in the number. Yadav (1999) and DIET (1992) reported the similar findings. It was also observed that equipments for education in visual and performing arts were not available in Narmada and Panchmahal DIETs; while manual slide projector and audio cassette player was less in number as recommended in DIET guideline. It was observed that other facilities were upto the mark as shown in DIET guideline and regarding the computer facilities, it was seen that more number of computer and its attachment were there in DIETs. All the DIETs have created web site of their DIETs. In relation to this findings of Gafoor et al. (1998) showed some contradiction with result, while Mehta (1999) and Yadav (1999) indicated that according to guideline the infrastructure facilities should be increased, especially blackboard facilities, toilet facilities and library facilities; while Lobo (1996) found that practical branch of the DIET was weak in its work, the reason might be the less availability of infrastructure facilities or the less use of the available facilities. This showed that except some facilities, most of the infrastructure facilities were there in DIETs.

With respect to expectation of teachers, resource persons and lecturers of DIET regarding in-service training programmes, it has been observed that teachers opined that resource persons should be trained and qualified and having effective skill of presentation and should be invited from different institutes of education. This finding was strengthened through findings obtained from teachers responded which indicated that if the resource persons were invited having effective presentation skill, teachers would be interested in in-service training programmes and teachers expected more knowledge from resource persons. These findings further strengthened findings obtained by Duggal (2005) and Yadav (1999). Duggal (2005) reported that guidelines for organization of in-service training programmes and their monitoring were not followed by the co-ordinators of in-service training programmes in terms of assessment and prioritization of the training needs, selection of resource persons etc., which in turn, demotivated the teachers to participate in in-service training programmes. Yadav (1999) reported that competent resource persons should be employed during in-service training programmes. The present study also revealed that teachers expected that the fund given to the Custer Resource Centers (C.R.Cs). should be increased for implementation of ideas learnt in in-service training programmes. Majority of teachers responded that school education suffers, when a place of in-service training programmes was not nearer to school, so time and place of in-service training programmes should be feasible to school programmes and teachers; while almost all teachers and resource persons felt that frequent in-service training programmes should be organized for improving quality of primary education. This finding was supported by Gadgil (1981), which indicated that most of the teachers desired to have continuing education in school subjects to get mastery over them; while some other teachers desired to have continuing education to improve their qualifications.

With respect to problem faced by teachers, resource persons and lecturers, it has been observed that sixty three percents responded that they had not faced any problem in implementation of ideas learnt in in-service training programmes in class room situation; while teachers faced problems regarding administration, crisis of teachers when they went for in-service training programmes but it was also cleared by them that they did not face any problems from school principal regarding in-service training programmes. Most of the teachers responded that the place of in-service training programmes was very far from school, so it was not possible to reach the place of in-service training programmes in time without the help of private vehicles and doing so, traveling expense increased than whatever they received from T.A. bills. In addition to this, most of teachers opined that more time was needed for fruitful discussion. This result was supported by DIET (1992), which indicated that one hour was too short time for explaining topic. The major problem faced by the teachers was regarding the resource persons invited in in-service training programmes, who were not able to justify the content matter of their topic and resource persons from department of education were not invited by DIET. This finding was supported by Yadav (1999), which indicated that teachers felt that the same resource persons should not deal with modules related to different subjects, so competent resource persons should be employed. The findings of present study also revealed that most of the teachers opined that due to frequent in-service training programmes, education of students had suffered. Most of the lecturers also opined that they have not faced any difficulties in organizing in-service training programmes. This result was contradictory with that of Mehta (1999) which showed that due to more in-service training programmes less attention was paid on the presentation of the programmes by the lecturers of DIETs.

With respect to selection of resource persons, it is seen that teachers opined that in a selection of resource persons, preference was given to female and it was also observed that resource persons invited were not only co-ordinators of C.R.C./Block Resource Centers (B.R.Cs). it seems that there was enough scope to invite resource persons from other sources. Majority of resource persons responded that they were invited by DIET. Lecturers of DIET opined that problems were their in selection of resource persons. It was felt that proper resource persons were not available. Most of teachers also opined that resource persons should be trained, qualified and having effective skill of presentation and should be invited from different educational institutes, along with this teachers also responded that same resource persons were invited by DIETs for different in-service training programmes. It was also observed that in the observation of in-service training programmes that majority of the resource persons were invited from the primary school and out of them sixty one percent resource persons having a P.T.C. This finding was supported by Yadav (1999). This clearly indicates that selection process of resource persons needs more attention.

It can be seen that in-service education is very well designed through various programmes theoretically. DIETs have tried to orient the teachers at various levels. Findings of few studies also support that such in-service programme have positive impact to classroom teaching. So it is recommended that as per need of society and emerging social context, a proper programme of in-service education be designed and implemented for better quality of education.

References

1. Baker, V.D. (2001). The Influence of a Professional Development Programme on Participating Educators in Oklahoma. (Doctoral Dissertation, Oklahoma State University) in Dissertation Abstracts International, Vol. 62, No. 8, 2450-A.
2. Blunck, S.M.S. (1993). Evaluating the Effectiveness of the Iowa Chautauqua Science In-service Programme: Changing Teacher Confidence Concerning Reculturing Behaviours (Doctoral dissertation, The University of Iowa).
3. Butala, M. (1987). A Critical Inquiry into In-service Educational Programme Conducted by Secondary Teachers Training Colleges of Gujarat State. An Unpulished Ph. D Thesis, Ahemadabad: Gujarat University in Buch, M.B (Ed) (1991). Fourth Survey of Research in Education. New Delhi: NCERT.

4. Casteneda, I.R. (2002). Teacher Perceptions of Effects Professional Development on Teaching Practice and Student Learning. (Doctoral Dissertation, University of Cincinnati) in *Dissertation Abstracts International*, Vol. 63, No. 5, 1789-A.
5. Chadwick, F.M. (1999). A Case Study of a Professional Development Programme in the Arts for Elementary School Teachers. (Doctoral Dissertation, University of La Verne) in *Dissertation Abstracts International*, Vol. 60, No. 7, 2450-A.
6. Dave, R.H. (1999). Towards Effective Teacher Education, Ahmedabad: IASE, Gujarat Vidyapith.
7. DIET (1992). A Project Report. Programme for the primary teachers. Vadodara: DIET.
8. Duggal, S. (2005). A Study of the Arrangement for In-Service Education for Assistant Teachers at DIETs. *University News*. 43(25), 13.
9. Gadgill, A.V. (1981). Expectations of Primary School in Poone Regarding Future Training Orientation and Continuing Education. Poone: Indian Institute of Education.
10. Gafoor, P.K. and Ayishabi, T.C. (1998). Availability and Utility of Physical Facilities of DIETs. *Educational Review*, CIV (3), 21.
11. Gupta, K.M. (1998). Learning Achievement of Primary Teachers–A Study of In-Service Education Programme. *Quest in Education*, XXII (2), 28-37.
12. Kishore, L. (1998) In-service Training Area Preferences of Primary Teachers. The Educational Review, CIV (12), 13-15.
13. Lobo, I. (1996). A Study of the opinions of DIET Trained Teachers of Four DIETs Centers of Kerala Towards Different DIETs functions, Published Project Report. Mangalore: Ann's College of Education.
14. Mangla, S. (2001). *Teacher Education: Trends and Strategies*. New Delhi: Radha Publications.
15. Mehta, I.D. (1999). A Critical Study of Working of D.I.E.T. in Gujarat State. Unpublished Ph.D Thesis, V.V. Nagar, The S.P. University.
16. MHRD (1986). National Policy on Education. New Delhi: Govt. of India.
17. MHRD (1992). National Policy on Education. New Delhi: Govt. of India.
18. MHRD (1986). Programme of Action. New Delhi: Govt. of India.
19. MHRD (1992). Programme of Action. New Delhi: Govt. of India.
20. MHRD (1989). District Institutes of Education and training (Guideline). Department of Education. New Delhi: Govt. of India.
21. MHRD (2012) Report to the People on Education. New Delhi: Govt. of India.
22. Ministry of Law and Justice (2009). The Right of Children to Free and Compulsory Education Act, 2009. New Delhi: Govt. of India.
23. NCTE (2008). B.Ed. (Two years regular) programme. New Delhi: NCTE.
24. NCTE (2009). National Curriculum Framework of Teacher Education (2009) New Delhi: NCTE.
25. NCERT (1964-66). Education and National Development: Report of Education Commission, Delhi: Ministry of Education.

26. NCERT (1988). The National Curriculum for Elementary and Secondary Education: A Framework New Delhi: NCERT.
27. NIEPA (1992). A Study of Identifying the Strength and Weaknesses of DIET in Hariyan, in Jha, M. (1996). A Study of District Institutions of Education and Training of Baroda with special reference to in-service training. Unpublished M. Ed. Dissertation, Vadodara: CASE, The M.S. University of Baroda.
28. Kothari, R.G. and Patel. J.B. (2011). In-service Teacher Education: Training Programme for Primary Teacher. VDM Verlag Dr. Muller GmbH & Co. Germany.
29. Ramana, K.V. (1997). Attitude of Teacher Towards Training. *Educational Review*, CIII (11), 189.
30. Ray, B.J. (2001). Impact of Staff Development Training on Technology Integration in Secondary School Teachers' Classrooms. (Doctoral Dissertation, Oklahoma State University) in Dissertation Abstracts International, Vol. 63, No. 1, 148-A.
31. Rao, R. (2003). Development of an In-service Training Programmes for Navodaya Vidyalaya Teachers in Meeting Students' Emotional Needs. An Un Published Ph. D Thesis, Vadodara: The M.S. University of Baroda.
32. Richmond, C.A. (1999). An Evaluation of How Teachers Implement Training Received in an Intensive Arts Staff Development Programme. (Doctoral Dissertation, Temple University) in *Dissertation Abstracts International*, Vol. 60, No. 7, 2453-A.
33. Shajoin, O.M. (1996). A Study on the DIET Training Modalities and its Impact on Primary School Teachers of Kerala. Collate Anns: Dissertation Abstracts. Karnataka: Poornima Power Press, pp. 213-214.
34. Sharma, P.S. (2004). *Teacher Education—Principles, Theories and Practices*. New Delhi: Kanishka Publishers.
35. Stewart, M.R. (2000). The Evaluation of Professional Development Training for Elementary Teachers in Urban And Native American Schools Using Design Technology and the Learning Cycles. (Doctoral Dissertation, The University of Akron) in *Dissertation Abstracts International*, Vol. 61, No. 2, 574-A.
36. Swaminathan, B.R. and Regarajan, V. and Gnanasundaratharasu, A.A. (2002). A Study on the Staff Development Programme for B.R.C. personnel in Pudukkottai DIET. *Educational Review*, Vol. 45, (2), 33.
37. Yadav, S.K. (1999). Quality of Primary Teachers In-Service Training. DPEP Calling, Vol. III, (4), 30.

5

Stress and Burnout among Primary School Teachers

K.S. Misra

Stress can be thought of as a response i.e. the stress response to an extreme stimulus; as a stimulus i.e. as the stressor itself; and as an intervening variable. Stress refers to the condition which arises when individual's perception of the demands made by the environment and his/her personal resources do not match. According to Fanner, Manahan and Heckler (1984) stress consists of any event in which environmental demands, interval demands or both, tax or exceed the adaptive resources of the individual, social system or tissue system. Lazarus and Folkman (1984) defined stress as a particular relationship between the person and the environment that is appraised by the person as taxing or exceeding his or her resources and endangering his or her well being. Groan and Bastian (1975) wrote that psychological stress refers to social situations that are frustrating (or threatening to frustrate) a group of individuals. The intensity and duration of stress may seriously upset and alter the homeostasis of communications among people in a group and disrupt their internal homeostasis i.e. their health. Quick, Quick and Gavin (2000) think that "stress is an individual's generalized, systemic mind-body response to demands and stressors. The environmental stress perspective focuses on external demands and stressors; the psychological stress perspective focuses on how the individual evaluates these demands and the biological perspective focuses on physiological responses".

Burnout is a state of emotional, mental, and physical exhaustion and diminished interest. It is caused by excessive and prolonged stress when one feels overwhelmed and unable to meet constant demands. The Maslach Burnout Inventory uses a three dimensional description of exhaustion, cynicism, and inefficacy Maslach, C., Jackson, S.E, and Leiter, M.P. (1996). Shirom and Melamed (2005) and Kristensen, Borritz, Villadsen and Christensen (2005) have argued for an "exhaustion only" model that sees that symptom as the hallmark of burnout. Engagement has been proposed as the antithesis of burnout. It is characterized by energy, involvement and efficacy, the opposites of exhaustion, cynicism and inefficacy. Worley, *et al.* (2008) studied the factor structure of scores on Maslach Burnout Inventory and found three factors namely-emotional exhaustion, personal accomplishment and depersonalization. The author is of the view that nonaccomplishment, depersonalization, emotional exhaustion, friction, task avoidance, distancing, neglecting and easy going approach may be the indicators of burnout among students and teachers in Indian settings.

It may lead to poor health, loss of interest in teaching, a motivation, helplessness, cynicism, hopelessness and resentment among pre-service as well as in-service teachers. Burnout in primary school teachers is an issue of concern for bringing about qualitative change in education. Various demands of school and social life to which teachers are exposed and their probable adverse impact on teachers' learning and teaching are responsible for burnout. It has a negative impact on the learning and health of teachers. Community members, principals and education officers pay less attention to burnout in college students and teachers.

The Right to Education Act has come into force. Attention is being paid to improve the infrastructural facilities, quality of teachers and teaching-learning resources. But if primary school teachers feel stress and exhibit the symptoms of burn-out, the quality of learning by students will be adversely affected. So, the present study was undertaken to find out stress among primary school teachers and find out how stress in different areas contributes to development of burn-out.

The objectives of the present study are as follows:

1. To compare stress among male and female primary school teachers
2. To compare stress among primary school teachers working in urban and rural primary schools.
3. To compare stress among primary school teachers of Government and private schools.
4. To compare burnout among male and female primary school teachers
5. To compare burnout among primary school teachers working in

urban and rural primary schools.

6. To compare burnout among primary school teachers of Government and private schools.
7. To find out how stress is related to burnout.
8. To find out the extent to which area of location of the school, gender, management and stress in various areas contribute to prediction of variance in burnout among primary school teachers.

Sample: The sample for the present study consists of 80 primary school teachers teaching in the primary schools of Allahabad. It included ten teachers belonging to eight categories based on the variables viz. male-female, urban-rural and Govt.-private.

Tools used: The following tools were used to collect the data:

1. Stress Scale for Teachers constructed by K.S. Misra and Poonam was used to measure stress.
2. Burnout Inventory constructed by K.S. Misra was used to measure burnout.

Statistical techniques used: t-ratio, product moment coefficient of correlation and step wise regression analysis were used to analyze the data.

Results and Discussion

It was hypothesized that urban primary school teachers do not differ those from rural areas on overall stress as well as all the five dimensions of it. A look at the Table 5.1 shows that all the six t-ratios are not significant at.05 level. So, the hypothesis can be accepted. It means that urban and rural primary school teachers perceive similar amounts of stress.

It was hypothesized that urban teachers do not differ from rural teachers on overall burnout as well as all the eight dimensions of it. A look at the Table 5.2 shows that all the nine t-ratios are not significant at.05 level. So, the hypothesis can be accepted. It means that urban and rural primary school teachers perceive similar amounts of burn-out.

It was hypothesized that male primary school teachers do not differ from female primary school teachers on overall stress as well as all the five dimensions of it. A look at the Table 5.3 shows that all the six t-ratios are not significant at.05 level. So, the hypothesis can be accepted. It means that male and female primary school teachers perceive similar amounts of stress.

Table 5.1: Mean, standard deviation and t-ratios showing differences in stress among Urban and rural primary school teachers

Stress	*Location*	*N*	*Mean*	*Std. Deviation*	*t-ratio*
Stress-Total	Urban	40	123.9000	29.2660	1.027
	Rural	40	131.6500	37.7125	
Interpersonal Stress	Urban	40	36.7000	12.3126	1.163
	Rural	40	40.1250	13.9801	
Working Conditions	Urban	40	17.8500	4.7206	.717
	Rural	40	18.8000	6.9289	
Physical Facilities	Urban	40	18.4000	5.1331	1.039
	Rural	40	19.7500	6.4201	
Teacher Role	Urban	40	20.3000	5.0697	.441
	Rural	40	20.8750	6.4972	
Student Role	Urban	40	30.6500	6.2983	.895
	Rural	40	32.1000	8.0854	

Table 5.2: Mean, standard deviation and t-ratios showing differences in burnout among Urban and rural primary school teachers

Burn Out	*Location*	*N*	*Mean*	*Std. Deviation*	*t-ratio*
Burn Out-Total	Urban	40	120.7250	32.9918	.101
	Rural	40	120.0250	28.8350	
Non Accomplishment	Urban	40	13.5500	4.9404	1.144
	Rural	40	14.8250	5.0275	
Depersonalization	Urban	40	15.2750	4.9819	1.532
	Rural	40	13.7250	4.0127	
Emotional Exhaustion	Urban	40	12.9750	5.9892	.229
	Rural	40	12.6750	5.7395	
Friction	Urban	40	15.5500	4.4947	.908
	Rural	40	14.5500	5.3202	
Task Avoidance	Urban	40	15.8500	5.4798	.617
	Rural	40	16.5750	5.0224	
Bo Distancing	Urban	40	17.8000	5.4217	.211
	Rural	40	18.0500	5.1885	
Bo Neglecting	Urban	40	13.6500	5.5909	.087
	Rural	40	13.7500	4.6945	
Bo Easy Going	Urban	40	16.0750	4.8536	.197
	Rural	40	15.8750	4.2256	

Table 5.3: Mean, standard deviation and t-ratios showing differences in stress among male and female primary school teachers

	Gender	*N*	*Mean*	*Std. Deviation*	*t-ratio*
Stress-Total	Female Male	40 40	16.6500 123.3750	4.8492 36.6310	1.168
Interpersonal Stress	Female Male	40 40	132.1750 36.2500	30.4630 13.88367	1.426
Working Conditions	Female Male	40 40	40.5750 18.4500	12.2764 6.7404	.188
Physical Facilities	Female Male	40 40	18.2000 18.1750	5.0291 5.9134	1.392
Teacher Role	Female Male	40 40	19.9750 19.5750	5.6454 5.3917	1.577
Student Role	Female Male Female	40 40 40	21.6000 30.9250 31.8250	6.0755 8.0236 6.4286	.554

It was hypothesized that male teachers do not differ from female teachers on overall burnout. Mean value for male teachers is 113.5 while for female teachers it is 127.25. The value of t-ratio is 2.037 which is significant at.05 level. It indicates that female primary school teachers exhibit more burn-out than their counterparts. Efforts were also made to find out whether male and female primary school teachers differ with regard to the eight dimensions of burn-out. A look at the Table 5.4 also shows that out of the eight t-ratios only one is significant at.05 level. For neglecting dimension of burn-out mean value for male teachers is 12.40 while for female teachers it is 15.00. The value of t-ratio is 2.329. So, it can be inferred that female primary school teachers exhibit more neglect behaviour than male primary school teachers. The values of non-significant t-ratios reveal existence of no significant difference between male and female primary school teachers on the remaining seven dimensions of burn-out namely-non accomplishment, depersonalization, emotional exhaustion, friction, task avoidance, distancing, easy going.

It was hypothesized that Govt. primary school teachers do not differ those from private schools on overall stress as well as all the five dimensions of it. A look at the Table 5.5 shows that all the six t-ratios are not significant at.05 level. So, the hypothesis can be accepted. It means that Govt. and private primary school teachers perceive similar amounts of stress.

Table 5.4: Mean, standard deviation and t-ratios showing differences in burn-out among male and female primary school teachers

	Gender	*N*	*Mean*	*Std. Deviation*	*t-ratio*
Burn Out-Total	Male	40	113.500	28.2207	2.037*
	Female	40	127.250	32.0438	
Non Accomplishment	Male	40	13.2500	4.0493	1.699
	Female	40	15.1250	5.6848	
Depersonalization	Male	40	13.9250	4.3523	1.129
	Female	40	15.0750	4.7468	
Emotional Exhaustion	Male	40	11.9000	5.1331	1.428
	Female	40	13.7500	6.3840	
Friction	Male	40	14.1250	5.1599	1.702
	Female	40	15.9750	4.5431	
Task Avoidance	Male	40	15.7750	4.7689	.745
	Female	40	16.6500	5.6909	
Distancing	Male	40	16.8250	5.5233	1.896
	Female	40	19.0250	4.8330	
Neglecting	Male	40	12.4000	4.61769	2.329*
	Female	40	15.0000	5.33974	
Easy Going	Male	40	15.3000	4.12124	1.342
	Female	40	16.6500	4.84927	

Table 5.5: Mean, Standard Deviation and T-ratios showing differences in stress among Govt. and Private primary school teachers

	Management	*N*	*Mean*	*Std. Deviation*	*t-ratio*
Stress-Total	Govt.	40	127.475	29.9605	.079
	Private	40	28.075	37.5726	
Interpersonal Stress	Govt.	40	37.9000	11.4124	.345
	Private	40	38.9250	14.9083	
Working Conditions	Govt.	40	17.7500	5.7763	.869
	Private	40	18.9000	6.0589	
Physical Facilities	Govt.	40	19.0000	5.5054	.115
	Private	40	19.1500	6.1796	
Teacher Role	Govt.	40	20.9500	5.5425	.557
	Private	40	20.2250	6.0913	
Student Role	Govt.	40	31.8750	6.4654	.615
	Private	40	30.8750	7.9877	

It was hypothesized that Government teachers do not differ from private teachers on overall burnout. Mean value for male teachers is 118.95 while for female teachers it is 121.80. The value of t-ratio is.412 which is not significant at.05 level. It indicates that Government and private primary school teachers exhibit similar amount of burn-out. Efforts were also made to find out whether Government and private primary school teachers differ with regard to the eight dimensions of burn-out. A look at the Table 5.6 shows that out of the eight t-ratios two t-ratios are significant at.01 level. For depersonalization and task avoidance dimensions of burn-out mean value for Government teachers are 16.00 and 14.675 respectively while for teachers

Table 5.6: Mean, standard deviation and t-ratios showing differences in burn-out among Govt. and Private primary school teachers

	Management	*N*	*Mean*	*Std. Deviation*	*t-ratio*
Burn Out-Total	Govt.	40	118.950	25.0793	.412
	Private	40	121.800	35.8752	
Non Accomplishment	Govt.	40	14.2000	4.1274	.022
	Private	40	14.1750	5.7863	
Depersonalization	Govt.	40	16.0000	3.6162	3.097**
	Private	40	13.0000	4.9458	
Emotional Exhaustion	Govt.	40	13.3250	4.9374	.765
	Private	40	12.3250	6.6308	
Friction	Govt.	40	14.7500	2.9677	.543
	Private	40	15.3500	6.3267	
Task Avoidance	Govt.	40	14.6750	4.3405	2.732**
	Private	40	17.7500	5.6421	
Distancing	Govt.	40	17.2000	4.10878	1.234
	Private	40	18.6500	6.19574	
Neglecting	Govt.	40	13.2250	4.76896	.827
	Private	40	14.1750	5.48605	
Easy Going	Govt.	40	15.5750	4.36118	.789
	Private	40	16.3750	4.69963	

of private primary schools the mean values for the two dimensions are 13.00 and 17.75 respectively. The value of t-ratios are 3.097 and 2.732 So, it can be inferred that teachers of Govt. primary schools exhibit more depersonalization but less task avoidance than their counterparts working in private primary schools. This points to a grave condition and demands urgent steps to be taken to reduce exhibition of task avoidance and depersonalization among primary school teachers. The values of six non-significant t-ratios reveal existence of no significant difference between Govt. and private primary school teachers on the remaining six dimensions of burn-out namely-non accomplishment, neglecting, emotional exhaustion, friction, distancing and easy going.

Efforts were made to study the relationship between stress burn-out. Product moment coefficients of correlations were computed between overall stress and stress related to various dimensions of it on one hand and overall burn-out as well as all dimensions of it on the other. Results have been shown in Table 5.7 to Table 5.13.

Table 5.7: Correlations between overall stress and burn out among primary school teachers

	Stress-Total
Burn Out-Total	.439**
Non Accomplishment	.523**
Depersonalization	.331**
Emotional Exhaustion	.435**
Friction	.079
Task Avoidance	.367**
Distancing	.271*
Neglecting	.289**
Easy Going	.363**

**/* significant at the 0.01/.05 level

Perusal of Table 5.7 shows that total stress is positively related to overall burn-out as well as seven dimensions of it. These dimensions of burn-out are non-accomplishment, depersonalization, neglecting, emotional exhaustion, distancing and easy going. Friction is not related to overall stress.

Perusal of Table 5.8 shows that out of nine eight correlations are significant at.01 level. They point to the existence of positive relationship between stress in interpersonal area and to overall burn-out as well as seven dimensions of it. These dimensions of burn-out are non-accomplishment, depersonalization, neglecting, emotional exhaustion, distancing and easy going. Friction is not related to interpersonal stress.

Observation of Table 5.9 shows that out of nine correlations three are significant at.05 level while one is significant at.01 level. These values reveal existence of significant positive relationship between stress related to working conditions and overall burn-out as well as three dimensions of it. These dimensions are non-accomplishment, emotional exhaustion

Table 5.8: Correlations between interpersonal stress and burnout among primary school teachers

	Interpersonal Stress
Burn Out-Total	.506**
Non Accomplishment	.589**
Depersonalization	.402**
Emotional Exhaustion	.486**
Friction	.090
Task Avoidance	.413**
Distancing	.319**
Neglecting	.356**
Easy Going	.409**

** significant at the 0.01 level

Table 5.9: Correlations between stress related to working conditions and burn out among primary school teachers

	Working Conditions
Burn Out-Total	.242*
Non Accomplishment	.308**
Depersonalization	.125
Emotional Exhaustion	.250*
Friction	.105
Task Avoidance	.258*
Distancing	.055
Neglecting	.164
Easy Going	.195

**/* significant at the 0.01/.05 level

and task avoidance. Five dimensions of burn-out namely- depersonalization, friction, distancing, neglecting and easy going are not related to stress in working conditions.

Perusal of Table 5.10 shows that out of nine six correlations are significant at.01 level while one is significant at.05 level. They point to the existence of positive relationship between stress in the area of physical facilities and overall burn-out as well as seven dimensions of it. These dimensions of burn-out are non-accomplishment, depersonalization, neglecting, emotional exhaustion, distancing and easy going. Friction and neglecting are not related to stress in the area of physical facilities.

Perusal of Table 5.11 shows that out of nine eight correlations are significant at.01 level while one is significant at.05 level. They point to the existence of positive relationship between stress in the area of teacher role and overall burn-out as well as eight dimensions of it. These

Table 5.10: Correlations between related to physical facilities and burn out among primary school teachers

Burn-out	*Stress in Physical Facilities*
Burn Out-Total	.391**
Non Accomplishment	.517**
Depersonalization	.301**
Emotional Exhaustion	.357**
Friction	-.031
Task Avoidance	.392**
Distancing	.270*
Neglecting	.220
Easy Going	.346**

**/* significant at the 0.01/.05 level

dimensions of burn-out are non-accomplishment, depersonalization, neglecting, task avoidance, emotional exhaustion, distancing and easy going. Friction is not related to stress in the area of teacher role.

Table 5.11: Correlations between related to teacher role and burn out among primary school teachers

Burn Out	*Teacher Role*
Burn Out-Total	.437**
Non Accomplishment	.437**
Depersonalization	.259*
Emotional Exhaustion	.409**
Friction	.219
Task Avoidance	.287**
Bo Distancing	.328**
Bo Neglecting	.351**
Bo Easy Going	.352**

**/* significant at the 0.01/.05 level

A look at Table 5.12 shows that out of nine values of correlations two values are significant at.01 level while three values are significant at.05 level. They indicate positive relationship between stress in the area of student roles is positively related to overall burn-out as well as for dimensions of it. The four dimensions are non-accomplishment, depersonalization, emotional exhaustion and easy going. Four dimensions of burn-out namely-friction, task avoidance, distancing and neglecting are not related to stress in the area of student role.

Step wise regression analysis was done to find out how area of location, gender, management and stress related to the areas of

Table 5.12: Correlations between related to student role and burn out among primary school teachers

Burn Out	*Stress In Student Role*
Burn Out-Total	.263*
Non Accomplishment	.347**
Depersonalization	.256*
Emotional Exhaustion	.325**
Friction	–.034
Task Avoidance	.203
Distancing	.156
Neglecting	.106
Easy Going	.226*

**/* significant at the 0.01/.05 level

interpersonal relations, working conditions, teacher role, student role, and physical facilities contribute to prediction of burnout among primary school teachers. Results of the analysis have been shown in Table 5.13.

Table 5.13: Values of R, R-square change, F and unstandardized B coefficients showing predictors of burnout among primary school teachers

S. No.	*Value*	*For interpersonal stress*	*For working condition stress*
3	R square change	0.256	.044
4	F (Change)	26.845**	4.817*
5	B	1.735**	-1.651*
6	Constant	83.980	

A look at Table 5.13 shows that stress related to interpersonal area accounted for 25.6 per cent of the variance (F = 26.845, df = 1,78) in burnout while stress related to working conditions accounted for 4.40 per cent of the variance (F = 4.817, df = 1, 77). Out of the seven variables only two emerged as the best predictors. They are interpersonal stress and working conditions stress. Stress related to teacher role, student role and physical facilities, gender, location of the school and type of management were excluded from the model of predictors. The value of constant is 83.98. The values of unstandardized regression coefficients for stress related to the two areas of interpersonal (IPS) and working conditions (WCS) are 1.735 and-1.651 (F = 16.488, df = 2, 77). So, the regression equation for predicting burnout may be written as given below:

Burnout = 83.98+ 1.735IPS-1.651 WCS

To sum up it can be said that male and female, urban and rural and Govt. and private school teachers do not differ from one another on overall stress and all dimensions of it. Similar is the case with urban and rural teachers with regard to overall burnout and all dimensions of it. Female teachers exhibit more neglecting and overall burnout than male teachers. Govt. teachers exhibit more depersonalization but less task avoidance than private school teachers. Stress related to various dimensions as well as total stress are positively related to overall burn out and various dimensions of it. Stress related to all dimensions as well as overall stress have not been found to be related to friction dimension of burnout. Stress related to interpersonal relations and working conditions contributed to 30 per cent of the variance in overall burnout. The findings imply that education functionaries involved in the work of implementing the Right to Education Act should pay attention to management of stress in these two areas.

References

Kao, Yueh-tzu (2009). Burnout in college student volunteers: a cross-level study. *College Student Journal.* FindArticles.com. 17 Mar, 2011. http://findarticles.com/p/articles/mi_m0FCR

Kristensen, T.S., Borritz, M., Villadsen, E., and Christensen, K.B. (2005). The Copenhagen Burnout Inventory: A new tool for the assessment of burnout. *Work and Stress*, 19, 192-207.

Liao, H. and Chuang, A. (2004). A multilevel investigation of factors influencing employee service performance and customer outcomes. *Academy of Management Journal*, 47, 41-58.

Maslach, C., Jackson, S.E. and Leiter, M.P. (1996). *MBI: The Maslach Burnout Inventory: Manual*. Palo Alto: Consulting Psychologists Press.

Schneider, B., White, S.S. and Paul, M.C. (1998). Linking service climate and customer perceptions of service quality: Test of a causal model. *Journal of Applied Psychology*, 83, 150-163.

Shirom, A. and Melamed, S. (2005). Does burnout affect physical health? A review of the evidence. In A.S.G. Antoniou and C.L. Cooper (Eds.), *Research Companion to Organizational Health Psychology.*

Worley, J.A.; Vassar, M.; Wheeler, D.L. and Barnes, L.L.B. (2008). Factor structure of scores from the Maslach Burnout Inventory: A review and meta-analysis of 45 exploratory and confirmatory factor analytic studies. *Educational and Psychological Measurement*, 68(5), *797823.*

6

Awareness of Primary and Secondary Teacher Towards Child Rights—A Comparative Study

Magre Sunita Vithalrao

Human Rights are the rights possessed by all human beings irrespective of their caste, race, nationality, sex, language etc. Human Rights are sometimes called fundamental rights or basic rights or natural rights. Besides protecting human rights, the universal declaration of human rights (1948) also comprises rights of children's. Article 26 of the declaration concerned to children's education specifically. According to the universal declaration a child has to be given 10 basic rights.

1. The child shall be brought up in a spirit of understanding, friendship peace and universal brotherhood and shall not be exposed to racial, religious or other forms of discriminations.
2. The child shall be protected against all forms of neglect, cruelty, exploitation and traffic and shall not be permitted to be employed before appropriate age.
3. The child shall, in all circumstances, be among the first to receive protection and relief.
4. The child is entitled to free and compulsory elementary education and such an education as in his best interest and for which parents are to be responsible.
5. The child is entitled to grow up in an atmosphere of affection and moral and material security, with public authorities taking care of children without families or other support.
6. The physically, mentally or socially handicapped child shall be entitled for special treatment, education and proper care.

7. The child shall have rights to adequate nutrition, housing recreation and medical services, including special health care and protection and parental and postnatal care for mother.
8. The child shall be entitled to a name and nationality.
9. The child shall enjoy special protection to be developed in every way in condition of freedom and dignity.
10. All children irrespective of their race, colour, sex and creed of their parents shall be entitled to these rights.

Right to Education

The right of children to free and compulsory education act, 2009 provides every child in the age group of 6-14 years the right to:

- Admission, participation and completion of elementary education.
- A stress-free school experience, no corporal punishment. No mental harassment. No detention and no expulsion.
- A child–friendly curriculum in conformity with the values enshrined in the constitution of India.

Levels of Right to Education

- Primary level of education which shall be compulsory, free regardless of their nationality, gender, place of birth or any other discrimination.
- Secondary level of education must be generally available and accessible.
- Higher level of education should be provided according to the capacity.

Significance of the Study

Education is widely understood as gradual processes of acquiring knowledge. The primary teachers are the future creator of the children's. Teachers know the rights of children's and they give the information and detailed of their rights through education using different kind of teaching methods and it is important for the future control of the corruptions. The child Right is recognized as the one which empowers the individual to cope with basic needs such as health and dignity and full and free development of his/her personality. Children's are empowered to act when they learn about their rights and can actively defend themselves from abuses, overcoming their lack of concern towards politics.

Empowerment through Human Rights Education develops the individuals' awareness of rights and obligation regarding his/her human condition and includes everyone in the citizenry. The implementation of human rights education goes beyond inclusion in the school curriculum, for it involves a whole commitment to human rights, from the training of teachers to a safe and healthy learning environment. Human Rights Education is not only a set of contents to be transmitted to learners but also understandings of how and where it will be done. Schools staff must be fully aware of child rights which should be incorporated in all strategies, procedures and activities developed and performed by them. Teachers become educators when they get fully aware of the surrounding world which influences every child. Therefore, there is a need to address teachers awareness about the child Rights

Article by Brian, H.R. and Katherine, C. concerns educating children in schools about their basic rights under the United Nations Convention on the Rights of the Child. The question address is the teaching of responsibilities. They point out that although there is no mention of children's responsibilities in the Convention; responsibilities are inherent in the concept of rights. Therefore, children's rights education requires that children learn responsibilities that go together with rights. But we also point out that although there is a conceptual linkage between rights and responsibilities, effective education requires that the central focus is on rights and that children are given the opportunity to discover for themselves the connection between rights and responsibilities. Sunita (2010) conducted the study on teachers' literacy towards the child rights and she found the secondary school teachers were aware about the child rights at satisfactory level. Fatima (2011) found that the male M.Ed trainees had higher awareness level of RTE. Karaman-Kepenekci, Yasemin found that the Children's rights are legally protected benefits for children to develop physically, mentally, emotionally, socially and morally with freedom and honour in a healthy and normal way. It is important that children know the rights they have. Works of high quality children's literature ensure the socialization of children.

Objectives

1. To measure the awareness level of primary teachers towards child rights.
2. To compare the awareness level of primary and secondary teachers towards child rights

Operational Terms

Primary teachers: Those teachers teaches only the standard first to standard eighth.

Secondary teachers: those teachers teach standard fifth to standard tenth.

Child rights: Following areas of child rights are selected–1) Child rights and universal declaration of human right and Indian constitution. 2) Child rights and laws for protection of child right. 3) Child rights and child development 4) Child rights and deprived class child. 5) Child rights and curricular and school activity.

Major limitation of the study was that, it is not a comprehensive one but is confined to primary and secondary schools situated in greater Mumbai.

Design of the Study

Survey method has been used in the present study because of investigating and describing the rights of children's in various aspects. 115 teachers were selected through simple random sampling. Self prepared tool was used. The scale has 47 statements belonging to the following areas. 1) Child rights and universal declaration of human right and Indian constitution. 2) Child rights and laws for protection of child right. 3) Child rights and child development. 4) Child rights and deprived class child. 5) Child rights and curricular and school activity. Each statement is set against four point scale of strongly agree, agree, disagree and strongly disagree. The scoring is of 4, 3, 2 and 1 are given. The reliability is 0.75. First area contains 11 statements, second contains 10 statements, third area contains 11 statements, fourth area contains 10 statements and last area contain 5 statements. The maximum score will be 188 and minimum score will be 47. Awareness level is fixed as indicated below:

Sr. No.	*Range of score*	*Awareness level*
1.	47-94	Low
2.	94-141	Average
3.	141-188	High

Data Analysis and Interpretation

Table 6.1 shows the Mean and S.D. of area-wise and Total Awareness of child rights of primary and secondary Teachers.

From Table 6.1, it can be seen that, there is no significant difference in the awareness level of primary and secondary teachers and this hypothesis is accepted. This hypothesis contain five more sub hypotheses and from that there is no significant difference in the awareness about Child rights and universal declaration of human right and Indian constitution, Child rights and laws for protection of child right and Child rights and child development. Significant difference exist in the Child rights and deprived class child and Child rights and curricular and school activity.

Table 6.2 shows Mean and S.D. of overall awareness score and area wise awareness score of rights of children of primary and secondary teachers.

It can be seen from Table 6.2 that the Mean overall awareness score about child rights of primary and secondary teachers were above the neutral point (94-141), indicating that all the teachers irrespective of level was aware about child rights. Similarly the mean awareness score of primary and secondary teachers were above the neutral point in the area

1) Child rights and universal declaration of human right and Indian constitution.
2) Child rights and laws for protection of child right.
3) Child rights and child development
4) Child rights and deprived class child.
5) Child rights and curricular and school activity.

It means that the primary and secondary teachers were aware with child rights.

Overall Awareness of Child Rights

Table 6.3 shows the Mean Score of whole group of teachers on different areas of rights of children and on overall awareness.

It can be seen from Table 6.3 that the mean overall awareness scores of the samples was 162.19. since the awareness inventory contain 47 items with the score on each item ranging between 1 to 4, the total score of the instrument could range between 47 to 188 with the neutral point of 94-141. A mean score above the neutral point indicates awareness with the child rights, while a mean score below the neutral point shows no awareness about the child rights. The obtained mean overall awareness score of 162.19 is above the neutral point this indicates that the teachers were aware about the child Rights in general.

Table 6.1: Area-wise and total awareness of Child Rights

Area/Total	*No.*	*Stage*	*Mean*	*S.D.*	*t-value*	*Significance level (0.05)*	*Null Hypothesis*
Child Rights and UDHR in Indian Constitution	80	Primary	38.54	3.02	0.98	Not significant	Accepted
	35	Secondary	39.17	3.47			
Child Rights and Law of protection of child rights	80	Primary	34.28	2.79	1.77	Not significant	Accepted
	35	Secondary	35.45	4.18			
Child Rights and Child Development	80	Primary	35.6	2.99	0.73	Not significant	Accepted
	35	Secondary	36.1	4.19			
Child rights and Deprived class child	80	Primary	31.48	3.12	3.72	Significant	rejected
	35	Secondary	33.9	3.44			
Child rights, curricular and school activity	80	Primary	16.88	1.69	3.61	Significant	rejected
	35	Secondary	17.68	1.96			
Total	80	Primary	156.8	9.33	2.41	Significant	rejected
	35	Secondary	162.31	14.74			

Table 6.2: Mean and S.D of Awareness scores

Area	*Primary*		*Secondary*	
	Mean	*S.D.*	*Mean*	*S.D.*
Total score	156.8	9.33	162.31	14.74
Child Rights and UDHR in Indian Constitution	38.54	3.02	39.17	3.47
Child Rights and Law of protection of child rights	34.28	2.79	35.45	4.18
Child Rights and Child Development	35.6	2.99	36.1	4.19
Child rights and Deprived class child	31.48	3.12	33.9	3.44
Child rights, curricular and school activity	16.88	1.69	17.69	1.96

Table 6.3: Mean scores of Whole group of teachers

Areas of child Rights	*Mean*
Total	162.19
Child rights and Universal declaration of human rights and Indian constitution.	39.15
Child rights and laws for protection of child rights.	35.49
Child rights and child development.	38.49
Child rights and deprived class child	33.34
Child rights and curricular activities	17.70

Summary of Findings

1) Significant difference was not found in the awareness level of primary and secondary teachers.
2) Significant difference was not found in the awareness about Child rights and universal declaration of human right and Indian constitution, Child rights and laws for protection of child right and Child rights and child development.
3) Significant difference was found in the Child rights and deprived class child and also the Child rights and curricular and school activity.
4) All the teachers were aware about the child Rights.

Discussion

The researcher also takes the interview of the primary and secondary teachers about the child rights. According to the that interview the researcher found out the theoretical knowledge about the child rights of the teachers are good but how to give the information and practical knowledge about child rights they don't know. In comparisons of the teachers, primary teacher are more knowledgeable than the secondary teacher. Primary teachers know how to implement the programme of the child rights.

Conclusion

From the above analysis, it was found that all the teachers were aware about the child Rights and primary teachers are doing well in giving the information about child rights.

References

Chauhan, R.S. (2009), Awareness of Working teachers and Prospective teachers to Human Rights: An Empirical Study. *GCTE Journal of Research and Education*, Vol. 4 (2) 8-14.

Dey, N. and Beck, B. (2010), "The Right of Children to Free and Compulsory Education Act, 2009: Teachers Perception". *Edusearch (Journal of Educational Research),* Vol. 2, No. 2, October 2011

Fatima J. (2011), "Right To Education—A Study on the Awareness of M.Ed. Trainees". *Edusearch (Journal of Educational Research)*, Vol. 2, No. 2, October 2011.

Kumar, D. and Sharma, S. (2011), "A Study of Parents and Teachers Awareness towards Right To Education Act 2009." *Edusearch (Journal of Educational Research),* Vol. 2, No. 2, October 2011.

Sunita, M. (2010), "Teachers Literacy towards the Child Rights". *Edusearch (Journal of Educational Research),* Vol. I, No. 2, October 2010

Sunita, M. (2011), "Awareness of B.Ed. Trainee Teachers towards Human Rights", *Horizon: The Journal of Education*, Vol. 1. January, 2011, pp. 15-21.

7

Elementary Education: Maladies and Remedial Measures

Prof. P.N. Muthiah

Children who develop an interest in learning before they enter elementary school are more likely to do well in school. Elementary Education should be preceded by a year or more of early childhood education which should pave a way for the development of desirable habits, knowledge attitude and skills.

Elementary education is base for the development of Higher Education. It is a proven fact Education development echoes in Nation's development. Having conceived this idea the Government of India has spent enormous money on elementary education in the successive years. For instance across India, investment in elementary education increased from Rs. 26,169 to Rs. 55,746 crores; per child allocation has increased from Rs. 2,004 (2009-2010) to Rs. 4,269 (2011-2012)

Incidentally fund allocation under RTE has doubled from Rs. 13,100 crore in 2009-2010 to Rs. 25,555 crore in 2012-2013, annual average drop out rate has come down from 9.1 per cent to 6.8 per cent, while enrolment has increased from 13.34 crore to 13.52 crore for the same period.

Inspite of huge expenditute on elementary education, participation of millions of teachers, the growth of enrolment, dropout, recruitment of teachers, expansion of education departments, growth of school buildings are uneven and lopsided. For instance the states which have seen a rise in drop outs include progressive ones like Tamilnadu and Gujarat. The number has even declined in states like Bihar, Jharkhand and U.P.

In other words, though funds are doubled, yet more primary children leaving in one third of states. Why this sorry state of affairs? Only one state i.e. Kerala boasts cent per cent literacy in Kottayam district. What about the rest of India? Statistics show that 29 per cent schools have pucca building, 23 per cent, teachers are untrained, 56 per cent schools have toilets for girls, 27 per cent schools don't have drinking water facility, 60 per cent schools are short of teachers, 09 per cent of schools have a single teacher for all classes. To cap it all, according to ILO estimate India has 45 million child labourers. The educationist, politicians declare this failure is due to vastness of this country, and huge population size.

The 2011 census suggests that about a fourth of India is illiterate. But the real number of people who can actually read and write is even lower. This needs to change. ASER reports that 51.8 per cent of standard V students cannot read text-books of standard II; 20.6 per cent standard VIII students cannot read standard II text-books; 75.9 per cent standard V students cannot identify numbers till 99; 43.2 per cent of standard V students cannot do simple mathematics.

The umpteen number of researches have been undertaken in the area of dropout and stagnation. The findings are not executed. Why do students dropout in spite of freebees? The reasons are enlisted as poverty and child labour; absence of toilets for girls; no potable drinking water; lack of play grounds; lack of teachers, caste discrimination, gender discrimination, lack of pre-schooling, lack of parental support in home, inadequate learning tools etc. It is complained that huge allocation of funds is drained in the form of salary, for school maintenance and for purchase of petty materials.

Even though educationists claim equity in education, increase in GDP, increase in literacy rate in some pockets of country education is in progress. Still India occupies 73rd rank in education in the world next to Kirghistan. Policy planners may pose as if illiteracy is being liquidated gradually and we are heading towards cent per cent literacy shortly, it looks like a distant dream.

The educationists should look into the lacunae in elementary education system. In other words educationists should plug holes and efforts must be taken to revamp elementary education system by way of changing curriculum in tune with technological development, reframing the teacher training programme.

Since, the whole higher education system is hovering around technology oriented society, the curriculum of elementary education must be thoroughly overhauled and consequently teachers must be oriented towards technology based training. In the name of feeding general knowledge, too many subjects are fed in elementary schools. The subjects must be minimized in curriculum.

With regard to curricular changes, following are the suggestions to revamp the system:

Educationists opine that even though education industry has grown leaps and bounds even educated people do not have values in life. It is because of absence of values in curriculum. So, values must be embedded in elementary education curriculum.

Since higher education centering round technology oriented education, and aims at entrepreneur oriented education, the elementary education curriculum must be changed with a view to prepare Technologists, and entrepreneurs.

To achieve, this goal the following steps can be immediately taken

- Present curriculum must be conceptually analysed.
- Psychological aspects related to the effective use of curriculum must be emphasised.
- Teaching–Learning Strategies must be developed suitable to the changing curriculum.
- Teaching skills must be identified to teach the new curriculum.
- Developing human values through curriculum at Primary stage.

While framing curriculum various psychological aspects must be taken into account with serious consideration. Hither to psychological aspects in elementary education curriculum was relegated to background.

For instance child's cognitive abilities must be identified through curriculum there must be provisions in the curriculum for suitable learning experiences to the child. Both interest and attitudes work as motivating forces that determine how far and in what ways the child will react to school life. So, Curriculum must help the child to build healthy interests and attitudes by way of curriculum experiences.

The role of needs and motives in the life of the child must find a place in curriculum.

Above all, in making effective use of curriculum the social needs of the child must be taken into account. Education is supposed to play an important role in harnessing the emotional energy of the child and guiding his emotional development. So, training of emotions must find a place in curriculum.

All the suggestions made so far are nothing but common sense. In other words, if the curriculum is redesigned with modern outlook, and learning strategies are modified, and teachers are adopting teaching styles with the focus of child psychology our elementary education will reap the desirable results.

8

Implementing CRC Norms in Schools: Supporting Actors and Structures Needed

Per Wickenberg

The aim of this article is to describe and explore what has happened and happens when international norms related to UN Convention on the Rights of the Child (1989) are meeting the normativity at very local school level in three countries in Asia-China (Inner Mongolia), India (Kerala) and Vietnam (Ho Chi Minh City, HCMC).[1] The time span in this chapter is 2003-2012 and the cases are connected to the Swedish International Training Programme "Child Rights, Classroom and School Management" funded by SIDA, the Swedish Development Agency and is carried out through Lund University. The programme started in 2003 and is oriented to target persons holding a position from where they could initiate processes of change in their home countries, schools and educational organisations. During 2003-2012 this training programme was arranged 16 times (17th time in September-October 2012) with some 500 participants completing it. Most of them are still working for child rights in their home countries and have formed national or regional networks (more on networks later in this chapter). In the new contract with SIDA in 2010 the training programme was slightly redesigned and is now arranged twice a year. Every batch has 30 participants and every country has three participants or *Change Agents* as they are called in the training programme. The three Asian countries mentioned above have had so far 86 participants of which China has: 26; India: 30 and Vietnam: 30 participants or change agents.

My aim is also to highlight what I have found in my research on norms: the "souls-of-fire-phenomenon" and the function of these dedicated, enthusiastic and important actors in the norm-implementation processes. Sometime you can see them as Change Agents in organisations, as they often pave the way for and establish new norms. Ellickson uses the term change agents for the people who first transmit new norms (Hechter and Opp 2001: 35). Bringing about change at schools are such that new norms set requires enthusiasts, movers or change agents who challenge old norms, who want to stake out new paths and establish new norms. One question involves the role that principals in schools play in building norm supporting structures and whether they may also serve as change agents with whom others can identify such that new norms are set. Implementation of new norms at the very local levels in schools, studied from sociology of law perspective, is important to the development of educational practice as well as adding new and useful knowledge in the understanding of social norms in implementation processes within schools and society.

Focusing Norms

Sociology of Law at Lund University has a special interest in and focus on the relation between norms, law and society and how the norms are communicated and socially reproduced. During the past few decades, theories and methods for studying norms and norm supporting structures at the individual and organisational level have been developed within the disciplines of sociology of law at Lund University (Hydén, 2002; Wickenberg, 1999; Svensson, 2008; Baier & Svensson, 2009; Leo, 2010; Persson, 2010; Larsson, & Svensson, 2012; Leo & Wickenberg, 2012). We would argue that sociology of law, given its focus on legal norms and other norms, offer a somewhat different perspective in studies that seek to explore, interpret and understand changes in the education system.

One problem with the word or concept "norm" is that it is used in so many different ways, both scientifically and in everyday language. In response, we proceeded based on a line of reasoning concerning the ontology of norms and what norms are. We use this sociology-of-law-based definition of the concept of norms, a definition that can meet the needs of both the social and legal sciences (Hydén & Svensson, 2008). This is also the definition with three core essences we use to identify norms: i) *Norms are action instructions*—norms are imperatives and thus directing actions, that is the very meaning of norms. ii) *Norms are socially reproduced.* Elster describes it as follows: "For norms to be social, they must be shared by other people" (Elster, 1992: 99). Wickenberg highlights the importance of communication and believes that the norms that are interesting to Sociology of Law are the ones that occur in a social context. They have social connections; social impacts and they are communicated in a social community (Wickenberg, 1999: 292). The direction for action must then be communicated and disseminated in a social community to live up to this essential attribute. In the our case, it means that the professional norms are reproduced in the school context. iii) *Norms represent the individual's perception of the expectations surrounding their own behaviour.* "Social norms cooperate expectations" (Elster, 1992: 97) and this is a widespread sociological starting point also expressed as a social pressure on individuals (Durkheim, 1895; Rommetveit, 1955).

Legal norms or laws are written (law in books) and most often visible and linked to the state and having a background in the political system. Social norms are based on relations among people, having a background in the interaction and communication that takes place between people. One criteria of a social norm is that it is not visible and not seen as written on a sign e.g. you are queuing in the shop, at the museum cinema or at the bus-stop—but there is never a sign saying that you have to queue up and take the last place in the line. But yet all of us know this and follow the social norm in this situation. It is spread between people in society—we learn it by imitating and seeing others doing so. Most often these social norms are related to the "lifeworld", talking by the wordings of the social scientist and social philosopher Jürgen Habermas (1981/1987). By professional norms we mean those norms that are communicated and socially reproduced within a certain professional context or local organisational culture e.g. among teachers in a local school. Professional norms are used to solve specific tasks, usually within a public authority or a private company, and having a background in knowledge developed by science or practical experience. Professional norms are often related to legal norms (law) and generated within political "system", using the concept used by Habermas (1981/1987). The main idea behind UN CRC is to establish a normativity in the states/societies that is based on values and norms according to Child Rights. Normativity, as argued by Reza Banakar (2012) is also more than merely social or moral norms. Normativity as such is very contextual. That is important in understanding the following on implementing new norms e.g. in schools and other social institutions.[2]

When new legal norms are introduced and implemented, starting in a top-down perspective, it is most often with an explicit purpose and intention to make changes of behaviour or action patterns in society or in organizations. I find these social phenomena most interesting from a sociology of law perspective in following the norm processes taking place at the very local level of implementation and application. My main research question have been for many years and still is: What will happen in the norm implementation processes at the very local level? This main question is followed by the sub questions: Why, how and where does the initiation of new norms take place? Who are the actors in these processes? And for the organization or school at stake: Which are the local supporting actors and structures that are working when new norms are taking root? Thus the sociology of law concepts in this article are norms and souls-of-fire or change agents in different organizational contexts, as well as norm supporting actors and structures at the local level in the implementation processes of new norms.

This sociology of law and norm approach have also and specifically been applied and developed in studies of implementation in education: Wickenberg 1999 & 2004; Hallerström 2006; Persson 2010 & 2012; Leo 2010 & 2012 (in this volume); Wickenberg & Leo 2012; Leo & Wickenberg 2012. These studies have contributed with new knowledge on norms and also about the vital function of education as an arena for formation of new norms. They also have contributed to the further development of the methodology on how to identify norms in organizations and to measure the strength of the norms. In the following I will use these sociology of law perspectives and apply them on three of the Asian countries in the above mentioned training programme on CRC and analyse how legal implementation of new CRC-related norms within different organizations in educational projects I am working in how are different new norms on Child Rights implemented by different key actors in the school and in educational organisations?

Implementation of New Norms on UN Child Rights Convention

The specific aim here is, as mentioned in the introduction part above, for me as mentor and lecturer during almost 10 years in the Advanced International Training Programme "Child Rights, Classroom and School Management", to reflect and analyze on the vast and rich empirical material and experiences from the implementation of legal norms related to the UN Child Rights Convention (CRC) in education and schools. I will do that especially from my own professional experiences 2003-2012 especially with schools in China, India and Vietnam using my Sociology of Law perspectives on educational processes. The overarching aim here is to analyze and reflect on the reported results of the implementations of CRC-related legal norms including my experiences. I will use material from the three countries (mentioned above) Project Reports written when completed the first year or cycle of the programme, and also using notes and reflections from my own Mentor Reports, written over the years when visiting the project sites and participating teams in their home countries and own educational contexts.

I will also use the empirical base constituted by e.g. the Report book, *Taking Child Rights Seriously*, written after the first five years of the programme, Wickenberg *et al.* 2009[3], but also to use all empirical material in the 30 final reports written by the country teams where I have been the mentor in the programme. During these ten years of work in the CRC Programme with 16 batches in training, I have made 36 separate field visits, each visit of about 6-10 working days, in "my" three countries and also participated in 15 Progress seminars including local school visits in as many countries. The programme as a whole today has 160 participating teams of three participants in each team. Most of the change projects—done by all teams as part of the training programme—in these three mentioned countries are focusing the right to "participation" related to CRC article 12, 13 and 14—respect for the views of the child; Child´s Right t freedom of expression; and Child´s right to freedom of thought, conscience and religion.

Points of Departure in the Implementation of CRC

In the reflections three levels of education in society, connecting to the recruiting of principles for the three participants forming the country teams in this ITP, have been used as the starting points: the local school and community level; the provincial/regional/district level; and the national/state level in society.[4] This is starting as a clear "top-down" process with a start at the international level. When starting to implement some new ideas, norms or policy documents on the very local level of a school or in society, you will soon find out (as we have noticed above) that you already existing social norms and dedicated people ("souls of fire" or change agents) and committed organizations (e.g. NGOs) working in the issue at stake (forming the local under-stream when new norms are to be initiated or to take root). The question is what is happening and has happened on the local level regarding CRC in the education sector the projects in this training programme have continued over the first year of the project in the training programme and then onwards. As mentioned before, establishing and new norms (legal and professional or social norms) can it be seen as a key feature of the empowerment of excluded groups (often most children and women), as they are an important steering mechanism towards values, behaviours, attitudes and action patterns in the society. I will finally sum up and focus some of the experiences and factors that are vital in the establishing of new norms based on the CRC-related legal norms.

I have identified and noted that very dedicated persons—or "souls of fire" or "change agents" (Ellickson in Hechter & Opp 2001:40)—are important as driving and/or supporting actors in transforming, mediating and supporting new norms in organisations. Those key actors were very vital in start making change of expectations and applying new in the investigated schools (Wickenberg 1999:451-). The souls of fire or change agents often challenge old norms, habits and routines in their search for new pathways in establishing new norms (Leo & Wickenberg 2012). I also noted that the key actors were bringing and transforming—using Habermas (1981/1987) wordings and interpretations—their values and social norms from "lifeworld into the school system". I will later get back to this interesting and crucial social phenomenon in these educational processes.

Establishing Professional Networks of Change Agents

Establishing professional networks of change agents is one of the most important steps in this competence and capacity building for supporting the new norms to take root. The CRC-network is one of the preconditions for sustainable implementation of new CRC-norms. Kerala state in the southwest of India is that one good example of autonomous networking. Today 26 professionals within education that are former participants, or change agents, continuing to work on the application of new norms related to CRC in the education in the state of Kerala. They are now working in six of the 14 districts in the state with some 35 million people. The change agents have now established a well-functioning CRC-network that has their regular meetings and workshops. They also support the state Education Department in Kerala on in-service training on CRC for teachers, principals, teacher trainers and education office. Furthermore they have initiated changes in curricula and written and published policy documents and books as teaching-learning guidelines on CRC in education for teachers and principals.

This Kerala network have some key persons (supporting actors)—being former participants in the programme—as change agents that are acting as coordinators in Kerala on further implementation of CRC-norms in schools and education. They have good contacts by personal meetings, by mobile phone or e-mail with all the other 23 change agents they meet regularly in the network. The network is supporting each other and other professionals applying and communicating new norms related to CRC in education. Three of change agents are now retired as educational leaders but they are still committed and convinced of their continued work applying CRC-norms in their education system in the districts of Kerala. They are also communicating the new norms to other professionals schools and education in their near districts. The participants are mostly doing this continued work on implementing new norm on CRC within their ordinary professional work positions on a district or at provincial level. The network and coordinators are very skilled in connecting to local media when they are presenting something new on norm implementation and other CRC-related news in schools and with in education. The change agents bringing their personal values lifeworld—as noted above—into the educational system and are socially reproducing new norms CRC.

Similar work on establishing networks and new norms on CRC by change agents are experienced in Vietnam and Inner Mongolia, China. The cooperation between LU and Inner Mongolia started in September 2003 when Mr. Sun Baijung, the Head of the Teacher Training Section of the Inner Mongolia Education Department in the regional capital Hohhot, participated in this SIDA funded ITP "Child Rights, Classroom and School Management" during 2003 and 2004. Since then, Mr. Sun Baijun has been a highly motivated key person in building a network of participants, so-called "change agents" or "solus-of-fire", on the CRC (Child Rights Convention) in the educational areas of Inner Mongolia with participants and teachers and headmasters from Hohhot city with some primary, secondary and high schools, Inner Mongolia Normal University (a Teacher Training University), Tongliao city with some High Schools (Middle Schools), Kunlun County with primary schools and Chifeng city with Chifeng University and Chifeng Middle schools. Mr. Sun Baijun also actively participated in the Seminars in Bangkok in 2009. He has been the Chinese coordinator who has been able to recruit new change agents from different parts of Inner Mongolia. After these has been finishing the training programme on CRC he has communicated with them to make them part of the regional network year by year which appeared to be a sustainable strategy. Sun Baijun also started spin-off-trainings with his own principals in primary schools in the countryside within Kulun County. These principals and local leaders in their turn continued the norm changing processes in their schools and with their teachers and parents. I was there on a follow-up visit in 2010 and the changes made in the schools. One of these principals now working as a district education officer spreading his experiences others as a change agent.

Some what different and the establishing of a CRC network there. In Hanoi it was done in a simple way and it still works as I was meeting the network in February 2011 some seven years after the first participants in the CRC-training programme (Ms Hahn coming from Save the Children Sweden in Hanoi). But the way to establish a network in HCMC in Vietnam was a bit different. Mr. Le Ngoc Diep, division Head at the Department of Education and Training in Ho Chi Minh City, was connected somewhat later to the training programme on one hand through Ms Hanh in Hanoi and on the other hand via one principal in Ho Chi Minh City, Ms My Hanh, in the training programme in batch 10 (2009). Then the participants followed by principals with the help of Mr Diep together with participants from the Teacher Training University in HCMC and District Education Office or Department of Education HCMC. Base and a critical mass of change agents on the right positions established. Mr Diep gave the change agents and the CRC-network support and the legitimacy that was the important norm supporting actor.

School Principals as Change Agents and as Supporting Actors

In the projects I also noted that the school principals of the local schools in Kerala—as seen above in Ho Chi Minh City in Vietnam—are important key persons or actors when supporting the establishing of new norms in the CRC implementation in schools. They are most often norm setters or norm breakers arenas. They also create different arenas for students, teachers and parents on meetings and communications on new norms on CRC within their schools. The examples heading for participation and ownership are class councils, schools councils and school parliaments, and PPTA (pupils-parents-teachers-association). Principals we have noticed are very important in these change processes regarding students influence real participation in decision making in the schools. Communication is as vital and important for creating and establishing the new norms (see the definition of norms above). That goes for teachers, students (student councils for active participation in decision making processes), parents (parents and students for participation) and also including persons from the local community and local government in the communication on new legal norms (Wickenberg *et al.* 2009:44).

At the same time it is essential to a critical view on especially the "souls of fire" that could "burn" only for herself or himself and not being connected to and in due pace with the processes in the rest of the school or the organization. They could sometimes have their own agenda based personal needs in this process and that could be a real problem regarding the sustainability of the new norms (Wickenberg 1999:451).

Similar experiences regarding norm setters and norm breakers in a constructive way, experienced in (26 participants and 23 change agents in Inner Mongolia) (30 participants and 14 change agents in Ho Chi Minh City 13 in Hanoi City). Inner Mongolia, an autonomous region in northern, new norms are initiated and established in three big cities with focus teacher training universities (IMNU, Inner Normal University in the Inner Mongolia capital, and Chifeng University) and Teacher Training Colleges, Tongliao Vocational College (see Change Projects 2012:29). Similar processes with in schools are experienced in, especially in Ho Chi Minh City. With real norm support from their leaders in the Education department—act change agent or souls of fire in initiating new norms creating processes with students, teachers and parents in their schools. The old norm on the disappearing some time after continuous work on the changes.

The networks and the change agents (or former participants) are now forming sustainable networks, new social arenas, student councils for communication and social reproduction of new norms on CRC. They have the driving force for change, and their key persons and education leaders are at a relatively high level and they have possibilities of making changes in opportunities for enlarging their space of action. The networks and the change agents are planning and producing teaching-learning materials and policy documents on applying CRC in local schools and education. They are involving other partners and testing new methods in local schools. In that way they are also testing and applying new norms in their local context. They are finding new ways to break old norms and introducing new norms based on CRC (Change Projects 2012:189 and Change Projects 2012:57-and 193-). Examples of this is clearly noted in Kerala (in six districts) and in Ho Chi Minh City and also in Kunlun County in the eastern parts of Inner Mongolia in China. When there is a norm supporting principal the teachers or other change agents ("souls-of-fire") were able to implement and develop new norms on CRC in the school or in education. We have also noticed that the CRC-related norms then could be disseminated to other parts of the local community through parents and the PTAs.

In the reflections on the examples from the different countries' and teams' projects for change work, the following have been noted and experienced: i) They have established norm supporting networks of change agents or programme participants with social arenas for communication and application of new norms. ii) The networks have dedicated key persons and principals (or other educational leaders in schools) who are supporting actors in organizing the continued and ongoing educational and social activities on new norms on CRC within the network. iii) The networks and the key persons are supporting initiation and establishing new norms and they are aware of and understanding what they are doing this and why. iv) The dissemination and communication of CRC-norms are being done horizontally on the local level i.e. outward from the pilot project or project school, partly to other schools and partly to the local community as such: parents, families, politicians, organizations and the different local media. This dissemination is called the horizontal primary dissemination. v) Here, the media, the local newspapers and television play an important role for the dissemination, communication and social reproduction of results and support of the new norms on CRC to be spread in schools and education. vi) It could be seen in this empirical material that there is ongoing interplay between legal norms and social norms regarding CRC. Professionals are bringing in their values from their life world to the educational system.

It has became empirically evident that implementation of CRC-norms with dedicated change agents and networks can be used as tools for establishing new norms and attitudes to children and adults (and teachers and parents). All these factors are supporting the children's rights at different levels in society which in turn could lead to changed behaviour or action patterns. They in fact constitute the social actors and competences which are the norm supporting actors and structures in implementing and applying new norms in organizations at the local schools in the mentioned three countries. Another important experience is the congruence between the new legal norm and the existing social norm at the local level. In the beginning there is a conflict between the old norms (traditional norms) and the new norms. A good example is the way parents and teachers are viewing *corporal punishment*, violating the CRC-norm on the right of protection from all forms on violence and maltreatment (CRC article 19). After some time and with good supporting examples, role models and social arenas for communication and discussions, the changes to a new norm according to CRC is noticed in the school and in the local community. The dissemination to other teachers in the schools is also vital in these norm spreading processes. The professional colleagues to the norm-breaking teacher is also crucial to offer a supporting structure as well as the social arenas supporting. All these factors are important findings to the development of educational practice as well as adding new knowledge to the understanding the function of norms in implementation processes in schools and education.

Conclusions

The following conclusions, as mentioned above, are based on the international—empirical based sociology of law themes in projects on implementation and application of new legal norms on CRC (UN Child Rights Convention) at the local level in society, in schools or organisations. My aim of this chapter was to describe and explore the similarities in implementation of legal norms in the international educational projects I have been involved in for many years. The results are in short the social reproduction as well as the essential norm supporting actors and structures that I have found in these research projects.

Leaders and Leadership and "Souls of Fire"

Including *principals* in different organizations is vital to the support change agents, key persons and other norm setters in the implementation and communication of new norms that can lead to changes in behaviour (see Leo 2012; Leo & Wickenberg 2012; Wickenberg 2012). *Key persons or dedicated actors* ("Souls of fire" or change agents) or even *principals* are those on one hand driving forces and on the other hand supporting actors who are trying to find ways to initiate and establish new norms or to break old norms, and making paths for new ones. They are often important role models regarding new norms for the teachers, for the parents, for the students and local community officials—and they have in most cases built up the legitimacy of the local norm leader. They are also the crucial actors who often are bringing their personal values and ideas from the lifeworld into the system, to use the concepts from Habermas 1981/1987 (Wickenberg 1999:451 ff). Creating or forming different and active *social and professional arenas* for communication, social reproduction of new norms and active participation by different actors in this processes is an important supporting structure in implementing new norms in organizations.

Social Arenas for Communication

The school's infrastructure for CRC or social reproduction of new norms by the mentioned supporting actors are seen to be one of the most essential factors in this process of establishing norms on the local level. Communication among actors in the organization and clear definitions—and thereby following understanding—of involved concepts like "sustainable development" or "public participation" or "child rights" are important support for the implementation and realisation of new norms in organizations as in schools. *Media*—including social media—play an important and supportive role in communication and social reproduction of new norms. To be able to communicate professionally one need to have established social arenas for those meeting places. On these arenas the new norms could be tested, verified and then spread out in the organisations or schools as professional norms. These arenas are vital to the rooting and to the social reproduction of the norms and those are also part of the infrastructure in the schools. We have also seen good examples of how big signs or wall papers in school yards have been built up to visually underline the importance and the vital content in Child Rights Conventions to be seen and read by the students. Those are part of the norm supporting structures in the schools.

External resources and *professional knowledge* are vital support to be used in implementation processes' on new norms on the local level. External resources could be—as we have seen in the three countries above—resource persons at the district or provincial level. We have experienced this in Kerala (DIET officers in the six districts), Ho Chi Minh City (Divisional Head at the Department of Education and Training and their officers) and in Inner Mongolia (director of Teacher Education Division at the Education Department of Inner Mongolia Autonomous Region). At these levels we have met many key person that are making a difference to the local level when they are acting as supporting actors to the change agents on the local school level. We often forget to realise these—to some extent to the local school external resources—active supporting actors.

Legal Documents and Policy Documents

These are is more important than we sometimes regard them. When the change agents or "the souls-of-fire" are active in taking initiatives in establishing new norms on a local level they use the law as a moral support for their work. Legal norms and legal documents with clear formulations are needed as a moral support for change agents in establishing and rooting new norms in organisations or schools. Another important experience and result in these studied and explored implementation processes is the important matching or congruence between the legal norms and the existing social norm at the local level. If the mutual fitting is too far away from each other it is difficult to get a sustainable application on the local level. On the contrary, if the legal and the social norms are congruent and near, the implementation process will work smoothly and it will be sustainable also.

All items mentioned are important supporting factors or aspects to be able to get a deeper understanding of the preconditions for implementing and establishing new norms, actions and action competences in educational or participation contexts in organizations at the local level. On the contrary, if the supporting actors and supporting structures are missing in the implementation processes of new norms at local level. It will of course be a clear hindrance for the creation and anchoring in the developing processes of new norms (Hydén & Wickenberg 2004:39) and that will be an evident loss of social capacity. When working with aim and ambition to establish new norms at local level in organizations, you have to be aware of and have knowledge of these mentioned preconditions and capacities when starting such processes of implementing and applying norm processes. A clearly formulated norm strategy is needed by the principals, the project leaders and/or the management when to start establishing new norms, otherwise this will not be successful.

As my main conclusion, these sociology of law studies have contributed with knowledge about the role of education and participation as (learning and) communicative arenas for supporting formations of new norms at the local level in organizations. To have a sustainable development in establishing new norms on the local level, the organization needs to have-or to build-supporting actors, or change agents and supporting structures for the norm-creating social processes. Those supporting factors as mentioned above are the vital knowledge, competences and prerequisites needed for successful implementing and applying new legal norms at the local level. This knowledge should be integrated as concrete and already useable part when making new laws or policies.

Notes

1. Norms in UNCRC are many but some core examples are: the right to nondiscrimination; the right to protection; the right to provision of food, shelter, education; the right to life and maximum survival and development; the right to participation in decision making regarding the child's own life; the right to freedom of expression; the right to freedom of thought, conscience and religion etc.
2. "Hence, the main argument of this paper that social and moral norms are not the only sources of normativity. Social systems and institutional settings of the law, polity, economy and the administration of society also exercise normativity, a form of normativity which should be understood

in its own right instead of being reduced to individual social or moral norms of behaviour." (Reza Banakar, 2012).

3. Parts of this programme have been published in the Indian International Journal *Academia*, No 1, 2012: 20-26. See also mentioned above Wickenberg, P. et al (2009) *Taking Child Rights seriously*, Lund: Lund University and in *Change Projects from International Training Programme: Child Rights, Classroom and School Management*, Batch 12, and later with the same title but regarding Batch 13 (both published in Spring 2012, at Lund University).
4. These words or concepts could be very different from country to country. The organizational principles of a State or a country, experienced, realised and learned so far, is very contextual. The same goes for Provincial and District levels in different countries.

References

Baier, Matthias and Åström, Karsten (eds. 2012), *Social and Legal Norms*, Ashgate (forth-coming)

Baier, Matthias (ed. 2009), *Participative aspects of law—a socio-legal perspective,* Lund Studies in Sociology of Law 31, Lund University, Sweden

Baier, Matthias, and Svensson, Måns (2009), *On normer* (About norms). Malmö: Liber

Banakar, Reza (2012), Can Legal Sociology Account for the Normativity of Law*?,* in Baier and Åström (eds. 2012), *Social and Legal Norms*, (Ashgate, forthcoming)

Change Projects from the International Training Programme Child Rights, Classroom and School Management, Final reports, Batch 12, Lund: Lund University, 2012.

Change Projects from the International Training Programme Child Rights, Classroom and School Management, Final reports, Batch 13, Lund: Lund University, 2012.

Durkheim, Emile (1982), *The Rules of Sociological Methods and Selected Texts on Sociology and it's Method.* New York: Free Press.

Ellickson, Robert C. (2001), The Evolution of Social Norms: A Perspective from the Legal Academy, in Hechter, Michael & Opp, Karl-Dieter (red) (2001), *Social Norms*. New York: Russel Sage Foundation

Elster, Jon (1992), *The Cement of Society, a study of social order*. Cambridge University Press

Habermas, Jürgen (1981/1987), *The Theory of Communicative Action*, Volume 1 and 2. Cambridge: Polity Press

Hallerström, Helena (2006), *Rektorer normer I ledarskapet för skolutveckling*, Lund Studies in Sociology of Law 23, Lund University.

Hechter, Michael and Opp, Karl-Dieter (red) (2001), *Social Norms*. New York: Russel Sage Foundation

Hydén, H. and Wickenberg, P. (2004), *Utvärderingsstudie av Venprojektet. Slutrapport.* Research reports in Sociology of Law 2004: 2, Lunds universitet.

Hydén, Håkan and Svensson, Måns (2008), *The Concept of Norms in Sociology of Law*, in Håkan Hydén and Per Wickenberg (eds., 2008), "Contributions in Sociology of Law. Remarks from a Swedish Horizon". Lund Studies in Sociology of Law 29. Lund University (this article is also published in *Law and Society, Scandinavian Studies in Law*, Volume 53, p. 15-32, Stockholm University, Law Faculty 2008)

Hydén, Håkan (2002), *Normvetenskap (*Science of Norms*). Lund Studies in Sociology of Law*. Lund University.

Leo, Ulf and Wickenberg, Per (2012), *Implementation of education for sustainable development—A study of the principals´ role in the work change* (forthcoming)

Leo, Ulf (2010), *Rektorer bör och rektorer gör. En rättssociologisk studie om att identifiera, analysera och förstå professionella normer* (Principals should and principals do. A sociology of law study on how to identify, analyse and understand professional norms). *Lund Studies in Sociology of Law* 34. Lund: Lund University

Persson, Lars (2010), *Pedagogerna och demokratin,* Teachers and Democracy: Developing Democracy in Education from a Perspective of Sociology of Law. *Lund Studies in Sociology of Law* 22. Lund: Lund University

Rommetveit, Ragnar (1955), *Social Norms and Roles, Explorations in the psychology of ending social pressures*. Minnesota: University of Minnesota Press

Svensson, Måns and Larsson, Stefan (2012), Intellectual property law compliance in Europe: Illegal file sharing and the role of social norms, in *New Media and Society,* Sage Publications, April 2012.

Svensson, Måns (2008), *Sociala normer och regelefterlevnad. Trafiksäkerhetsfrågor ur ett rättssociologiskt perspektiv.* (Social Norms and Observance of Law. Traffic Safety in the Perspective of Sociology of Law.) *Lund Studies in Sociology of Law* 28. Lund University.

UN Child Rights Convention, UN General Assembly resolution 44/25, November 20, 1989, Entry into force September 2, 1990.

Wickenberg, P., Norm supporting structures in environmental education and education for sustainable development. In: P. Wickenberg, *et al.* (eds. 2004): *Learning to change our world? Swedish research on education and sustainable development*. Lund: Studentlitteratur.

Wickenberg, Per (1999), Norm Supporting Structures. Environmental Theme is beginning to take root in schools. *Lund Studies in Sociology of Law* 5. Lund University

Wickenberg, Per (2009), The unknown but well-known wells in Holma, in Baier, Matthias (ed. 2009) *Participative aspects of law—a socio-legal perspective, Lund Studies in Sociology of Law* 31, Lund University, Sweden, p. 167-183.

Wickenberg, Per (2010), "The unknown but well-known wells in Holma—Public participation in the City Tunnel Project in Malmö", in *Retfaerd*, 2011, 34, Nr. 2/133:42-58

Wickenberg, Per (2012), Souls of fire and implementing new norms in organizations. The importance of norm supporting actors and structures, in Baier and Åström (eds. 2012) "*Social and Legal Norms*" (Ashgate, forthcoming)

Wickenberg, Per *et al.* (2009), *Taking Child Rights Seriously. Reflections on five years of an International Training Programme*. Lund: Lund University

Wickenberg, Per, and Leo, Ulf (2012), *Rättslig reglering av miljö och hållbar utveckling i svensk* skola. *Vad hände på lagstiftningsarenan mellan 1990-2011?* (forthcoming)

9

In the Best Interest of the Child: Change Agents' Efforts to Reduce Drop-Out in Malawi

Ulf Leo

Malawi is a sub Saharan country with approximately 15 million people and a lot of challenges. This is a description of efforts to make change, promoting children's rights, in a rural area in Malawi and it is also an attempt to analyze an intervention with a theoretical perspective based on a concept of norms.

The intervention is primarily based on the United Nations Convention on the Rights of the Child (CRC) and that is also the legal point of departure for the theoretical Sociology of Law perspectives. The leaders of the world decided in 1989 that children under 18 years needed a special convention and most of the countries in the world soon ratified it. Today 193 countries have committed themselves to undertake the obligations of the 54 articles. The four core principles of the Convention, according to UNICEF, are non-discrimination; devotion to the best interests of the child; the right to life, survival and development; and respect for the views of the child.

The study is focusing the implementation of CRC in education, especially Article 28 about the child's right to education. The ratifying states have agreed on an education on the basis of equal opportunity; with free primary education; to encourage the development of different forms of secondary education including general and vocational education; to make them available and accessible to every child, and to take appropriate measures such as the introduction of free education and offering financial assistance in case of need; and to take measures to encourage regular attendance at schools and the reduction of drop-out rates (from Article 28 UN Convention on the Rights of the Child).

Challenges in Education

A lot of people in Malawi are poor. According to UNICEF data of 2010, 74 per cent of the population is living below the international poverty line of US$ 1.25 per day. This is, of course, affecting education a lot.

The Millennium Development Goal number 2 is to achieve *Universal Primary Education* by the year 2015. In Malawi two national initiatives have been successful—abolition of school fees and promoting education for girls[1]. But still there is a long way to go (Table 9.1)

Table 9.1: UNICEF Data Refer to the Most Recent Year Available During the Period 2007-2010

Primary education, standard 1-8	*Female*	*Male*
Gross enrolment ratio per cent	121	118
Net enrolment ratio per cent	94	89
Attendance ratio per cent	79	76
Secondary education, form 1-4	*Female*	*Male*
Net enrolment ratio per cent	24	26
Attendance ratio per cent	20	19

(www.unicef.org)

In Malawi there used to be a gap, with more boys in school, but the data is showing that the gap between female and male students have been closed, perhaps as a result of the special efforts of promoting education for girls. But the figure also shows the great number of drop out in Malawi, and there are several reasons. Poverty is a reason for drop out and the abolition of school fees is one way to reduce the dropout rate.

Another reason for dropout is *teenage pregnancies*. In Malawi 9 per cent of the girls are married by the age of 15 and 50 per cent by the age of 18 (UNICEF, 2010).

A third reason for drop out is child labour. The term child labour is often defined as work that deprives children of their childhood, their potential and their dignity, and that is harmful to physical and mental development. The International Labour Organization (ILO) refers to child labour as work that:

- is mentally, physically, socially or morally dangerous and harmful to children; and
- interferes with their schooling by;
- depriving them of the opportunity to attend school;

- obliging them to leave school prematurely; or
- requiring them to attempt to combine school attendance with excessively long and heavy work.(www.ilo.org)

The Convention concerning the Prohibition and Immediate Action for the Elimination of the Worst Forms of Child Labour, known in short as the Worst Forms of Child Labour Convention, was adopted by the International Labour Organization (ILO) in 1999 as ILO Convention No 182. As of April 2012, the convention had been ratified by 175 out of 183 ILO members and Malawi had ratified the convention already in November 1999.

In Malawi, as many as 26 per cent children from 5 to 14 years of age, are involved in labour activities (UNICEF Survey 2010). A child is considered to be involved in child labour activities under the following classification: (a) children 5 to 11 years of age during the week preceding the survey did at least one hour of economic activity or at least 28 hours of domestic work, and (b) children 12 to 14 years of age during the week preceding the survey did at least 14 hours of economic activity or at least 42 hours of economic activity and domestic work combined.

In conclusion the official data is pointing at three big challenges and reasons for dropout; poverty, teenage pregnancies, and child labour.

The Change Effort

The project for change, in focus here, started 2008 by a team of three Malawians taking part in an international training programme, Child Rights Classroom and School Management. The programme is given by Lund University in Sweden and funded by the Swedish Development and cooperation Agency (SIDA). 30 participants from 10 different developing countries form a batch, and since the start in 2003 there have been 16 batches trained so far. The first phase was three weeks of training in Sweden that ends with a project plan where each team is elaboration on the question—what is to be different in our context concerning implementation of children's rights in education? The team members represent different levels—local, district and national level of the educational system.

The First Team

The Malawian team of batch 8 chose to work in a rural area west of the capital Lilongwe, close to the border of Zambia. Teenage pregnancies and child labour is more frequent in this district than in the rest of the country thus, the drop out ratio in general is higher. The data in the figure below is showing that the dropout rate due to pregnancy is considerably higher in the rural schools, but in dropout schools is slowly decreasing. One explanation is an increased knowledge of family planning. The data in the figure below is revealing the fact that a lot of girls, especially in rural areas, are denied their right to education and that was a point of departure for the project.

Table 9.2: Drop Out Due to Pregnancy, Data from the Respective Schools

	Dropout due to pregnancy	
	Urban secondary school (Lilongwe)	*Rural secondary school (Project area)*
2008	1-2	12
2005	2-4	10-12
2000	4	14-15
1995	6	17
1990	7-8	17

The aim of the project was to promote Children's Rights and to increase access and equity to quality education of learners in line with CRC Articles 28 and 29; Millennium Development Goal 2; Malawi Growth and Development Strategy (MGDS) and Malawian National Educational Sector Plan (NESP).

By the end of the project, 2010, the following was expected:

- Learners' enrolment increased
- Reduced dropout rate due to pregnancy
- Increased awareness in Child Rights by all stakeholders
- Learners had acquired knowledge on sexual reproductive health and life skills

It is of course a great challenge to reach objectives like those in such a short period.

Activities Led by the First Team

The team started with resource mobilization in their organisations, and seeking alliances with local NGO's and community leaders. The team continued with the sensitization process by holding meetings and workshops for all stakeholders. The content was focusing children's right to education (Article 28) as well as the aim of education (Article 29). In this area a lot of parents do not see what good education will bring to their daughters and sons, so the first step in the intervention was to enhance and show the meaning of education. To reach parents and key persons in the community the team of three change agents also used media, radio and television. In this way information about children's rights could be communicated and panel discussions were organised. Local NGO's were invited to support and strengthen the change efforts.

In the schools the information meetings on the content of the convention were followed by drama and debate in the classrooms. A new subject, Life Skills including sexual reproductive health, was introduced. Life skills teachers were trained in the capital city, Lilongwe, and they were also taught new and more learner-centred teaching methods to use in the classrooms.

The Second Team

Another team of three followed in 2009. The aim was the same, to reduce drop out, but this time the focus was to reduce the child labour that caused dropout. The target area was the same and the project was placed at the same secondary school but this time another secondary school and a primary school were included in the project. The second team could, of course, benefit from the work of the first group. Traditional leaders and other key persons in the area had a positive effect on parents and students on all the schools in the area.

A baseline study on the three project schools gave the same biggest reasons for drop out as other studies; poverty, child labour and pregnancy. These three factors could, of course, be linked to each other given that poverty could lead to child labour or pregnancy. The results in this area indicated child labour as the main reason for dropping out of primary school and pregnancy as the main reason in secondary school. Farm work is the main type of employment for children in the area, followed by household work and cattle herding. A problem in rural area, west from Lilongwe, is children working on big estates growing tobacco. A surprising, and disturbing, finding was that most of these children are paid less than 200 Malawian kwacha (much less than 1 US$) a *month*. This reveals the strong link between child labour and poverty, where 1.25 US$ a *day* is the limit. It was also found out that most of these children start working at the age of ten. The specific objectives expected to be achieved by this second team are:

- Reduced absenteeism in schools around Mkanda area.

- Children in the area will be able to positively and actively participate in school activities.
- Reduction of school dropout.
- Children in Mkanda area will be able to know their rights and claim them once abused.
- The community of Mkanda will be able to offer full support to children's activities both at school and outside school environment in order to safeguard the rights of children in the area.

Activities Led by the Second Team

The second project started in October 2009 followed the same structure as the predecessors by awareness and sensitisation meetings with the traditional authority of the area, traditional leaders, religious leaders and other key persons in the community, parents, PTA (Parent, Teacher Association) and the Mothers Group[2]. The same activities were conducted in the school and classrooms with principals[3], teachers and students followed by debates, drama and other activities involving students.

A Norm Perspective on Change Efforts to Reduce Drop-Out Rate

Working as a teacher in the training programme, Child Rights, Classroom and School Management, I followed both teams, first during a 3-week training in Sweden, then on a 2-week follow up session, and finally after a year, on location in the project area west from Lilongwe. My analysis and conclusions as a researcher, below are built on interviews and observations with the six change agents, teachers, principals, students, parents, traditional leaders, and religious leaders in the area and on the targeted schools. The theoretical framework used is a Sociology of Law based perspective with a special focus on the relation between legal and other norms.

Theoretical Framework-Culture and the Norms Within

The two projects aim at reducing drop-out rate in the schools in a rural district. They have initiated change in the schools as organisations and doing so they also had to consider the "extended" organisation since so many external factors affect the school as an organisation. This means that parents and community leaders are closely linked to the schools and thus closely linked with the school organisations. In this case it is not possible to totally separate the school as an organisation from the surrounding community—it seldom is. Never the less the main focus is on the schools, with the aim of reducing drop-out rate, and that is the reason for using theories linking culture, organisations and norms with each other.

The image of organisations as cultures (Morgan, 2006; Alvesson, 2002) is used as a theoretical approach to support the study to identify and analyse norms in the two combined projects aiming at reducing drop out. Cultures are generally described as development patterns of the organisation in terms of knowledge, values, rituals, ideologies, actions, laws and norms (*ibid*). Hemmelgarn refers Organizational Culture to the shared norms, beliefs, and behavioural expectations that drive behaviour and communicate what is valued in organizations and organizational culture is which often described as the "way things are done around here," (Hemmelgarn *et al.* 2006). Hoy and Miskel (2008) give a general definition of organizational culture as a "system of shared orientations that hold the unit together and give it a distinctive identity" (2008:177). In this case I have a special focus on the norms guiding Implementation of the UN Convention on the Rights of the Child (CRC) in the schools.

Culture as Shared Norms

According to Alvesson "Culture is a tricky concept as it is easily used to cover everything and consequently nothing" (2002:13). He means that culture often refers to surface phenomena rather than explores the meanings and ideas behind them. In this study is on focus the norms in the school culture.

The influence culture has on the members in the organisation varies, and there are often several sub-cultures in an organisation. A problem with studying organisational culture and the norms in it is that norms and culture is often unconscious and covert (Elster, 1992; Rommetveit, 1955). Norms play an important role in human interaction, they reduce uncertainty about how to act in different situations, they set standards and specify what appropriate behaviour is, and there are different expectations of different people (students, teachers and principals) in the organisation (Giddens, 1989:31). Norms are usually unwritten which are affected by informal expectations and they directly influence behaviour. Norms determine for example the way people talk in the organisation, the way participants respond to authority, conflict or pressure and how they balance self-interest with organisational interest (Hoy and Miskel, 2005: 78).

The norms of a work group define a big part of the culture of the organisation and that it is important to be aware of social and professional norms that influence the organisation. One problem is the intertwined relation between culture and norms as they are stated as functions of

Culture according to Robbins (1998) and as functions of Norms according to Elster (1992), Alvesson (2002), and Baier and Svensson (2009). Culture and Norms provide standards of behaviour, creates distinctions among organizations, provides the organization with a sense of identity, enhances stability in the social system, social glue that binds the organization together (*ibid*). The conclusion is that both strong cultures (Hoy and Miskel, 2008) and strong norm systems (Elster, 1992) can promote or impede development and change processes.

One problem with the term "norm" is that it is used in so many different ways, both scientifically and in everyday parlance. In response I proceeded is based on a line of reasoning concerning the ontology of norms and what norms are. I use this sociology-of-law-based definition of the concept of norms, a definition that can meet the needs of both the social and legal sciences (Hydén and Svensson, 2008). This is also the definition I use to identify and to analyse norms in this case:

Norms are action instructions—norms are imperatives and thus directing actions, that is the very meaning of norms. *Norms are socially reproduced.* Elster describes it as follows: "For norms to be social, they must be shared by other people" (Elster, 1992: 99). Wickenberg highlights the importance of communication and believes that the norms that are interesting to Sociology of Law and are the ones that occur in a social context. They have social connections; social impacts and they are communicated in a social community (Wickenberg, 1999: 292). The direction for action must then be communicated and disseminated in a social community to live up to this essential attribute. Norms represent the individual's perception of the expectations surrounding their own behaviour. "Social norms do cooperate expectations" (Elster, 1992: 97) and this is a widespread sociological starting point and is also expressed as a social pressure on individuals (Durkheim, 1895; Rommetveit, 1955).

According to sociologist Therborn we may follow a norm out of our *identification* with the norm source and its values (2002: 869). Ellickson uses the term 'change agents' for the people who first transmit new norms (Hechter and Opp 2001: 35). Bringing about change at schools are such that new norms are set which requires enthusiasts or change agents who challenge old norms, who want to stake out new paths and establish new norms. One question involves the role that the Change Agents in the CRC-programme play in building norm supporting structures in schools and communities, but there is also a need for new local change agents with whom others can identify old norms which are changed or new norms are set.

Discussion and Conclusion

The outcomes of both projects are difficult to measure. It takes time to change norms both in schools and in communities and it is, of course, hard to understand relations between cause and effect in these kinds of projects where so many factors are interrelated. As of 11th June, 2012, four years after the launch of the first project, the enrolment ratio is as follows in the first targeted school:

Table 9.3: Enrolment Ratio the First Project School in the Beginning of the Academic Year 2011-2012

Sex	*Form 1*	*Form 2*	*Form 3*	*Form 4*	*Total*
Boys	53	56	43	68	220
Girls	41	41	29	26	137
Total	**94**	**97**	**72**	**94**	**357**

The national selection in form 1 is on the basis of 50-50 boys and girls and on this school the numbers of girls are on the lower side from the beginning. The data shows that the national and local efforts to support girls to start secondary education have had effect even if it's not 50-50 yet. But the data from form 4 gives a totally different picture, revealing the challenges, especially for girls with the enrolment ratio of 68 boys and 26 girls. According to the principal two girls dropped out because they couldn't afford the school fee and 28 girls dropped out during the academic year due to pregnancy. Out of these 28, as many as 14 were in form 1 being the youngest and most vulnerable girls. One problem for the students, especially the girls, is the four month gap between the academic years, between standard 8 of primary education and the beginning of form 1, secondary education. During this period a lot of girls get pregnant. The numbers of teenage pregnancies raises a big question of how to change norms that are denying children the right to be children and the right to education.

According to the principal of the project school there are no drop-outs due to child labour. Could this be right, and if so what could be the reason? From the baseline study we learnt that the drop out due to child labour is high in primary school and perhaps that explains the lack of drop-out from secondary school. The working children perhaps never start secondary education, thus they cannot drop out?

An important factor for the teams in the training programme is that the projects are not funded by the Swedish International Development and cooperation Agency (SIDA) at all. It means that the resources the team could bring into the project are what they themselves could allocate from the Malawian system. This creates problems since teachers and people in the community expect some gratification or reimbursement for coming to meetings and taking part in the activities. To overcome this, the most important input from the team members is perhaps one's own belief, the conviction that children have rights and that these must get translated into action. This leads to the question what role norms play in the change of the culture of the school and what kind of support is needed to be able to be successful as a change agent to promote children's rights. First there are the legal norms; law and other policy documents that could be used such as; the International UN Convention of the Rights of the Child, the Millennium development goals and of course in this case the Malawian laws and policies. One example is the re-admission plan, introduced in 1993 by the Government of Malawi and revised in 2006. The policy is allowing girls to come back to school after giving birth. Before the re-admission plan, pregnant girls were expelled and after giving birth they didn't come back to school. In the same way the team could point at laws and policies against child labour as the Worst Forms of Child Labour Convention (1999 ILO convention no. 182). There are legal norms and policies, but they are not working in practice in this area of Malawi.

Legal Norms as a Part of the Solution

Is law the solution to problems related to children's rights? UNICEF is arguing that the power of the Convention lies in three fundamental strengths. First, it is a legal instrument, defining unequivocally the responsibilities of governments to children within their jurisdiction. Second, it is a framework for the duties borne by different actors at different levels of society to respond to the rights of children, and it helps us understand the knowledge, skills, resources or authority needed to fulfill those duties. Third, it is an ethical statement, both reflecting and building upon core human values about our commitment to collectively provide the world's children with the best we have to give (www.unicef.org).

One could argue that there is a need for more and stronger international and national laws regulating children's rights, in this case prohibiting child marriages, child labour and other forms of child abuse. I will argue that there is also a need for changing old social norms in the community and for establishing new professional norms for teachers and principals of the schools.

Norms are Action Instructions

One conclusion is evident; social norms against teenage pregnancies and child labour are not strong enough in the targeted rural area. From my point of view the strongest norm should be: All children have the right to qualitative and relevant education. If this norm always comes first it could have a great impact in all communities.

One solution, in my opinion, is in establishing new norms in the community to support education and my conclusion is that the best arena to create new norms is in the school by changing the school culture and the norms in the school culture.

Changes within the School—Professional Norms Guiding New Learner Centered Methods

To change the culture of a community is very difficult, and it takes a long time. It is also difficult to change the culture of an organization, in this case school cultures. I claim it is easier to change some norms, and I have observed the change of some professional norms in the schools. The old norm of teaching according to the "talk and chalk-method" has been changed for a lot of teachers in the area. The training of teachers and the new subject Life skills brought new learner centered methods to the schools. The new professional norm[4] guiding some of the teachers; I should use learner centered methods in the classroom, is gradually spreading. It means; there are new action directives on how to teach and involve students; the new methods have led to improved learning and a reproduction of new norms among the teachers has taken place; and the teachers now feel surrounding expectations from students, other teachers, principals and parents that they should use learner centered methods. As of today, four years after the launch at the first school, the principal notices an improvement of the results of the students. The district education manager of the area states: "The learner centered activities are good and I am of the opinion that they must continue because this helps in increasing the pass rate at national examinations."

I claim that this is the most important result of the two projects in regards to the CRC Article 29, the aim of education. As I see it, change in the community often starts in the school and improved teaching and learning will benefit the community and in the long run fight the poverty that gives teenage pregnancies and child labour.

Apart from giving new teaching and learning methods, the new subject Life skills came with facts about sexual reproductive health. Talk about these issues had been avoided and a lot of myths about pregnancies existed in the community e.g. you cannot become pregnant the first time, during day time, and so on. One of the tasks of the school is to give facts about various things that effect life. I observed lessons, interviewed students, teachers, parents, and religious leaders; and there has been a considerable change in attitudes regarding teenage pregnancies and sexual reproductive health. In a session at the first project school, a year after the launch, there were deliberations, poetry, drama, singing and dancing on the theme of sexual reproductive health. Students, sometimes together with parents, were acting out on the stage. At the end the Traditional leader declared Mkanda district a child friendly district and she gave full support to the continuation of the project. In my opinion this is an example of a strong link from changing norms in the school as an organization to changing norms in the community, in the area.

Social Reproduction and Surrounding Expectations on Teen Age Pregnancies

Surrounding expectations and social pressure plays a major role in norm-setting; for example, collective expectations influence individuals to engage in correct or culturally desirable behaviour (Durkheim, 1895; Rommetveit, 1955). The school principals and teachers in the project schools say that social pressure of early and forced marriages are strong in the area and the peer pressure and sexual activity is high. Awareness is raised because of the project, and the campaigns still continues; the attitude of community leaders is positive and they are involved; people in the community have started to talk about the problems of teenage pregnancies and what could be done to reduce them. However the culture, or the norms, is still too strong and the drop out due to teenage pregnancies has not decreased. One explanation could be that it is so secretive and it is being influenced by a lot of complex factors like poverty, peer pressure, cultural practices like early or forced marriages and lack of positive role models.

Often role models are functioning as change agents in setting new norms. In the case of teenage pregnancies a lot of different role models are needed. It is about giving re-admitted girls the opportunity of being role models, being able to function both as a mother and as a student. But it is also about teachers, fellow students, and key persons in the community being role models in their behaviour against pregnant and re-admitted girls. In this case local NGOs, with young people that just had completed secondary education, were invited to function as role models, and to support and strengthen the change efforts.

Another important factor is the motives of the individual or the driving forces. What if education becomes the strongest motive for a better life for all the girls in the area? Now early marriages have a very strong influence in the community and that norm is still supported, but hopefully it is gradually changing due to awareness campaigns and other activities started by both teams on the importance of education and the effects of teenage pregnancies and child labour.

Social norms to Reduce Drop-out Rate Due to Child Labour

The issue of child labour is totally different from teenage pregnancies, because child labour is more evident, observable behaviour thus easier to stop on the spot, according to the principals. There are no reported cases of child labour from the schools in the area at the moment and the principals say that the attitude of the community and the traditional leaders is very good. The leaders help in disseminating information on the negative effects of child labour as well as the importance of educating girls. As mentioned before, it is difficult to interpret this information, probably there is still a lot of child labour in the area, but those children are not enrolled and they do not appear in the data from the schools. We can at least identify a new norm in the community; children should not be involved in child labour, even if there is reason to believe that a good number of children in the area are denied their right to education. The conclusion is that there is a new norm, but there is a need for further *social reproduction* and the creation of stronger *surrounding expectations* to enforce the norm to create a norm that also leads to actions.

Social Reproduction and Surrounding Expectations on Child Labour

In the case or child labour perhaps the best role models are students who get employment and a good salary after completing secondary school. This would show all in the community that there is a meaning with education and that studying actually pays off. With the current salary for child labour a child has to work more than a month to earn the sum of 1.25 US$ the poverty limit of one day. In a strict economic sense it would be better for the individual, for the family, for the community and for the country to give all children an opportunity to complete secondary education.

A question raised is how to reach the working children, the ones not enrolled. From an organizational change point of view, the school is where the project and the intervention starts and if you don't reach these children or their parents, how can you make change and change the existing norms?

Based on the theory of norms and role models in the schools and in the community will function as role models or change agents. In this way there can be a social reproduction of new actions, promoting education, and the social pressure in the community can change in favour of new norms promoting children's rights.

Support Used by the Change Agents in the Projects

Finally, I will turn to the role of the change agents with a summary of the support that has been used in the efforts to implement children's rights in schools and to reduce drop-out from schools. To be able to face challenges and ensure the child's *right to education* the six change agents in the two teams have used support from:

- *Legal norms* and policies as a starting point to give a kind of authority to the change agents and to the projects.
- *School authorities and supervisors* from the Ministry of Education, the Division of Education and the District Education Office.
- *Key persons in the school* as principals and teachers who gradually become spokespersons for the local project and who can take the role as local change agents to make it sustainable.
- *Students,* are the main target group in the projects and once students realised the power of their rights they could support the efforts and give a very effective pressure to establish new norms.
- *Key persons closely linked to the school*, as parents in the PTA (Parents and Teachers Association) and the mothers group.
- *Key persons in the community* from leaders representing the Traditional authority to Village head men, and religious leaders.
- *Network* as the national network for Child Rights in Malawi with Change Agents trained in the programme: Child Rights, Classroom and School Management.
- *Governmental organisations*, as the Malawian Law Commission who could assist with competence and material.
- *Non Governmental Organisations (NGOs),* both national and international who could also assist with competence and material.
- *Media,* by the use of radio and TV the change agents were able to reach far beyond the schools—out in the community—to give information about CRC.

The role of Change Agents is multifaceted and a lot of people are involved in complex processes that need to be managed. It is quite obvious that Change Agents have to be leaders with a special mission to change old norms and establish new ones. In this case the mission is to give all children their right to education and new norms are arising; norms guiding actions-in the best interest of the child.

Notes

1. *The Millennium Development Goals Report 2010,* United Nations
2. Mother Group is an organisation linked to FAWEMA (Forum for African Women Educationists in Malawi). Mother Group follows up and protects the girl child at school. It discusses with parents on the children who have dropped out of school and encourages the children to come back to school.
3. The word *Principal* refers to the responsible leader of the school. In Malawi the title is head teacher.
4. A professional norm is generated in the professional system; in this case teachers' norms are generated in schools, by teachers and guiding the work of teach three Rs.

References

Alvesson, Mats (2002), *Understanding Organizational Culture*. London, Sage.

Baier, Matthias and Svensson, Måns (2009), *Om normer.* Malmö, Liber.

Durkheim, Emile (1982), *The rules of Sociological Method and Selected Texts on Sociology and its Method.* New York, Free Press.

Elster, Jon (1992), *The Cement of Society, a study of social order.* Cambridge University Press.

Giddens, Anthony (1989), *Sociology*. Cambridge, Polity Press.

Hechter, Michael and Opp, Karl-Dieter (red) (2001), *Social Norms*. New York, Russel Sage Foundation.

Hemmelgarn, Anthony L; Glisson, Charles; James, Lawrence R. (2006), Organizational culture and Climate: Implications for Services and Interventions Research. *Clinical Psychology Science and Practice V13 N1, Spring 2006.* Published by Blackwell Publishing.

Hoy, Wayne and Miskel, Cecil. (2008), *Educational Administration, Theory, Research, and Practice.* New York, The McGraw Companies.

Hydén, Håkan and Svensson Måns (2008), The Concept of Norms in Sociology of Law. *Law and Society, Scandinavian studies in Law*, volume 53. Stockholm, Stockholm Institute for Scandinavian Law.

International Labour Organization (ILO), Convention No. 182.

Morgan, Gareth. (2006), *Images of Organization.* Thousand Oaks, CA, Sage.

Robbins, Stephen (1998), *Organizational Behaviour*. Englewood Cliffs, N.J. Prentice Hall.

Rommetveit, Ragnar (1955), *Social Norms and Roles, Explorations in the psychology of ending social pressures*. Minnesota, University of Minnesota Press.

Svensson, Måns (2008), *Sociala normer och regelefterlevnad: trafiksäkerhetsfrågor ur ett rättssociologiskt perspektiv*. Lund: Lund University.

Therborn, Göran (2002), Back to Norms! On the Scope and Dynamics of Norms and Normative Action. I *Current Sociology*, November 2002, Vol. 50(6). Sage Publications, London, Thousand Oaks, CA and New Delhi.

UN Development Programme (UNDP), *What Will It Take to Achieve the Millennium Development Goals?—An International Assessment 2010,*

UNICEF,www.unicef.org

UNICEF. UN Girls' Education Initiative, (www.ungei.org)

United Nations *The Millennium Development Goals Report 2010,* UN MDG Database (mdgs.un.org); MDG MonitorWebsite (www.mdgmonitor. org)

Wickenberg, Per (1999), *Normstödjande strukturer: miljötematiken börjar slå rot i skolan*. Lund, Lund University

10

Challenges of Transforming an African into a Child Rights Change Agent

Some Reflections

Anthony Mugagga Muwagga

Child rights violation and failure by most African countries to implement the Child Rights Convention both at home, in the community and at school remains a big challenge to all Child Rights advocates especially in Africa. The colonial, post colonial economic, political and social instability have had tremendous negative implications to the quality of life for most people especially the child. Different organisations such as Swedish International development Co-operation Agency SIDA have tried to provide short and long term interventions in the form of Child Rights Education but their efforts were hampered by the philosophy, nature and environment in which the Child Rights Change Agents operate. This paper using two school contexts namely Uganda in Eastern Africa and Sweden in Europe tries to provide a reflection on the challenge of transforming an African into a Child Rights Change Agent.

Uganda is located in East Africa and it borders Kenya in the East, Tanzania and Rwanda in the South and the Democratic republic of Congo in the West and Sudan in the North, while Sweden is located between Finland and Norway in Northern Europe, Denmark and the Baltic Sea. Sweden unlike Uganda uses Swedish as the official language, while Uganda uses English and Swahili as the official languages but both are foreign. Sweden has enjoyed over 500 years of relative peace on the other hand Uganda has been at war for the last 100 years, first during the pre-colonial inter-tribal wars, colonial wars of conquest by Britain and the post independence, civil strife and misrule. In Sweden both the school and home complement each other in fostering a child friendly society which may not be the case in Uganda.

Design and Methodology

The study adopted a descriptive cross-sectional research design. It involved making meaning from responses and discussions with Child Rights trainee Change Agents and their mentors in a SIDA sponsored Child Rights School and Classroom Management Programme held in Lund University, Sweden September 20-October 14 2010 and in Hohhot, Inner Mongolia China—June 5-16 June 2011. It also examined a cross section of Ugandan Child rights Agents who have attended and completed the Child rights training programme since 2006 to 2011. The paper also purposively selected 3 schools that is Buganda Road Primary school in Kampala, Kiziba Primary school in Wobulenzi Primary School in Luwero District and Nakaseke Core Primary Teachers training College. These are the schools in which the Change agents had carried out their study projects. On the other hand in Sweden the paper draws its findings from a focus group discussion with teachers and students in two schools namely Viking Skolan pre-school/Elementary school and Gymnasie Skolan Spyken Lund. In trying to decipher the seen/said and unseen/unsaid in the two contexts, the discussions and findings were guided by following questions:

> Can we have a uniform or a global approach to child rights?
>
> What are some of the intrinsic and extrinsic challenges one may encounter when trying to transform an African into a Child Rights Change Agent?
>
> What makes Sweden succeed in areas of Child Rights Education?

Though the findings are not drawn from the whole of Africa and Europe, the paper using documentary analysis and focus group discussions examines the challenge of child Rights in Africa before contextualising the Ugandan Child Rights challenge. Preliminary investigations from the discussions with the different stakeholders, both in Sweden and Uganda, revealed that in both Countries there very many good policies on child rights. They are well implementation and adhered to in Sweden and on the other hand in Uganda they remain only in books and the minds of policy makers.

Conceptualising and Contextualising the Challenge of Child Rights in Africa

Child rights education involves training and getting information aimed at building in the trainee a universal culture of human rights through sharing of knowledge, imparting skills and molding of attitudes directed to; respect human rights, fundamental freedoms, human dignity, tolerance of other peoples' philosophies, beliefs and ideologies, gender equity, peaceful coexistence, sustainable development and social justice (Wickenberg, *et al.*:2009:9). Convention on the Rights of the Child (CRC), on the other hand is the legally binding international instrument meant to incorporate a wide range of Children's civil, cultural, economic, political and social rights (Hodgkin and Newell, 2007). While a child is every human being below the age of 18 years a Child Rights Change Agent in the context of a Lund University SIDA Sponsored Child Rights, School and Classroom Management Programme is any person who has under gone training in both child rights theory and practice, school and class management so as to develop skills, understanding and attitudes in favour of right based educational work at classroom, school and community level.(Hartmann and Stenelo, 2007). On the other hand a mentor is any person engaged in the programme but at the level of management and transmitting good practices meant to foster Child Rights Education in theory and practice. The Child Rights SIDA sponsored Child Rights programme in this paper is in response to the question

> Why are developing countries home to poverty, unending wars, violence, social and economic unrest.? Could these maladies be a result of a society which abuses its young?

Many African countries in-spite of the over 40 years of political independence seem to be in a worse off situation today than they were in the 1960s. Africa unlike other continents seems to be always in a vicious circle of political, economic and social challenges (Davidson, 1991 and Curtin, 1990). These challenges have had tremendous negative implications to the African child, women and the disadvantaged. Different scholars such as Fanon (1961), Mbiti (1980), Rodney (1982), Mamdani (1990), Nabudere (1990) provide varying reasons and solutions to these challenges.

Some, for example, within the neo-socialistic, pan-African and the African Renaissance paradigm attribute these challenges to colonialism and neocolonialism. They argue that colonialism murdered Africa's traditional approaches to child rearing and parenting thus disorienting the African with very dire consequences for the Child and the entire society. They further argue that the introduction of formal education and Judeo-Arabic spirituality in the 1870s intentionality or unintentionally ended up creating persons with no sound social bases, void of clear moral stances and pivots. The education in Africa did not grow from the African environment but the Euro-theistic and capitalistic stances with their many distortions for example; blind obedience which was taught to most new Christian converts (Fanon, 1961, Faupel, 1962 and Rodney, 1982). This initial formal education in Africa did not take child rights as salient issues. The African Child was given an education which had a dual intention namely:

- to drive him/her away from his/her culture which they deemed pagan and uncouth and
- to instil in him/her new Christian or Islamic values befitting a true human being (Davidson 1991, Curtin 1990, Ssekamwa 2000)

Unfortunately, in eroding the African's traditional values the missionaries enabled the creation of a person who is very foreign to himself/herself. A person who cannot comfortably transmit globally acceptable values because his/hers are long gone and those which are taught to him in the school and the Church are foreign to him/her.

On the other hand, scholars within the liberal and critiques of African traditional philosophy argue that Africa's challenges are a result of the intrinsic and extrinsic factors within Africa's culture, norms, politics and economics in the pre and post independence era. (Nsereko, 1997 and Mamdani, 1999). These argue that within African there traditions, cultures and norms, which demean the human person. They cite practices such as polygamy, in extreme cases child sacrifice, child marriages, child labour and out right violence towards the child in form of corporal punishment, carrying heavy loads many at times twice their body weight, female genital mutilation in east, central and parts of northern Africa.

It also noted that in almost all parts of Africa both in current and pre-colonial Africa, a child was deemed as a property of the family and the parents in particular. The child had no say in how he/she lived, was disciplined or fed. The elders, members of the extended family and parents had all the say to mould the child spiritually, morally and socially. It was therefore a social duty to discipline children in any way possible to achieve the goal of moulding the child. Studies by Roscoei 911, Kaggwa 1952 and Mbiti, 1982 seem to suggest that violence and aggression towards the child could be the course of violent culture in Africa. Different history books on pre-colonial, colonial and post colonial Africa allude to the fact that there seem to be a correlation between constrained childhood and adult psycho-pathetic behaviour. They cite examples: Shaka King of the Zulu in Southern Africa and Idi Amin of Uganda: East Africa both who were abused by their parents and community and ended up notorious violators of peoples' rights (Ibingira, 1973; Karugire, 1980; Karugire, 1989; Curtin, 1990 and Davidson, 1991)

Cases of Child Abuse in Africa

Different reports by UNICEF and ILO indicate that the African child has been greatly impacted by the past and prevalent conditions in Africa. For example children under the age of 14 work for more than ten hours a day for example in report by African Recovery (2001), it is revealed that in West Africa, Burkina Faso 51 per cent of all children in Burkina between the ages of 10 and 14 work, even though the labour code bars employment under 14. Child labour takes many forms namely; prostitution, pornography, child soldiers and sex slaves (ILO, 2005). This ILO report also indicates that Africa has the highest incidence of child labour in the world specifically 41 per cent of all African children, between the ages of 5 and 14, do support themselves or their families economically. A similar situation also occurs in Uganda, Kenya and Tanzania. It is also reported that in Tanzania a constrained education system pushes children to work at a very early age, while, poverty and conflict has pushed over 50 per cent of the children below 14 years of age to work.

There many reported and unreported cases of defilement of children in most African countries. According to Lirri (2009), in Uganda 16 children were sexually abused daily in the first six months of 2009. Between January and June 2009 a total of 9480 children were abused and out of these 2594 were defilement cases, 1259 of child disappearance, and of 1089 child stealing. Other cases of child abuse are child torture, neglect, assault and child trafficking. In spite of the prevalence and purported public profession to Christian faith with over 60 per cent of the popuiation professing to be Christian, values such as monogamy are in most cases ignored. Many Ugandan men are polygamous. (Muwagga and Kaahwa, 2009). The existence of polygamy leads to child neglect, school drop-out, early marriages and perpetuates a vicious circle of poverty.

It is also alleged that there religious practices demean the child. For example in Ugandan Muslim communities they select some children and declare that these should not attend formal schools but instead go to Koranic schools. This practice is prominent in the West Nile part of Uganda at the Uganda-South Sudan boarder. It is also practised at the Tanzania and Kenya coast towns and on the Islands of Zanzibar and Pemba in East Africa. Children who go to these Koranic schools miss out on formal schooling, can not speak and use standard English which is the official language in these countries (Rowe, 1991). It is also alleged that though Roman Catholic and Anglican founded Schools profess to open up to students of other denominations in reality they are not. They force all students to pray in their ways, and attend their spiritual activities. (Rujumba, 2011; Muwagga and Genza, 2011).

The worst reported case of Child abuse and violation of Children's rights is conscription of children into the army or into rebel soldiers. This has been the case by the Lord's Resistance Army (LRA) in Northern Uganda, SPLA in Sudan, Liberia, and Sierra Leone civil wars, Congo Rwanda, South Africa during the anti apartheid struggles, in Angola and currently in Somalia.

Unlike other continents Africa has continued to witness coups, counter coups, civil strife and an expansion in the number of African military men who took political power by force, perpetuate corruption, violence and violation of human rights in order to stay in power for example; Idi Amin of Uganda, Fernando Macias Nguena of Republic of Equatorial Guinea, Mobutu Sese Seko of Zaire, Mengestu Haille Mariam of Ethiopia, Said Barre Somalia of Kamuzu Banda of Malawi, Hussen Mubarak of Egypt, Do Santos and Savimbi of Angola, Mugabe Robert of Zimbabwe Gadafi of Libya, Museveni of Uganda, and many others. These and their protégées manipulate their country's constitutions to stay in power. At the same time their long stay in power becomes a recipe for violation of human rights especially of children and women. The leadership styles of most of the contemporary African leaders (1970 to date) has distorted and eroded values which upheld their societies by way of truthfulness, respect for life and property. As a result the African child has been the greatest victim. It has become very hard to exercise proper parenting and child rearing amidst a good value stance vacuum.

Uganda's Education System

There are three types of sub systems in Uganda's education system. These are—Formal Education (FE), Non-formal Education (NFE), and Informal Education (IE) sub-systems

Formal Education (FE)

The Formal school system runs from pre-primary (1-5 years of Age); primary (6-12 years of Age); secondary (13-18 years of age) tertiary and higher education (25 years). It should be noted that over 30 per cent of the children do not have access to formal education.

Non Formal Education (NFE)

In this paper Non Formal Education refers to an education system which was introduced to solve the gap created by the void in formal education. It mainly targets the school drop out, post conflict educational needs and rural girls and women. It is mainly an education offered by NGOs. This type of education though very useful it is not popular because it is not graded and offers no certificates.

Informal or African Indigenous Education (IE/AIE)

Informal Education is a home based education. It is largely responsible for the existence and survival of many African traditional beliefs, values and knowledge stance. Most children over 60 per cent especially for most rural areas in SSA spend their first years of life between one and four at home with their parents, grand parents or members of the extended family. Most children learn values and norms informally at home. These values stances are resident in the African proverbs, idioms, African music dance and drama and in cultural practices right from naming of a child, initiation into adulthood ceremonies and burial of the dead. When reflecting on Child rights it is imperative to think about this informal education. It is this which in most cases might be that which dictates how most people behave most especially in their homes in private practice, how they parent or rear their children. It may also be a major determinant of the African's attitude towards the children and women. Though the contemporary African's mind, beliefs and values are infused with many foreign philosophical underpinning we can not totally ignore the role played and implications of the indigenous/traditional education transmitted at home and in his community. Hence in reflecting on child rights it is very important to candidly think about non-formal education in Africa. The above are dramatically represented in Figure 1:

Fig. 1 suggests that there is limited enrolment at pre-primary, high enrolments at primary, secondary implies high drop out from primary and low enrolments at tertiary levels. Figure one illustrates that informal education influences all levels of education in Africa. It also shows that only 20 per cent of the children receive meaningful pre-primary education, which is corroborated by the *Education for All Global Monitoring Report* (UNICEF, 2010). Many of the children stay at home with their mothers or other relatives until the age of 6 when they get enrolled in formal primary schools.

Challenges to Child Rights Implementation

Under normal circumstances the home and school would have

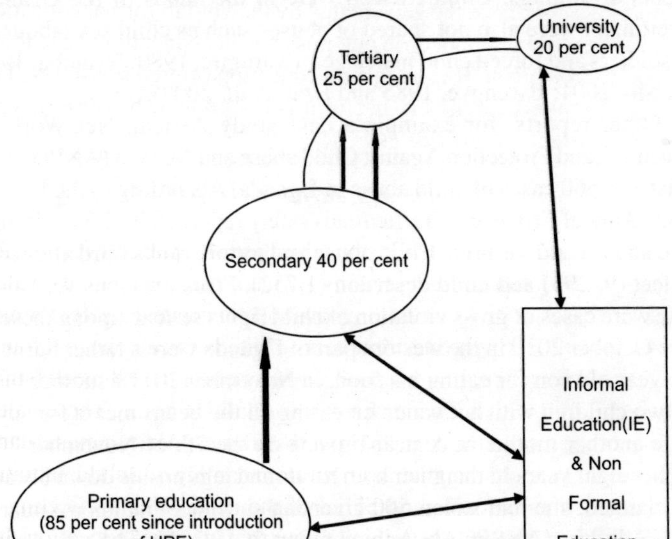

Fig. 1: The Educational Path of a Ugandan Child

* The percentages indicate the approximate number of pupils who access education at that specific level.

complemented each other in the implementation of the CRCs but this is not the case in Uganda. War and civil strife has disintegrated the traditional Ugandan family thus eroding most of the acceptable social norms. The violence and out right abuse of peoples' rights has greatly affected the child, for example, during Obote's regime between 1981-1985 soldiers were in the practice of invading the supposedly opponents of the government to either rape women and girls, force boys to have sex with their sisters or mothers while the rest of the family was watching (Karugire, 1980; Kyemba, 1997; Tarcisio, 2001). In extreme cases the LRA during the 1986-2007 civil war in Uganda, Children were forced to kill and drink the blood of those they had killed who in most cases were their parents or siblings. Children who were in the hands of the Ugandan government were also not spared of abuses such as child sex labour for the soldiers and forced child marriages. (Karugire, 1980; Kyemba, 1997; Tarcisio, 2001; Bwengye, 1985 and Ezati *et al.* 2008).

Other reports, for example a case study African Net Work for Prevention and Protection Against Child abuse and Neglect (ANPPCAN), registered 660 cases of child abuse in Uganda. According to the Uganda Police Annual Crime and Traffic/roads safety report 2010, 1,315 children were abused and tortured. Child abuse and torture ranks third after child neglect (9, 293) and child desertion (1,732). From previous year alone there were cases of gross violation of child rights salient among these on were October 2010 in the western part of Uganda were a father burnt his five year old son for eating his food, in November 2011 a mother burnt his two children with hot water for eating all the beans meant for super, while another mother in central Uganda on the 7th of November 2011 tied her eight year old daughter both hands and legs upside down because she claimed, she had stolen 500 Ugandan shillings that approximately 0.2 US dollars (ANPPCAN Annual report 2010/2011. The worst abuse so far has been the 19 year step mother in Wakiso district who used a sharp object to pierce her 5 year old step daughter in her private parts. (Ssebuyira 2011) while it was also reported that one John Otebati a traditional healer cut off the penis of a 5 year old child Geofrey Mukisa (Namboga, Musingo and Mudoola, 2011). The Uganda Child rights NGO network also carried out a study and in its report where it was revealed that the key child abuses in Uganda are denial to majority of children meaningful education, sexual exploitation, child forced marriage-children are married off between the age of 9 and 10 to men above the age of 35 years, abductions, defilements and child labour. (http://www.ucrnn.net 28/11/2011) The Uganda demographic and health survey 2006/2007 (http://www.ubos.org 28/11/2011) also revealed that the girl child is the most abused child in Uganda. It was revealed that 16 per cent of the Ugandan girls are forcefully married at the age below 15 years and 53 per cent before the age of 18 years and teenage pregnancy stands at 25 per cent.

The above child abuses create an unstable and very constrained environment for the child. The troubles at home and in the community are in most cases transferred to the school. From the study schools the following were revealed.

- It was revealed that most schools, especially rural schools, have inadequate and at times very constrained both in and out of class overheads for example all the study schools the toilets were not disaggregated and pupils studied in dilapidated infrastructures.
- Children between the ages of 5 and 12 years walk very long distances—between 3 to 15 Kms from home to school.
- Children go and stay at school for a whole day without food. One teacher in a focus group discussion lamented and said: "A hungry teacher teaching very hungry and sleeping children. If one calls this education then there is something wrong in his/ her head" Discussion with a Primary school teacher in (Statement from one of the teachers in Nakaseke Core PTC).

The above lamentation is supported by the United Nations Annual Report 2007, which reveals that Sub Saharan Africa is not on track to achieve most of the (MDGs) education (27th 03, 08 http://unstat.un.org). This is also supported by Ndeezi (2000) who further notes that in practice Universal Primary Education is not yet universal. It has had a number of challenges especially the implementation phase. In countries where there are conflicts, extreme poverty and deprivation the challenges facing access to real education are even more compounded and this is the case with Uganda. Uganda ratified the Convention on the rights of the Child (CRC) in 1990. There was a commitment to ensure each child receives appropriate nurturing and protection within the frame of the minimum standards set up by the convention. Laws have been put in place to facilitate the implementation of this convention. These include: the 1995 Ugandan constitution,

Children's Act of 1992 and Children's statute: In order to make operational the above laws, Uganda introduced Universal Primary Education (UPE) in 1997, which saw a drastic rise in primary school enrolment exceeding 120 per cent. Unfortunately the actual implementation of the CRC seems to be problematic cases of gross violation of children's rights seem to be on the increase. The overwhelming response to Universal Primary Education (UPE) created very many challenges. These include high dropout rates of nearly 50 per cent especially of the girl child. The teacher-pupil ratio 1: 110, infrastructures are also inadequate, disadvantaged children are not yet fully benefiting, class rooms are too congested and in some areas classes are still conducted under trees.

Reflection on the Encounter and Learning Experiences from Lund Swedish Schools

The venture to reflect on any European system makes it imperative to think critically about the philosophical underpinning resident both in the past and currently for it is these which have moulded and formed the current debates on the human person and the child, in particular. The debate on the rights of the person and human being as such dates as far back as the time of the Sophists (pre-Socratic philosophers) Socrates, Plato, Aristotle and later finds a pivot in the Existentialists, such as Jean Paul Sartre, culminating in the great debates on the existence of God and his relationship with man either as a subordinate or slave of God and fellow men; for example, Copleston's (1965) thesis on Friedrich Wilhelm Nietzsche works on the Birth of Tragedy, Beyond Good and Evil and the Joyful Wisdom in which Nietzsche declared that "God is dead" His attack on Christianity implies an attack on Christian moral standards and values which he argued had a diverse effect on man. Whom he thinks it renders weak, submissive, resigned, humble or tortured in conscience and unable to develop or actualize his/her true self. The death of God to Nietzsche is the death of European absolute values to be replaced by new philosophies and values which in turn were transmitted to Africa by the missionaries. Current Europe an beliefs including those of Sweden in particular have also been influenced by the post modernists, liberal Euro-American philosophies such as the phenomenological movement anchored in the philosophy of Edmund Husser coupled with the mild socialistic paradigms found in some Scandinavian countries (Russell, 1996).

Venturing into the Unknown (On Becoming a Change Agent)

From the focus group discussions with Child rights Change Agents and trainee Change Agents the followings are revealed: Many of them come to Lund not knowing what awaits them. Come loaded with their African beliefs and values necessarily not to become zealous advocates of the child but out of curiosity, in anticipation of new connections and visiting Europe for the first time. The curriculum, pedagogy and package in the Lund University's Child Rights programme is not known 99 per cent of the prospecting change agents but being accepted in the programme means a venture into the unknown. This was evidenced by what some said after reflections during a child rights discussion sessions at Lund University 2010. One Trainee Change Agent student said:

> "When I applied and was accepted I thought to my self let me go to Europe and tour see new areas and enjoy but on reaching and beginning the study every day made feel that I needed more studying and getting to know the issue of the child and his/her rights" *(Discussion contribution by one of the child rights student change agent.)*

However, on reaching and embarking on the study all the candidates end up becoming zealous advocates of the child rights both at home, work places and in their communities. This is reflected in what many change agents said while having a plenary discussion in Inner Mongolia hotel in June 2011, one said:

> The Child rights programme taught me to feel that also my wife gets tired, she needs to rest. It also taught me that it is our duty I and my wife to see to it that our children are comfortable in our home *(One African Trainee Child rights and School Management participant in China inner Mongolia, June 2011)*

While another said:

> I thought cooking is only done by women and men whose wives have bewitched them with some African love portion. Back at home it is not the normal practice for a "real" man to cook, wash utensils, clothes or even sit down and play with children. A man has to go to drink alcohol and converse with other men not children. If a man stays with children then what will the women do? *(One Trainee African Child Rights and School Management participant in China Inner Mongolia Autonomous region, June 2011)*

The above statements point to a real change in attitude towards life, the child and a turn from the African norm. It is therefore imperative that we now reflect and try to establish the intrinsic and extrinsic factors within the programme which are responsible for this conversation.

Factors Within the Programme which Initiate Change among the Participants

In this section I will try to reflect on the possible extrinsic and intrinsic factors within the programme that are intentionally or unintentionally placed therein to facilitate or transform persons into child rights change agent. These are identified from the experiences of the different participants either within the study, in the students' hostel at Sparta Lund and the experiences back in their homes. It may be hard to identify or demarcate the intrinsic from extrinsic factors. These, however, can be deciphered from the statements made and revealed by the different change agents both while studying in Lund and after completion. The experiences are drawn from the very first day of the training. They seem to be resident in the *bonding between the trainee agents, the students hostel and pedagogical environment during the CRC study sessions, visits and experience with the mentors, Swedish schools and cultural sites.*

The Bonding

On the first day of the training there is a lot of excitement which is coupled with fear by almost all candidates enlisted in the CRC class in Lund University. The fear stems from the entry into a new county, meeting new people of very diverse cultures, colours and many of whom speak languages unknown to many of their colleagues and other speak inaudibly. To this the different child rights change agents in June 2010 had this to say and getting used to each other and in the class discussions.

For example one said:

> "Many participants looked much older on the first day but I am very surprised that actually they are not; probably I was looking at most of the participants with fear." *(Child Right agent student Lund, September 2011)*

While another student change agent in an out of class discussion with another student change agent said:

> "Many of the student change agents looked or seemed to be

> persons who can never initiate serious debates but I am very surprised at the level of intellectual maturity people exhibit in the different discussions. (Out of class discussion by one Colombian Child agent student, September 2010)

While another said

> "My first day in Lund was very hard I had never been away from my children for over a weak. (*Out of Class discussion with a female Indian student Change Agent, October 2011)*

On the other hand another said:

> Every body looked strange, even the meals were strange, the cold break fast on a very cold morning made every thing look as if I had made a mistake to come to Lund, but now after a week I am feeling as if I am at home with friends and I even miss the cold breakfast of Sparta." (*Out of class discussion by one Female Asian child Agent Student Lund, September 2010)*

Another said

> "Many of the participants spoke and it was very hard to comprehend what they were saying because of their accents but now I can understand almost 99 per cent of what they are saying" *(Out of class discussion with one Malawian student change agent)*

These statements show the gradual opening up by the different Trainee Change Agents. The opening up eventually leads to a bonding or a feeling that all the change agents are pursuing the same vision and mission, i.e. the good of the child.

There seem to some 'magic' in the programme which ends up bonding the entire group together. In this section I try to highlight some of the means through which this bonding takes place. These include;

- Team work and bonding begins in the change agents' home country when they begin working on their projects and prepare to come to Lund University. They get to know each other and begin tolerating each other. On reaching Lund the first days of the training is a bit problematic because of the cold, walk in the cold and the cold break fast but as the days go on the following were noted:

- Many change agents especially the African male and head teachers on many occasions back at home do not cook, wash their clothes or even clean their offices. Therefore, the humbling experience of cooking, washing and even cleaning the utensils after eating runs counter to the acceptable norms back at home. Norms are behavioural instructions, socially reproduced and are the individual's uderstanding of surroundig expectations regarding their own behaviour. For example for most of Africans cooking, washing and cleaning the house or household utensils was supposed to be work done by girls, women and children especially the girl child. On a number of occasions the boy child was exempted from most of the domestic chores (Kagwa, 1952 and Mbiti, 1987). It should be noted that with the introduction of formal schooling, urbanization and out right social change these practices are diminishing but are still cherished in some societies especially in rural parts of Africa.
- In most parts of Africa it is a common norm to greet and address teachers, elders and academicians by their titles and actually one would run a risk of missing out on an issue if an elder was addressed by his/her without a title. This many of us found as a new practice. The use of lecturers' names without using their titles makes the candidates to think as loser to them.
- Walking from the students hostel (Sparta) for those accustomed to using a car, accustomed to teaching others and thinking I knew but here I was being taught and getting to know that I actually did not know.
- Learning with people some of whom did not have university degrees and yet their contributions were priceless was a very humbling and great learning experience.
- The humility and yet knowledge rich mentors greatly humbled me. Warmth of both the mentors and Mother Nature the bonding between the participants comes from:
- Sharing of food stuffs back in the residence.
- This was one of the greatest bonding factor among student change agents. Each group from their respective countries came with their local dishes to supplement the food to be bought in Lund so every evening in the dinning hall each group would prepare

and apart from sharing they would also share with people from other countries. Many shared or accepted the food stuffs out of politeness and curiosity. But ended up creating a bond. This is in line with the African tradition of sharing foods with strangers so that they become brothers and sisters.

- Every evening some change agents who smoke would converge in some place and share a cigarette, this bonded them and one of the participants had this to say:

"The sharing of a cigarette brings us together as friends and humans" (Discussion with one Change agent in Uganda)

- Curiosity about other cultures (conversations) form the classroom discussions curiosity and interest develop as such after class many would again converge and continue with the class discussions but this time is in a non formal way.
- Team work by both the mentors and students. In almost all activities there was a call by the mentors for team work, this thus bonded people together.

The change is not very fast it comes gradually but eventfully the change agents become so convinced of what is taught to them that many, if not all, open up especially in the discussions and conversations. The programme devised a motto of Give and Take.

The Environment at the Students Hostel, Pedagogical Approaches and Classroom Environment

In reflecting on the pedagogical and non pedgaogical over heads of the programme I am humbly reflecting on issues of Quality asurance as noted by Maria Löfgren Martinsson while discusing isues of quality assurance to the programme particiapnts in (Lund 2010 September) we need to clearly see that part of quality management focused in providing the confidence that quality requirements are being fulfilled. The planned and systematic review process of an institution or programme to determine that acceptable standards of education, scholarship and infrastructure are being maintained and enhanced.

Being a teacher and a teacher trainer, the lectures in the Pictura (*this is a lecture room on top of Lund university administration block). This room gave* a great learning experience to all trainee Child Rights Change Agents. It is a very cold room and at times its warming systems were not working. This also became a big source for "*real reflection*". I come form a back ground where professors and PhD holders are in the habit of introducing themselves with their academic titles. The mentors in spite their great academic sophistication, exhibited great humility and pedagogical expertise. They employed a multi pedagogical approach which catered for the diverse cultural, educational levels and the English by some participants.

This is a very big challenge to many teachers at all levels in Africa whose approaches do not aim at transforming the learner into a critical and reflective individual. This is prominent in Africa where, as Paulo Freire noted, the teacher is just like a Banker or a knowledge depositor. Who expects nothing new from the learner but to store and reproduce the facts given to him/her by the omniscient teacher. However, in the Lund programme the mentors or lecturers give each participant learner a chance to make his/her point.

The specific pedagogical approaches used in the programme were unorthodox they did not follow the conventional teaching approaches. They included; participant-observations, discussions, talk and listen, inclusive, dramatisation, singing, reciting of experiences and stories by both the mentors and students, meditating as a ground for reflective practice, field work and school visits and country side excursions. These when used for pedagogical purposes seem to have a number of implications to the transformation and learning of the trainee Change Agents namely;

Teaching them to critically observe for the seen and unseen in given situations such as:

(i) Teach the participants to discuss issues maturely,
(ii) Learn to listen and allow others to talk,
(iii) Teach and allow all even those who did not have much to say to also participate in the class and out of class discussions,
(iv) Engage the entire class, namely the mentors and students, in a bonding session through music dance and drama,
(v) Learn to accept other people, views, beliefs, values even if they may be offending to your.
(vi) Learn to think before talking,
(vii) learn to participate in discussions.

The pedagogical approaches employed it was hoped would have a multiplier effect on both, home, community and school approaches to the child. This was also noted during the visits to the mentors' homes in which the trainee Change agents learnt hospitality.

Reflections on Education in Sweden

Reflecting or philosophising on anything from without one runs a risk of misinterpreting and misreading what lies therein. However, in a humble way I would like to make the following observations about the Swedish education system.

The Swedish education Act dictates that all children and young persons shall, irrespective of gender, geographic residence and social and financial circumstances, have equal access to education in the national school system for children and young persons. The education shall be of equal standard within each type of school, wherever it is provided in the country. The education shall provide the pupils with knowledge and skills and, in co-operation with the homes, promote their harmonious development into responsible human beings and members of the community. Particular attention shall be paid to pupils who need special support. School activities shall be structured in accordance with fundamental democratic values. Each and every person active in the school system shall promote respect for the intrinsic value of every human being and for common environment. Education in Sweden is mandatory for all children between ages of 1-9. It is noted that children between ages 1 to 5 are also admitted in pre-schools (Forskola). These schools aim at providing an environment in which children's psyche is stimulated which enables parents to combine parenthood with work or studies.

Between the ages 6-7 these are compulsory and comprehensive Pre-school compulsory school and leisure-time centre (Grundskola). These all aim at providing Child care for school children. These coupled with the Swedish culture have a bearing on the current trend towards the child. There are allegations that there are significant number of divorces and remarrying by the male partners while the ladies remain single mothers. These have a bearing to the child.

Reflections on Child Rights in Swedish Schools

Experiences from Visits of Swedish Schools in Lund

Discussion in this section is the change agents' observations from study of school visits. We note that from the various visits and focus group discussions with both the teachers and students in the project schools namely at pre secondary level VikingaSkolan, Klostergardsskolan,

Ostratornskolan, Tunaskolan and the pre University GymnaSieskolan Spyken. It is revealed that CRCs are cultivated in schools and nurtured at home where both the school and the hidden curriculum propagate the following: Peaceful Relations, Communication, Participation, Inclusive education, Democratical values, Gender Critical thinking and Problem solving.

Evidence of this lays in the different CRC organs in all educational institutions right from pre-primary to University level for example students councils, discussions and debates in schools and at home. In these debates and discussions issues affecting people's lives such as paying of tax, public and private morality are discussed. Discussions enhance the confidence of the learners "ipso facto" that of the child.

This was seen in the discussions the CRC study group had with students of GymnaSieskolan Spyken in Lund where students preparing for their pre university philosophy lessons had discussion on a number of topic but all aiming at the freedom of the child. For example one student said:

> "These discussions help us grow into responsible citizens". *(Student discussion in GymnaSieskolan Spyken)*

While another said:

> "When we discuss topics like suicide, surrogate motherhood we are able to make informed choices (*One of the students in GymnaSieskolan Spyken)*

The most interesting thing seen in these discussions was degree of reflective practice by both the teachers and students for example some students in their debates especially in GymnaSieskolan Spyken revealed as noted by one female student when she said:

> "The loose moral imperatives resident both at school and at home are a recipe for drug abuse and sexual adventurism since the divine as deterrent fence was killed by the advent of a non spiritual society reminiscent of the Swedish society".

This debate was taken on by one teacher in GymnaSieskolan Spyken who said:

> "It is true that our society and approach to the child and other human rights are advanced, however there are things which indicate challenges to the very existence of a sober society namely: instances of suicide, non orthodoxy sexual practices, the rampant divorces all might deprive the Swedish child of a human face" *(Discussion with a teacher from GymnaSieskolan Spyken Lund 2010)*

While another revelation was made by one Principal who said:

> "Our education system is good but at times it is a bit unfair to the teacher. Actually too much is expected from the teacher but little from the child and the parents. The parents. many of them are very bad role models they divorce all the time and we the teachers have to deal with the challenge of managing these children from collapsed families in our school we have to deal with at least 5 cases per term of children whose parents have separated or are divorced. These seemingly small things will in the long run kill the entire effort placed on education of children" (A *principal in one of the study visit schools)*

These statements by the student and teacher may look innocent but could be pointing to the unseen in the education of the Swedish child both at home and in the school, the role of the family both nuclear and extended family which in the case of Africa were more pronounced in the past but today in some societies they are gone. On the other hand, the concern of the student at Gymna Sieskolan Spyken should also not be ignored as it could be a call for more implicit and explicit moral imperatives and need for more reflections on the Swedish society and its cultural influences.

The Success of the Child Rights Lund University Programme

It is important to establish the reasons within the Swedish culture which makes Child rights training programme a success. From the observations, discussions in Lund University, visit to the different Swedish cultural cites, Museums and with the programme mentors the following are revealed about the Swedish people namely:

- Swedes are egalitarian in nature that is they hold the belief that all persons deserve and hold equal rights and opportunities. This value position is continuously passed on to their children.

- Swedes are taught at an early age to listen to others to ensure that others in turn will listen to them. This is the cradle of their humility and respect for others' views.
- Swedes people speak softly and calmly this enables other people to follow and pick the message.
- Majority of Swedes love to pay their taxes.
- The Swedes are very critical and analytical. This is drawn from the influence of philosophers such as Edmund Husserl 1859-1938, Rene Descartes 1596-1650, Alf Ahlberg 1892-1979. Emanuel Swedenborg 1688-1772 and many other philosophers.
- Swedes do not take hospitality and kindness for granted. Children are taught to thank for every thing given to them as a pivot for hospitality and kindness to other beings even the non human beings.
- Swedes prefer to do things in moderation and this is also taught to their children.
- In as much as these divorces and remarrying the Swede take the family as a very important micro unit in their society the entire society, as an imperative, ensures that all children are protected. This is evident in the Swedish labour laws and the marital obligations of both male and female towards the child. For example parents are obliged to reduce on their work load by 25 per cent up to the time the child reaches eight years of age. This is done with an aim of enabling the parents to nurture and offer attention to the child.
- From my observations there is a mathematical perfection which the swedes exhibit in execution of their duties. This observation was validated by what one male child rights mentor when asked about parenting said:

  "We try to give the best and do the best so that our children can emulate that which is the best ensures that the good Swedish practices are passed and transmitted from one generation to another" *Discussion with one Swedes Child Rights male mentor, October 2011)*

There have been arguments that the divine (religion) is very far in the minds and practice of majority of Swedes. This seems to be true if we are to measure spirituality in terms of reading the bible, attending church services and reciting prayers. This unfortunately debases and tends to reduce God to a mere being without an anchor in man's axiomology or life experience. When one looks and critically reflects on the conduct, attitude and open hearts of the majority of Swedes people one discovers that they are very religious. Here religion is taken to mean "man behaving like a true human being, humble, respectful of others and their views, in short according others their due rights. This definition fits very well with what the majority of the swedes do and practice in every day life.

> "We in Africa deceive our selves that we are God fearing and condemn people who do not pray or go to Church such as the Swedes, but upon close examination our conduct, attitude towards each other and especially our children is that of vampires and mammals. While those who do not go to Church do treat each other, including strangers, in a very humane way it defeats what we call being God fearing. Actually those we think are not God fearing are the most God fearing people one can ever meet" *(Statement made by one Child Rights Agent in a Child rights discussion in Uganda 2010)*

On the other hand many of what the Swedes do cherish and adhere to, are conspicuously missing for most of Africans. There are things which enhance obnoxious norms in Africa, for example corruption, violation of human rights by African presidents and their protégées, These send a message to the child that; it is normal to do the same since leaders who are supposed to be the models are doing the same hence a big challenge to Child Rights Agents in Africa.

Conclusion

As we conclude this reflection we may need to ask our selves an important question: Has the Lund University SIDA sponsored Child rights, Classroom and School Management programme succeeded in fulfilling its overall objective, which is to improve participating countries capacity to offer and ensure everyone right to relevant and quality education, an education that is safe and secure, inclusive, child-centred, democratic, problem-solving that creates opportunities for all, regardless of background to participate in community life as an active citizen. Apparently in all African countries, where the project has change agents, for example Africa: Burkina Faso, Egypt, Ethiopia, Liberia, Malawi, Mali, Mozambique, Namibia, Sierra

Leone, South Africa, Tanzania, Uganda, Zambia and Zimbabwe, there are tremendous changes and successes in all study schools and departments. The good experiences are the new approaches to the issues of values in the South African context as spearheaded by the different Change Agents in the Orange province, South Africa, there is a change in Ugandan Teacher-training which has taken on and infused issues of Student-Centred Pedagogy and Child Rights, in both, the graduate and primary teacher training programmes. The project has not only enhanced the CRCs, it has been a pivot for the repositioning of the school for most of the African conflict prone countries. In this case the repositioned school becomes an anchor to rejuvenate the human person and his inalienable rights. It is worth noting that making a comparative reflection on two or more significantly different contexts gives one a chance to learn, adopt or copy the good in other people's systems or discard that which may not positively apply in his/her context. There is an imperative to use what is already on the ground so as to better what is already in existence for example the religious structures, the good and at times modified values and beliefs. We also need to note that in order to enhance and create a more child friendly community we need to have the home and school complement each other in fostering a child friendly society.

References

Aguti, N.J. (2002), *Facing up Challenges of Universal Primary Education, UPE in Uganda through Distance Teacher education programmes*. Makerere University, Kampala.

Bwengye F. (1985), *Agony of Uganda, From Idi Amin to Obote*. Regency Press, London

Curtin, Phillip (1990), *African History*. Longman, London.

Davidson Basil (1991), *Modern Africa; A Social and Political History;* second edition. Longman, London.

Ezati Betty A., Caul Leslie, Ssenkusu Peter, Muwagga M.A. Ssempala Cornelius, Memunatu Pratt, Nyamurasa Moses and Maani John (2008) *Capacity building for teachers in post conflict areas the Case of northern Uganda, Northern Ireland, Rwanda and Sierra Leone*. DFID/Delphe British Council; sponsored project.

Education For All Global Monitoring Report (www.efareport.unesco.org)

Hartmann Annelie and Stenelo Richard (2009), The Convention on the Rights of the Child cited in Wickenberg, Flinck, Leo, Rasmusson Stenelo and Yebio eds., (2009) *Taking Child Rights Seriously: Reflections on Five years of an international Training Programme*. Media-tryck Lund Sweden.

Hodgkin and Newell (2007), Implementation Handbook For the Convention on the Rights of the Child, Unicef.

Freire Paulo, (1970), *Pedagogy of the Oppressed*, Penguin books.

Furley, Olive (1991), Education in post independence Uganda: Change amidst strife Cite in Hansen Bernt H and Twaddle Michael eds (1991) *Uganda Now between decay and Development Heinemann Nairobi.*

Franz Fanon (1961), *The Wretched of the Earth.* A Negro Psychologists study of the Problems of racism and Colonialism in the World Today.

Ibingira Grace (1973), *The Forging of an African Nation, the Political and Constitutional Evolution of Uganda from Colonial rule to Independence (1894-1962),* Viking Press, New York.

International Labour Organization. Child labour in Africa page 10. Http://digital commons.ilr.edu/child/10

Kagwa Apolo (1952) *Empisa za Baganda The Customs of Baganda in the Luganda language*. Macmillan and Co. London.

Karugire R. Samuel (1980), *A Political History of Uganda*. Heinneman, London.

Karugire R. Samuel (1985), The Roots of Political Instability and Violence in Uganda. New vision printing press Kampala.

Kyemba, Henry (1997), *A State of Blood.* Fountain Publishers. Kampala.

Lirri Evelyn (2009), Sixteen Children defiled Daily Says New Report. *The Daily Monitor,* News Paper Uganda 29th September 2009. http://www.monitor.co.ug

Mamdani Mahmood (1999), *Politics and Class Formation in Uganda.* Fountain Publishers, Kampala.

Mbiti John S (1982), *African Religions and Philosophy*. Heinemann, London.

Mbiti John S (1985), *Love and Marriage in Africa*. Longman, London

Muwagga Mugagga Anthony and Genza Gyaviira Musoke (2011), The Dilemma of Teacher Professionalism and Commitment in Roman catholic Founded secondary schools in Uganda http;//www.interesjouranls.org/ER

Muwagga Mugga Anthony (2009), *A study of Traditional and Modern Child Rearing Practices in Selected Communities in Central Eastern and western Uganda.* (2009) Sponsored by Plan international

Nabudere Wadada Dani (1990), External and Internal Factors in Uganda's continuing Crisis cited in Hansen Bernt H and Twaddle Michael eds. (1991), *Uganda Now between decay and* Development, Heinemann, Nairobi.

Namboga Jackie, Musingo, Doreen and Mudoola Patride (2011), Man gets 15 years for Chopping off a Boys Penis. *Saturday Vision* News Paper, Uganda. November 26 2011.http://www.newvision. co.ug

Ndeezi, A., (2000). "*Focus on Policy: Universal Primary Education In Uganda.*" *Enabling Education Network Newsletter* No. 4: United Kingdom.

Munakukaama, N (1997), *Secularisation of Post Independence education in Uganda and its significance for moral Education in Public Primary and Secondary Schools 1963-1985* un published PhD Thesis. Makerere University, Kampala.

UNESCO's 2010, *Education Report.*

John, R. (1911) *The Baganda. An account of the customs and beliefs of the Baganda.* Macmillan and Co., London.

John, R.A. (1990), Islam Under Idi Amin; A Case of deja vu cited in *Hansen Bernt H and Twaddle Michael eds. (1991), Uganda Now between decay and Development.* Heinemann, Nairobi.

Rujumba AS., (2011), *Administrative Challenges posed by Born Again Students in Catholic Founded Schools in Kampala Arch-diocese*. Unpublished MED Dissertation Makerere University.

Russell B. (1996), *History of Western Philosophy and its connection with Political and Social Circumstances from the Earliest times to the Present day*. Routledge, London.

Ssebuyira M (2011), Mother sent to Jail for defiling five year old daughter. *Daily Monitor November 21, 2011 news paper* http://www.monitor.co.ug

Stasavage, D., (2005), The role of Democracy in Uganda's move to Universal Primary Education. *The Journal of Modern African studies* 43:53-73 Cambridge University Press.

Umoh M.E., (2003), A Policy Analysis of the Uganda's Commitment to Universal Primary Education. *Senior Edge*-Spring Qtr June 2003

Wickenberg, Flinck, Leo, Rasmusson Stenelo and Yebio eds (2009), *Taking Child Rights Seriously: Reflections on Five years of international Training Programme.* Media-tryck Lund, Sweden

http://cva.stanford.ed/peple/davidbs/Swedish_facts.htm

http://www.kwintessential.co.uk/resources/global-etiquette.sweden.html

www.eenet.org.uk/newsletters/new4/p7.shtml

From *Africa Recovery, Vol. 15 #3, October 2001, page 14*

www.un.org/ecosocdev/geninfo/afrec/vol15no3/153chil4.htm 18/11/2011 at 14;06

11

Elementary Education in Malawi

Grace Kafulatira Mulima

Malawi is located along the southern part of the East Africa rift valley of and bordered by Mozambique to the East and South, Zambia to the West and Tanzania to the North. It has an area of 119,140 square kilometers of which 20 per cent is water, which is Lake Malawi. Malawi has a population of 13 million with 63.5 per cent living under the poverty line and 28 per cent in absolute poverty.

An estimated 5,787,769 million persons are in gainful employment in all sections of the economy including agriculture, both in urban and rural areas.

Over 70 per cent of Malawi's population lives in rural areas. This translates that the majority live in absolute poverty who need interventions such as the Millennium Development Goals (MDGs) for sustainable poverty reduction. It its urged that MDGs help the human development that is not based solely on income but priotizing interventions that can be established with obtainable objectives. Prioritizing interventions help developing countries with limited resources like Malawi to make decisions about where to allocate its resources and through which public policies. The MDGs also strengthen the commitment of developed countries in helping developing countries, and encourage the flow of aid and information sharing. The joint responsibility of developing and developed nations for achieving the MDGs increases the likelihood of their success, which is reinforced by their 189-country support (the MDGs are the most broadly supported poverty reduction targets ever set by the world). Malawi also uses the Malawi Development and Growth Strategy paper which is also in line with the MDGs. However, Malawi is among countries in the sub-Saharan Region that need the most reduction, and it is essential to make drastic changes in improving people's quality of life. The MDGs were developed out of the eight chapters of the Millennium Declaration, signed in September 2000. There are eight goals with 21 targets and a series of measurable indicators for each target. Malawi through Ministry of Education, Science and Technology (MoEST) has concentrated on goal No. 2 (Achieve Universal Primary Education (UPE) by 2015.

During the one party era under the leadership of Malawi Congress Party (MCP), the education system covered the whole country in order to cater for the needs of the labour market and white collar jobs which were readily available but the workforce was inadequate. These efforts resulted into the primary education system which expanded from a total enrolment of 359,841 in 1964 to 847,157 in 1980 and to 1,895,423 in 1994. When Malawi changed to multiparty system of Government, introduced FPE in the 1994/95 academic year, partly in response to the Jomtien conference on Education for All (EFA) which was held in Thailand in 1990. In respect to MGD goal number 2, (Achieve Universal Primary Education), Malawi has intensified Free Primary Education as an effort to endorse the right to education in the Child Rights Convention (CRC) to which Malawi is also a signatory.

Globally, 570 million children are enrolled in schools. The number of children of primary school age, who were out of school, fell from 103 million in 1999 to 73 million in 2006. In that year, primary school enrolment in developing countries reached 88 per cent on an average—up from 83 per cent in 2000.

In sub-Saharan Africa, the net primary school enrolment ratio has only recently reached 71 per cent, even after a significant jump in enrolment that began in 2000. Around 38 million children of primary school age in this region are still out of school (UN 2008).

Malawi is no exception. There are numbers of children who are not in school despite the declaration of UPE with respect to Education for All (EFA) goals and the right of the child to education. The Malawi Government through the Ministry of Education, Science and Technology, (MoEST) outline some of the education plans in the National Education Sector Plan (NESP).

National Education Sector Plan (2008-2017)

National Education Sector Plan2 (NESP) draws on the first and second education development plans, PIF and the Long-term Development Perspective for Malawi (Vision 2020). Subsequent to these development policies, it is also drawn from the current medium-term national development strategy (the Malawi Growth and Development Strategy—MGDS). Furthermore, the NESP reflects the Government of Malawi's commitment to both regional (Southern African Development Community and the African Union) and international (the Millennium Development Goals) targets and priorities, and it incorporates the ideals of Education For All (EFA) National Plan Action 3, in order to respond to the Fast Track Initiative (FTI). Consistent to the above and based on the Paris declaration on donor assistance, the NESP paves the way towards a Sector Wide Approach (SWAP) to planning, development and financing of the education sector. In essence, the detailed NESP is the long-term programme from which the MTEFs, District Education Plans (DEPs) and Annual Implementation Plans (AIP) will be drawn.

1. The NESP operationalizes the MGDS broad educational development priorities, which recognizes education as a catalyst for socio-economic development, industrial growth and an instrument for empowering the poor, the weak and the voiceless. It is also cognizant of the positive role of education in enhancing group solidarity, national consciousness and tolerance of diversity. Furthermore, it ratifies the facilitating role of education in the development of a culture of peace, which is conducive and critical for socio-economic, political and industrial development and appraises education as being critical and necessary for economic and industrial growth and development.
2. NESP states specific details and costs for primary, secondary, teacher education (primary and secondary), technical vocational and higher education sub-sectors only.
3. In footnote 1 the EFA Plan of Action gives comprehensive details and their related costs for early childhood development, primary, out-of school youth and adult literacy as per responsible institution/ministry.
   (i) To equip students with basic knowledge and skills to enable them to function as competent and productive citizens in a free society.
   (ii) Students with disabilities are able to live an independent and comfortable life.
   (iii) To provide the academic basis for gainful employment in the informal, private and public sectors, and
   (iv) Provide high quality professionals in all fields.

As stated earlier in the preamble, the NESP covers Basic Education (Early Childhood Development, out-of-school youth, complementary basic education and adult literacy as non-formal education and Primary Education), Secondary Education (Open and Distance Education and Formal), Teacher Education Development for Basic and Secondary education; Technical Education and Vocational Training (formal, village polytechnics and distant learning) and higher education (private, public and open universities). Thus it is envisaged that NESP will have a wide coverage in the course of implementation and will involve key players (stakeholders) in the private and public sector.

NESP Priority Areas

Priority 1: Access and Equity

(i) Promote stimulation-learning activities at an early life for all children,
(ii) Promote early detection, intervention and inclusion for children with special health and education needs, and
(iii) Promote early childhood care for orphans and vulnerable children.

Priority 2: Quality and Relevance

(i) Improve quality Early Childhood Development (ECD) services for children in Malawi,
(ii) Design a curriculum for children with disabilities, and
(iii) Improve training of ECD teachers/educators/trainers.

Priority 3: Governance and Management

(i) Develop ECD data base including on SNE and gender segregation,
(ii) Strengthen the institutional framework for the delivery of ECD services,
(iii) Promote the profile of ECD,
(iv) Develop an ECD Act,
(v) Improve implementation of the ECD policy, and
(vi) Provide parental education and support groups on early childhood.

The following guiding principles will be adhered to between 2008 and 2017 for developing and sustaining an effective and efficient ECD:

(i) At least 80 per cent of children aged 5 years and below will have an opportunity to access ECD by 2017,
(ii) The average annual growth of ECD, as a whole, will be 17.5 per cent,

(iii) The increase coverage of ECD services will be based on the current basis of 84 per cent CBCCs, 4 per cent day care centres and 12 per cent pre-schools,

(iv) Each ECD centre will increase the number of minimum classes from two to three in order to curb underage enrolment and prepare five year olds for entry into standard one (primary education) at an appropriate age of six years. Thus, three classrooms will still be of levels 1 and 2 although level 2 will have separate classes for ages 4 and 5 with a relatively modified syllabus/course content,

(v) Communities, such as Community Based Care Centres (CBCC), will be encouraged to establish ECD centres through grants which will be accessible upon meeting minimum standards,

(vi) Each education district will have an ECD resource centre to offer the necessary services to CBCCs and,

(vii) By 2018, the average care giver to child ratio will be 1:20 and the helper to child ratio will be 1:40.

Education System: 8-4-4

Malawi is divided into 6 Educational Divisions, and 36 Educational Districts. For administrative purposes, Malawi is divided into three regions (North, Centre, and South) which cover 28 districts. English is the official language and, used for communication in business and commerce, and it is also used as the language of instruction in all levels of education except in Standards 1 to 4 of primary schooling. Local language of the area in which the school is located is used as the medium of instruction. English is taught as a subject in all Standards. (SACNEQ II: 2000).

Learners are supposed to spend 8 years at primary school, which is divided into three sections namely: infant, junior and senior sections. The infant section comprises Standards 1 and 2; junior section comprising Standards 3, 4 and 5 and senior section comprising Standards 6, 7 and 8.

Elementary Education—Methods and Practice

Pre-school education provides an important foundation for learning and development. The Malawi government encourages communities to set up their own pre-schools, but does not support them financially. In most rural areas pre-schools run without funds for support and they are run by volunteers. Teachers work for free and have no resources for teaching and learning, hence they lack the very basics like chalkboards, chalks, books and toys which are commonly used in in pre-school education in developed countries. Pre-schools do not have their own buildings, and many share facilities in churches or other buildings meant for different purposes. It is not all children that have access to pre-school education since this depends on the location and community initiatives and involvement. Most of the pre-schools are unregistered and the probability of being handled by unskilled professionals is likely to be very high. In cities and towns the trend is different because pre-schools are very expensive and are privately owned. Some operate in already existing schools which include; a day care for infants (1 to 24 months olds), a Nursery school (24 to 36 month olds), and a pre-school age—those between 36 to 48 months old. This group has an added advantage to the on-set of primary school because they are expose to learning facilities at a very tender age than those in the rural areas let alone those who do not even have a chance to attend any pre-school activity.

The official entry age for primary level education is 6 years but there are wide variations in the ages of pupils, ranging between 4 years in Standard 1 to 18 years in Standard 8. The wide variations are mainly due to late and multiple entries into schools and multiple grade repetitions. The Malawi government maintained a policy of open access (but not compulsory) to primary education for a long time. Until the introduction of the FPE policy, this access had been severely hampered by the charging of user fees, the requirement to wear school uniform and the many other contributions which parents were expected to make towards the education of their children.

Primary School Education

Primary school education in Malawi is made up of eight years (referred to as Standard 1 to 8). Although the official primary school age group in Malawi is categorized as 6-13, it is very common for students of varying ages to attend primary school, as many students have to repeat some primary years. There are three school terms a year for primary schools in Malawi, running generally from September to December, January to April, and April to July. Primary school students in Malawi learn a variety of subjects, and take examinations in English, Chichewa, Mathematics, Science, and Social Studies. A Primary School Leaving Certificate (PSLCE) based on their standard 8 final examination results in order to progress to secondary school.

Implementation of Child Rights in Elementary Education

Gender Equality

Malawi cites gender issues as an integral part of its national strategy for growth and development. The National Gender Policy (NGP) supports this national strategy and aims at promoting gender mainstreaming throughout the public sector. In the education sector, the NGP advocates reduced repetition, absenteeism, and dropout rates for girls, especially in the higher classes where the gender parity index decreased from 1.04 in the first four standards of primary education to 0.96 in Standards 5 to 8 (MOEST, 2008). The policy also advocates the increased enrolment of girls in science and technology and the implementation of a gender-responsive curriculum. To effectively coordinate and monitor the implementation of gender-related programmes, the Ministry of Education, Science and Technology (MOEST) has a Gender Coordinating Unit. As a policy requirement, all education institutions under the ministry are required to identify a gender focal point person. Most of the policies and programmes addressing gender inequalities in education focus on access and participation, as seen in the following examples:

- Free primary education which reduced gender disparities in enrolment.
- The readmission policy which was put in place in 1993 (the procedures were revised in 2006) and that allowed school-aged mothers to return to school after giving birth. The policy benefited a lot of girls.
- The child-friendly School programme. Included in this programme are the provision of water and sanitation facilities for both boys and girls, with an emphasis, in particular, on girls.
- Grant programmes targeting orphaned girls and boys. There are also specific grants aimed at girls in difficult circumstances.
- Gender Balance in standard 6

Provision of Additional School Blocks Additional Teacher Training Colleges and Programmes

In order to achieve universal primary education and reach the recommended teacher pupil ratio of 60:1 per classroom, 50 additional schools have been targeted to be built every year as stipulated in the NESP. It is expected that the total number of schools will increase from 4,932 in 2004 to 5,392 in 2010 and that during the six year period, the average number of 77 per year will be achieved exceeding the NESP target.

However, the issue on the ground is that there were actually 69 more primary schools (5,461) in 2008 than in 2010. The reason being a decrease from 343 to 142 between 2008 and 2010 in private schools which did not meet the required minimum standards, financial problems or operational problems. In public school primary schools increased from 5,118 in 2008 to 5,191 in 2010 (see Table 11.1). This did not meet the NESP target of 50-schools-per-year.

MoEST has added Liwonde Teachers Training College as a way of reaching the pupil teacher ratio and has also introduced Initial Primary Teacher Education (IPTE) and Open Distance Learning

Table 11.1: Number of All Schools from 2005-2010

Year	*Primary schools*		
	Public	*Private*	*Total*
2005	5004	155	5159
2006	5041	190	5231
2007	5086	221	5307
2008	5118	343	5461
2009	5106	298	5404
2010	5191	201	5392

Source: Key EMIS Indicators Analysis 2004-2010: MoEST.

(ODL) programmes for student teachers in all the teacher training colleges. There is need to increase the number of qualified teachers in order to fill the primary school teaching positions where vacancies have occurred because of primary school teachers who leave for other professions and upgrading into secondary school teachers.

School Health and Nutrition (SHN)

The strategy targets all school-aged children (between 2 and 18 years). The learning institutions and targeted Ministries, are:

Table 11.2: Targeted Learning Institutions and Responsible Ministry/ Department

Learning Institutions	*Ministry/Department Responsible*
1. Childcare centres	MoGCCD; Early Childhood Development
2. Government Primary Schools	MoEST Basic Education
3. Complementary Basic education	MoEST Basic Education
4. Government Secondary schools	MoEST Secondary Section
5. Private or faith based schools	Management and staff of those institutions
6. Out-of-school youth	MoGCCD: Social welfare

Source: National School Health and Nutrition Strategic Plan 2009-2018: MoEST.

The National School Health and Nutrition Strategic Plan indicates that, "*Malawi's health situation, including that of school aged children, as measured in terms of child mortality rate, and malnutrition is unsatisfactory. The multiple Indicator Cluster survey of 2006 indicated that the child mortality rate was at 118/1000 live births. The main causes of the child deaths being malaria, diarrhoeal diseases, and acute respiratory infection.*"

Current School Health and Nutrition Interventions

The health services are currently being provided by the MoH and MoEST and health training institutions. The health package which was improved in 2006 has the following components:

- Assessment of the school environment
- Health and nutrition assessment (physical examination)
- Prevention and treatment of minor illnesses and emergencies
- De-worming for intestinal worms and bilharzias, with a strong education component on personal hygiene, water and sanitation.

(a) School Meals

SHN was officially launched in 1999 and in 2007 MoEST began to provide meals to about 16 out of 33 Educational Districts, covering approximately 900 out of 5,200 primary schools. The meals encouraged children to be in school and brought the hard to reach children to be alert in class which also brought about an increase on more children especially girls doing better in school. It also led to better selection of secondary schools and a reduction in drop-out rate due to early marriages.

(b) Micronutrients

There is an aspect of nutrition education and dietary diversity, with an emphasis on micronutrients (Vitamins and minerals). The package includes vitamin A, iron/folate and iodine. In 2007 MoEST covered the 5,200 primary schools in the country by providing:

- Vitamin A supplements once every six months
- Iron with folate tablets once a week for children up to 10 years of age
- And promoting the use of iodised salt and testing household salt once every six months. (Learners were asked to bring in the salt they use at home).

(c) Productive School Environment

This intervention aims at improving the whole school environment and the results have been more food, healthier soil, water supplies, improved sanitation, additional fuel wood, building materials and income for schools, along with a cooler, cleaner environment in which to learn. (Moest, SHN, 2009).

Instead of relying on outside donors, schools since 2006 embarked on more approaches focusing on what the school can do using their own resources such as; Teaching and Learning Using Locally Available Resources (TALULAR) and Permaculture.

Water, Sanitation and Hygiene (WASH) in Primary Schools

Improved Water, Health and Sanitation (WASH) was introduced in primary schools by following the guiding documents such as the National Water Policy (2007); the National Decentralization Policy (2005), and the national Gender Policy (2004) and the National HIV Policy among others. The introduction of WASH in schools is to provide safe water, sanitation and hygiene in schools as one way of promoting child rights in the area of provision. The positive effects of WASH are as follows:

- Reduced disease burden among children and staff.
- Improved school attendance and retention.
- Improved gender balance in education.
- Improved attraction and retention of teachers.
- WASH is for universal school feeding.
- Effective learning through a Conducive environment.
- School children as agents of change.

Challenges

As opposed to EFA goals and UPE, children's earnings play a vital role in most low income households' survival strategies. It is an uphill task for MoEST to encourage school attendance and discourage children's work among families living in absolute poverty. Exposure to socio-economic shocks such as the recession which has its after-shocks being felt in Malawi has brought about retrenchment, devaluation of the kwacha, therefore, having, influence on child labour in the most affected households. Natural disasters such as flash floods, earthquakes bring about loss of property and crops and if the victims are not given assistance fast enough; this brings about high probability of child labour and less probability of attending schools despite all the policies and initiatives by the Government to keep children in schools.

Poverty and Orphanhood due to the impact of HIV and AIDS has brought about double orphans who grow up in child-headed families with siblings looking after one another. These children often are vulnerable to sexual abuse, early or unwanted pregnancies and if policies aimed at reducing household vulnerability are not implemented then child labour becomes the order of the day which may hinder MoEST efforts to achieve Education For All (EFA) by 2015.

Free Primary Education though not compulsory, has helped to keep children from poor families in school and has seen many proceeding to secondary education. The drop-out rates have decreased over the years and work that could have compromised children's education in Malawi, due to lack of school fees, is being tackled by adults as a result of awareness campaigns by MoEST. Kamlongera A.F. stated that Free Primary Education (FPE) in 1994 has led to:

- Increased net and gross enrolment rates approximately over 70 per cent of school-age children enrolled in school.
- Improved equity for girls and the Orphans and Vulnerable Children (OVCs) (41.1 per cent of the total enrolment in 2006 were orphans), and

Deteriorating education quality, due to high enrolment rate which brought about congestion especially at primary school level, need for more school blocks, teaching and learning materials and training more teachers; a thing which MoEST has embarked on in its recent projects.

Overview on CRC in Elementary Education

Malawi being a signatory to CRC has made sure that the central pillars of CRC namely, provision, participation and protection have been catered for in the NESP priority areas which are:

- PRIORITY 1—Access and Equity
- PRIORITY 2—Quality and relevance
- PRIORITY 3—Governance and management

MoEST in conjunction with international NGOs has worked so hard in the implementation of CRC by providing additional classrooms, school blocks, Teacher Training College and programmes such as Initial Primary school Teacher Education (IPTE) and Open and Distance Learning (ODL) for student teachers to meet the teacher-pupil ratio of 1:60. There also has been provision of food through SHN and protection through WASH and Information, Education and Communication.

Despite all the efforts by MoEST towards the Elementary Child Development as stipulated in the NESP, there is still need to do more as the enrolment numbers in primary schools continue to swell due to the introduction of Free Primary education (FPE) as one way of achieving Universal Primary Education (UPE) by 2015 and the much improved child mortality rate.

There is need to bring awareness to all stakeholders on the rights of a child especially to education in both private and public sectors; reach the OVCs who usually do not have access to education if there is no proper care, especially in the child headed families, due to the impact of HIV and AIDS pandemic and Orphan hood.

References:

Bruns, B, *et al.*, 2003, Achieving Universal Primary Education by 2015: A chance for every child, Washington D.C., The World Bank.

Colclough, C, and Lewin, K, 1993, *Educating all the children: Strategies for primary schooling in the South*, Oxford, Clarendon Press.

Education Statistics 2010: Education Management Information System. Ministry of Education, Science and Technology

Kamlongera A.F., 2009, *Reaching out-of-school children in Malawi*, Lilongwe

Key EMIS Indicator Analysis 2004-2010: Department of Monitoring and Evaluation. Ministry of Education, Science and Technology

Malawi School Wash 2008: A Status Report on Water, Sanitation, and Hygiene in Primary Schools. Ministry of Education, Science and Technology.

MOEST. (2008a), The National Education Strategic Plan 2008-2017, a statement. Lilongwe.

National School Health and Nutrition Strategic plan: School Health and Nutrition Response in the Education Sector 2009-2018. Ministry of Education, Science and Technology

Paris, UNESCO. 53

Saito, M. (2010). Has gender equality in reading and mathematics achievement improved? SACMEQ

United Nations (2006), The Millennium Development Goals Report 2006. New York.

—

12

Elementary School English Teaching in Multilingual Context

Implementation in Indonesian Rural Classrooms

Ngasbun Egar, Rahmawati Sukmaningrum and Siti Musarokah

In much of Asian countries, included Indonesia, English is claimed as the language of education, business, culture and even regional cooperation. This is not just a political statement but is simply a descriptive remark concerning the current state of the English language in this part of the world. Thus, students are becoming more and more aware that English is a dispensable Asian language (Honna, 2003). The likelihood of using English with other Asians motivates an increasing numbers of students to learn the language better.

In Indonesia, English as a foreign language is taught as a compulsory subject from junior secondary school up to the university level. In response to the need for developing human resources, the teaching of English as a foreign language has been extended to reach the elementary school level. Starting from the year of 1994, English is also taught to elementary school students. Unlike other levels of school, in elementary level, English is taught as elective subject or local curricular content. It means that students in the elementary school level will not have the same burden in learning English as the other elementary school compulsory subjects. As a consequence, English is given less attention and portion than other subjects. To put in line, this is a contradictive policy to the need of that language in the real world. Based on the theory of psycholinguistic, human brain is not fully developed at birth. Rather, it matures gradually over a period of several years (Locke, 1983). Related to the language and other cognitive skills acquisition, the brain can easily absorb any information from age two to puberty, which is called critical period. Thus, it is very important to teach English to our children as early as possible since they are in their most valuable critical period. Thus, we have seen that the proficiency in English of every school level graduates still create disappointment among teachers themselves, as well as parents. The unsatisfying quality of English teaching is, of course, related to different variables. In line with the need to get a detailed picture and investigate the problems encountered in the English teaching in elementary schools, especially in rural areas, the writer conducted the research.

Role and Function of English alongside Other Language in Indonesia

Talking about cultural background related with EFL teaching learning, it is so much relevant to discuss first about the role and function of English alongside other languages in Indonesia. Indonesia comprises of 17, 000 islands is stretched across 3200 miles of Equatorial Ocean. Indonesia is the world's most populous (current population over 200 million) country with its variety of ethnic and a densely multilingual nation. Indonesia has more than 500 ethnic groups, each with its own regional language such as Javanese, Balinese, Sudanese, Aceh, Batak, etc. Most of Indonesian children speak regional language as their first language (mother tongue), while Indonesian is served as the second language. English and other languages are assumed as foreign or international languages for almost all Indonesians. Thus, making generalization about the social function of English is not easy since it is not a first language, although English is an international language. Huda (2000: 68) mentions five factors that have made English an international language:

(a) Its internal number linguistic feature.
(b) The large number of English speakers.
(c) Its wide geographical spread of where it is used.
(d) Its importance in field such as politics, international diplomacy, business and economics, science and technology and culture.
(e) The use of English by countries which currently dominate world affairs economically, politically, and culturally.

Though English has now been widely used in the society, yet it is not used as a medium of communication in official domains like government, the law courts, and educational system, and is not accorded any special status in the country legislation, it is still seen as a priority, as the most important of foreign languages to be taught. Crystal (2003: 106) categorizes the reasons a person, for whom English is not a mother tongue, might want to learn English as historical, political, economical, intellectual or related to entertainment. Those factors, and the large number of speakers who use English worldwide, can be considered as valid reasons for its special status in Indonesia. Commentators on the use of English in Indonesia have seen it as *potentially* serving a number of important purposes (Huda, 2000: 65-66):

- as a means of international communication in practically all fields or walks of life
- as a medium through which scientific knowledge, and new technologies can be accessed implemented with a view to succeeding in the global marketplace
- as a source of vocabulary for the development and modernization of Indonesian
- as a way to get to know native speakers of English, their language, culture and literature, or as a means of expanding one's intellectual horizons.

The position of English in Indonesia can be seen in the Fig. 12.1.

This issue influences to the English teaching learning process and its success of the learning outcomes. This is particularly based on the idea that the language habits of the children will influence the proficiency of the targeted language itself. From the investigation toward the language habit of the elementary students in Demak district (one of a rural areas in Central Java, Indonesia), it was found out that all the students use Javanese as their first and daily language. They almost never use English outside the classroom. The rare use of the language causes the learning as almost never effective.

A. Method

A case study approach was used in order to investigate the implementation and the challenges of English teaching learning in a specific characteristic that is in rural areas with its multilingual context of the learners. According to Nunan (1992), the case study is generally concerned with the specific features of an individual entity such as a class or a school. Hence, it is ideally suited to the in-depth investigation of a particular group, which may provide a fertile ground to make generalizations of the broader population of which the group is a member (Cohen & Manion, 1985, as

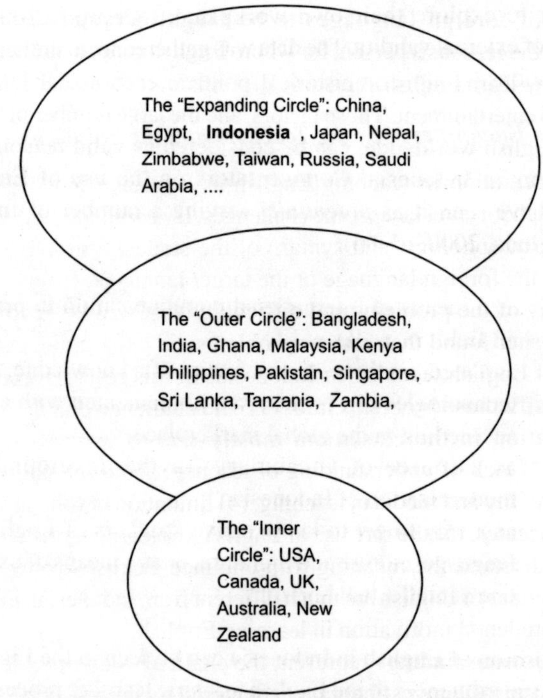

Fig. 12.1: Kachru Three-Circle of World Englishes

Source: (Kachru, 1992: 356) reprinted in (Jenkins, 2003:16).

population of which the group is a member (Cohen & Manion, 1985, as cited in Nunan, 1992). A case study methodology is also, particularly, suited to the individual or a particular group of teachers, since it is easily accessible and its findings can be put to practical use in the classroom. Nunan (1992) also refers to the centrality in the case study and this is the key reason why this method has been selected in this research, since the context described is broadly reflected throughout the English teaching in multilingual classrooms in rural areas.

The research undertaking was carried out involving a sample of 30 elementary teachers in Demak district (one of rural areas in Central Java, Indonesia). The research was designed to investigate the teachers' language teaching strategy from the perspective of students' cultural backgrounds. Besides that, the investigation was also carried out to discover the challenges and problems toward the implementation in the classroom context. The case study also provides means for the individual practitioner to explore their own workplace, thereby lessening the importance of external validity. The data was gathered from the interviews and observations.

B. Problems Encountered by the Teachers and the Solutions

The implementation in teaching English as a foreign language in the elementary school level faces some challenges. By comparing the structure (phonology, morphology, and syntax) of the students' native language with that of the foreign language or the target language, it is possible to predict many of the problems and difficulties that will be encountered. Thus, the writer found that various problems did exist in the context of multilingual English teaching in Indonesia. In this research report, the writers classify those problems into: (1) The challenge dealing with the implementation in the classroom mostly due to teaching learning strategies, (2) lack of understanding of teachers about the children are, (3) lack of facility and media in teaching, (4) limitation of time in teaching learning processes, (5) the rare use of English, (6) learners find it difficult to spell, understand the meaning to pronounce English words, (7) the complicated rules of English are much different from Indonesian language, (8) lack of students' motivation in learning English.

The following findings represent the challenges and problems that were found from the investigation encountered by the teachers.

1. Teaching Learning Strategies used by the Teachers

This study revealed that the teachers in elementary schools face difficulties to use appropriate strategies in teaching. 87 per cent from 30 teachers reported their difficulties in designing the appropriate strategies in teaching English to their elementary school students. The writers identified many teachers who teach English focusing on grammatical rules and vocabulary mastery. This condition might be based on the 1994 curriculum that said "the assessment focus of learning language at elementary schools is in language skill achievement, especially in speaking". Because of that determination, in English teaching learning activity, the teachers focus on speaking ability which is understood in mastering as much vocabulary as possible.

In fact, it is not considered as a good method to use. The focus of teaching learning in speaking does not mean that students should master 'a bulk' of vocabulary and know all grammatical rules without knowing its uses in context. The teacher should understand that though focusing on speaking, the knowledge of vocabulary and grammatical rules are learned to support the development of students' ability in speaking. They may learn vocabulary and grammatical rules subconsciously. The activities in language teaching, learning in the elementary classroom, should be contextually embedded. As stated by Brown (2001: 90), context-reduced language in abstract, isolated, unconnected sentences will be much less tolerated by children's minds.

Dealing with teaching the children, Cameron (2001: 93-94) proposed some general principles of helping the children to learn. These principles can be applied by EFL teachers in the classroom:

(a) Teacher can model how to use strategies and draw children's attention explicitly to aspects of strategy use. For example, teachers can show how to find clues to the meaning of a new word in a picture or in other words in the same sentence.
(b) Teachers can teach the sub-skills needed to make use of strategies. For example, to use dictionary efficiently requires knowledge of alphabetical order and lots of practice with it.
(c) Classroom tasks can conclude structured opportunities for using strategies. For example, when reading a story, teachers can explicitly encourage prediction of the meaning of new words.
(d) Independent strategy use can be rehearsed in classrooms. For example, children can be helped to prepare lists of words that they want to learn from lesson which can be shown which ways of learning from the lists and later can be put in pairs to test each other.
(e) Children can be helped to reflect on the learning process through evaluating their achievements. For example, at the end of the lesson, they can be asked how many words they have learned and which words they need to learn more about. Through regular self-evaluation, children can understand more about what they are learning and how.

The teaching learning strategies, as has been reported by some researches undertaken, have powerful impact on the students' learning outcome. Teaching learning strategies are specific actions, behaviour, steps, or techniques that the teacher and students employ, often consciously, to improve students' progress in internalizing, storing, retrieving and using the language (Oxford, 1990). The most common findings is that the use of appropriate language teaching learning strategies leads to improve proficiency or achievement of overall or in a specific skill areas (see O'Malley and Chamot, 1990; Oxford and Crookall, 1989; Wenden and Rubin, 1987). Thus, it can be stated that the appropriate strategies in teaching will lead to the satisfying achievement or proficiency of the students.

2. Lack of Understanding of the Teachers about the Children

Dealing with the first factor proposed by McKay next influential problem might have large contribution to the unsatisfying achievement of elementary students in EFL teaching learning process. The major concern here is from the teachers' point of view. From the investigation, the writers found that 87 per cent of the sample of the elementary teachers seems to have a misconception about how the children learn the language. The children here have been wrongly assumed as being a miniature of an adult, in which the way they learn English as a foreign language exactly the same as the way adults do. This misconception leads them to use inappropriate teaching learning approach in English. They tend to use the same teaching learning approach in English as they would teach adults.

However, teaching children is different from teaching adults. Children have less complicated view of the world than older children and adults, but this fact does not imply that teaching children is simple and straightforward. On the contrary, the teacher of children needs to be highly skilled to reach into children's worlds and lead them to develop their understanding toward more formal, more extensive and differently organized concepts (Cameron, 2001: 3). This concept should be understood by the elementary teachers. Thus, the elementary teachers need to understand how the children make sense of the world and how they learn. They also need skill of analyzing learning tasks and using language new ideas to groups and class of children.

The misconception problem might occur generally based on the wrong assumption of the teachers that teaching English at the elementary level is a simple matter. As stated by Huda, the elementary schools teachers are generally willing to teach, but they are not actually prepared to teach English for young learner, in particular. Teaching English has never been part of the curriculum of elementary school teacher education programme in Indonesia (Huda, 2000). The wrong assumption has grown in Indonesia. Teaching children is assumed as an extension of mothering rather than an intellectual enterprise. The primary or elementary teachers, therefore, are often given less training, lower status, and lower pay, than their colleagues in the same educational system who teach more adult learners. This wrong assumption should be changed. Everyone should understand that teaching languages to children needs all the skills of the good primary teacher in managing and keeping them on task, plus knowledge of the language, of the language teaching, and of language learning. And this is even more complicated in teaching a foreign language. The English elementary teachers, therefore, need more training and appreciation toward their professionals.

Language teaching has always been, and remains, more of an art that a science. That is to say, it is largely intuitive and dependent on the personal abilities and convictions of the teacher (Prator, cited in Croft, 1980: 18). It appears that most of teacher's success is the result of such qualities as enthusiasm, intelligence, and love for the students. Understanding the students' natures and their needs in learning the foreign language should be the teachers' great concern in teaching. It is important—perhaps more important—for a teacher to understand the nature of the students as it is to understand the nature of the language itself. The language teachers, therefore, have much to learn from psychology, the discipline which studies how the language is acquired and the personal variables that may affect its acquisition.

3. Lack of Facility and Media in Teaching

The next issue is concerning the facility of the schools. The investigation dealing the facility of the schools shown that most of the elementary schools do not have enough facility to support the teaching learning activities. From 30 schools to be investigated, there are only 4 schools that have a language laboratory, while the rest reported the non-existence of language laboratory. This condition is getting even worse because the teachers are not creative to use media in teaching. From the classroom observation, it was found that the teachers never use any kinds of media in teaching learning process. The use of media in teaching children is, however, essential particularly to the need of providing the students with good modeling in the targetted language. How can the children be able to identify the pronunciations of the word correctly if they have never been heard in their native sound?

The development of listening and speaking is as important as the development of reading and writing skills. The more the learners listen to and speak English, the better will be their language use. By listening the native speaker talks, the learners will be given large opportunities to expose a wide variety of spoken texts in order to develop listening and speaking competences to communicate effectively and appropriately according to purpose. Teaching media, however, does not always deal with the expensive facility. As stated by Gandini, as cited in Karen (1997: 178), a teacher can use materials around him/her to enhance the learning experience of young children by opening new avenues for discovering, creating, and constructing. There are many materials that have that potential all around us; they can be brought inside the classroom together with the usual crayons, markers, chalks, paper, and glue. And even the variety and the use of crayons, markers, chalks, paper, and glue themselves can be expanded and transformed into a powerful mine of idea, as our first story tells us. Let us just observe the crayons we used. How can teacher puts, side by side, combining and contrasting its shape, colours, and size to enhance their learning of vocabulary. Later on teacher can expand students' writing skill by asking them to make simple sentence from those words. It is helpful to look around and observe what is available or search for things that can be used, combined and transformed. It is not obvious or easy at the beginning, but when teachers start to pay attention, their eyes will see better and detect more paths to potential materials that our environment offers for their work and pleasure.

4. Limitation of Time in Teaching Learning Process

Time limitation is also considered as another problem of teaching this foreign language. As stated in advance, at elementary level, English is taught as elective subject or as local curricular content. It means that Indonesian students in the elementary level will not have the same burden in learning English as the other elementary compulsory subjects. As a consequence, English is given less attention and portion than the other subjects. At elementary level, English is only taught one or two times a week (35 minute per lesson). This is not significant number of hours devoted to a foreign language. With a very limited time of teaching learning process in class, teachers find it more difficult to explore the students' ability in four language skills (i.e. speaking, listening, reading and writing).

5. Limited Use of English

The lack exposure to English use in everyday life is also important issue. According to the investigation concerning the issue of exposure to English in everyday life, it was found out that all the learners from those 30 elementary schools almost never use English outside the classrooms. This finding can be used to make a general assumption that learners mostly think that English is only a lesson in the classrooms. This is one of the biggest challenges that children in elementary schools may come across.

The adults' language habit around the children might give a great contribution to this condition. As we know in Indonesia, as an implication of positioning English as a foreign language, it is just learned in the classrooms, and not widely used as a means of communication by people across the region. This lack of exposure makes children difficult to see English learning as being functional and useful for them. They might think that English is no more than one of the lessons that must be learned at school only, not as something useful and should be used in their everyday life. This problem should be prevented by giving learners the information that English is useful for their future life to face globalization era. The adults should also give them a modeling of language habit by using this foreign language in their daily uses.

6. Learners' Difficulty to Spell and Understand English Words

The next problem is that the English writing and its complex grammatical rules which students find it difficult to spell, understand the meaning and pronounce English words, and the complicated rules of English which are much different from Indonesian language. As we know, English words are written differently as opposed to the way they are pronounced. Different to English, the Indonesian language has the phonetic writing system wherein the writings clearly consistently reflect the sounds. From the investigation, students reported that they find the problem to read or write a word by dictation in English. For example the word "bus" is pronounced [b?s], while in Indonesia it is pronounced [bis] which represents the same phonetic writing of the word "bis". Children would find it difficult to learn English since its writing system is confusing considering the fact that there is no direct one-to-one correspondence between the pronunciation of a word and its spelling. This problem can be solved by the time they are learning.

7. Lack of Students' Motivation in Learning English

The last problem to be investigated is that the lack of motivation in learning English as a foreign language. From 30 teachers to be investigated, 22 teachers reported that students are not really motivated in learning English. This statement was strengthened by the result of the class observation. It was found that the elementary students were not really engaged to involve the class activity.

Motivation is generally assumed as their interest to join a certain programme. It naturally has to do with students' desire to participate in learning process. But it also concerns at the reasons and goals that underlie learners' involvement and non-involvement in academic activities (Stipek, 1998).

In language teaching-learning context, learners' motivation is defined as their active participation to use the language and improve their competence in it. Motivation can also be defined as the impetus to create and sustain intensions and goal-seeking acts. Ames suggested that motivation is very important because it determines the extent of the learner's active involvement and attitude toward the learning (cited in Hussein *et al.*, 2000). Motivation, therefore, can be the students' power in the learning process.

Fostering students' motivation is not easy. Hussin Maarof and D'Cruz (2000) in their paper presentation suggested that a persistent problem faced by the teachers, especially non-specialists, is the attempt to sustain genuine interest in continuing to learn the subject and to use it once the examinations are over. The challenges also occur due to the energizing students' motivation to create a real supportive effort to their learning process. Besides providing conducive classroom climate, teacher can also foster students' motivation by creating various activities and tasks dimension. Ideally, tasks should be challenging but achievable and relevant. It should also be able to promote motivation, as does 'conceptualizing' learning; that is helping students to see how skills can be applied in real world.

C. Conclusion

Given the above explanation of the research findings, there are several points to be concluded. The conclusion point is followed by the writers' suggestion concerning each issue. Those points are:

1. English teaching for children is different with the adults. Thus, teachers should apply different teaching approach also. The appropriate approach in teaching will lead to the successful of students' proficiency to the target language. The *whole language* approach, therefore, is essential. If language is broken into too many bits and pieces, students will not see the relationship. Language teaching learning should be firmly context embedded. Story lines, familiar situations and characters, real-life conversations, meaningful purposes in using language—these will establish a context within which a language can be received and sent and thereby improve the language achievement contextually.

2. It takes a very special person to be able to teach children effectively. Along with this guideline, an elementary school teacher should develop a certain intuition with increasing months and years of experience. She/he then, should be the one who can really master both the knowledge content and children' language acquisition development. If there is no other solution except using class teacher, at least she/he should be trained to teach that language effectively to the children. Empowering classroom teacher in technique of language teaching will support the learners' outcomes.
3. The next issue is concerning the facility of the schools. Most of urban elementary schools in Indonesia do not have enough facility to support the teaching learning activities. From the investigations, it was found that there are only four schools that have a language laboratory. This condition is getting even worse because the teachers are not creative to use media in teaching. From the classroom observation, it was found that the teacher never uses any kinds of media in teaching learning process. The use of media in teaching children is, however, essential particularly to the need of providing the students with good modeling in the target, language. English elementary teachers can solve this problem by providing innovative and creative media in teaching.
4. Limitation of time is also considered as a problem in teaching English. As elective or local content English is only given once or twice a week (35 minute per lesson). With a very limited time of teaching learning process in class, teachers find it more difficult to explore the students' ability in four language skills.
5. From the students' perspectives, it was found that the lack exposure to English use in everyday life and the complicated English phonetic writing system became the major problems faced by the students. The problem concerning the issue of English exposure should be prevented by giving the learners information that English is useful for their future life to face up the globalization era. The adults should also give them a modeling of language habit by using this foreign language in their daily use. The English writing system problem can be solved by the time they are learning. Thus, they need more practices in English. The lack of students' motivation in learning English is also considered as a big challenge in teaching EFL in Indonesia.

References

Allwright, D. and Bailey, K.M. (1991), *Focus on the Language Classroom: An Introduction to Classroom Research for Language Teacher.* Australia, Cambridge University Press.

Brown, H.D. (1994), *Principles of Language Learning and Teaching,* 3rd Edition. New Jersey, Prentice Hall.

Cameron, L. (2001), *Teaching Languages to Young Learners.* Cambridge, Cambridge University Press.

Croft, Kenneth. (1980), *Reading English as a Second Language,* 2nd Edition. Canada, Little, Brown and Company.

Crystal, D. (2003), *English as A Global Language*, 2nd Edition. Cambridge: Cambridge University Press

Honna, N. (2003), English as a Multicultural and Intercultural Literacy. *Southern Review*, Vol. 1, No. 18.

Huda, N. (2000), *The Position and Function of Foreign Language.* Jakarta, Pusat Bahasa Departemen Pendidikan Nasional.

Hussin, S, Nooreiney M, dan JV D'Cruz. (2000), *Sustaining an Interest in Learning English and Increasing the Motivation to Learn English: An Enrichment Programme.* http://www.findarticle.com/ 2000annual/ article.html

Jenkins, J. (2003), *World Englishes: A Resources Bool for Students.* Routledge English Language Introduction Series. London and New York, Routledge.

Kachru, B.B. (1992), *The Other Tongue: English Across Culture,* 2nd Edition. Urbana, IL, University of Illinois Press.

Karen Menke Paciorek (1997), *Early Childhood Education*, 18th Edition. USA, McGraw-Hill.

Lepper, M.R. (2001), *Motivational Consideration in the Study of Instruction.* http://www.cyc.net.org/today/today100801.html

Nunan, D. (1992), *Research Methods in Language Learning.* Cambridge, Cambridge University Press.

O'Malley and Chamot, A.U. (1990), *Learning Strategies in Second Language Acquisition.* Cambridge, Cambridge University Press.

Oxford, R.L. (1993), Research on Language Learning Strategies. *Annual Review of Applied Linguistic,* Vol. 13, 157-158.

Stipek, D. (1988), *Motivation to Learn: From Theory to Practice.* New Jersey, Prentice Hall.

Wenden, A. and Rubin, J. (1987), *Learner Strategies for Language Learning.* Englewood Cliffs, NJ, Prentice Hall.

III

Child Rights in Different Countires

III

Child Rights in Different Countries

13

Child Rights in India

Introduction

Every nation whether developed or developing links its future with the status of the child. A child of today cannot develop to be a responsible and productive member of tomorrow's society unless an environment, which is conducive to his social and physical health, is assured to him. Neglecting children means loss to the society as a whole. If the children are deprived of their childhood-socially, economically, physically and mentally the nation gets deprived of the potential human resources for social progress, economic empowerment, peace and order, social stability and good citizenry.

India has the largest number of children in the world. India's heritage of a stable family life and traditional joint family system helped children grow into an atmosphere of warmth and affection into a secure future. However, with the changing socio-economic vertices weakening of the institution of joint family and resulting 'nuclearization 'of the families children were deprived of that enabling atmosphere and were propelled into an atmosphere where the parental care to the childhood started being shared with the institutions like school. In the rural set up too, there has been a trend towards the nuclearization undermining the emotional, psychological and the social support, which used to go into the child's upbringing.

History of Child Rights in India

The Indian Constitution has a framework within which ample provisions exist for the protection, development and welfare of children. There are a wide range of laws that guarantee children their rights and entitlements as provided in the Constitution and in the UN Convention.

It was during the 50s decade that the UN Declaration of the Rights of the Child was adopted by the UN General Assembly. This Declaration was accepted by the Government of India. As part of the various Five Year Plans, numerous programmes have been launched by the Government aimed at providing services to children in the areas of health, nutrition and education. In 1974, the Government of India adopted a National Policy for Children, declaring the nation's children as 'supremely important assets'. This policy lays down recommendations for a comprehensive health programme, supplementary nutrition for mothers and children, nutrition education for mothers, free and compulsory education for all children up to the age of 14, non-formal preschool education, promotion of physical education and recreational activities, special consideration for the children of weaker sections of the population like the scheduled castes and the schedule tribes, prevention of exploitation of children and special facilities for children with handicaps. (Rao,1979)

The policy provided for a National Children's Board to act as a forum to plan, review and coordinate the various services directed toward children. The Board was first set up in 1974. The Department of Women and Child Development was set up in the Ministry of Human Resource Development in 1985. The Department, besides ICDS, implements several other programmes, undertakes advocacy and inter-sectoral monitoring catering to the needs of women and children.

In pursuance of this, the Department formulated a National Plan of Action for Children in 1992. The Government of India ratified the Convention on the Rights of the Child on 12 November 1992. By ratifying the Convention on the Rights of the Child, the Government is obligated "to review National and State legislation and bring it in line with provisions of the Convention". The Convention revalidates the rights guaranteed to children by the Constitution of India, and is, therefore, a powerful weapon to combat forces that deny these rights. The Ministry of Women and Child Development has the nodal responsibility of coordinating the implementation of the Convention. Since subjects covered under the Articles of the Convention fall within the purview of various departments/ ministries of the Government, the Inter-Ministerial Committee set up in the Ministry with representatives from the concerned sections monitor the implementation of the Convention. Ensuring that child rights are met for every child is a daunting challenge for India but also a testimony to the Government's commitment to the cause of children.

National Commission for Protection of Child Rights (NCPCR)

The National Commission for Protection of Child Rights (NCPCR) was set up in March 2007 under the Commission for Protection of Child Rights Act, 2005, an Act of Parliament (December 2005). The Commission's Mandate is to ensure that all Laws, Policies, Programmes, and Administrative Mechanisms are in consonance with the Child Rights perspective as enshrined in the Constitution of India and also the UN Convention on the Rights of the Child. The Child is defined as a person in the 0 to 18 years age group.

The Commission visualises a rights-based perspective flowing into National Policies and Programmes, along with nuanced responses at the State, District and Block levels, taking care of specificities and strengths of each region. In order to touch every child, it seeks a deeper penetration to communities and households and expects that the ground experiences inform the support the field receives from all the authorities at the higher level. Thus the Commission sees an indispensable role for the State, sound institution-building processes, respect for decentralization at the level of the local bodies at the community level and larger societal concern for children and their well-being.

The historical process, and its social, economic and political priorities from mid-nineteenth to mid-twentieth century, paved the way for shaping a more coherent concept of childhood located within the family as the principal institutional influence and as the prime site for socialization. Further, it determined the nature of the relationship between the child, the family and the State and thus created the essential foundations of a national childhood for all children. Correspondingly, the Constitution of India, which came into force in January 1950, contains provisions for survival, development and protection of children. These are included both in Part III and Part IV of the Constitution pertaining to 'Fundamental Rights' and 'Directive Principles of State Policy'.

Being one of the world's largest democracy, India has a federal system of government, with the States having their own democratically elected governments. The relative jurisdiction of the Central and State Governments over different matters has been indicated in the Seventh Schedule of the Constitution of India under the Union, State and Concurrent Lists. The survival, development and protection of children fall either in the Concurrent or in the State List. However, the implementation of schemes, including those of the Central Government, is carried out by the States.

Major Constitutional Provisions

Fundamental Rights

- Article 14: ... shall not deny to any person equality before the law or the equal protection of the laws within the territory of India.
- Article 15: ... shall not discriminate against any citizen... (3) Nothing in this article shall prevent the State from making special provision for women and children. (4) Nothing ... shall prevent the State from making any special provision for the advancement of any socially and educationally backward classes of citizens or for the Scheduled Castes and the Scheduled Tribes.

Chapter 2

- Article 17: "Untouchability" is abolished and its practice in any form is forbidden. ...
- Article 19: (1) All citizens shall have the right–(a) to freedom of speech and expression; ... (c) to form associations or unions; (d) to move freely throughout the territory of India; (e) to reside and settle in any part of the territory of India.
- Article 21: No person shall be deprived of his life or personal liberty except according to procedure established by law.
- Article 21 A: ... shall provide free and compulsory education to all children of the age of six to fourteen years...
- Article 23: Traffic in human beings and begar and other similar forms of forced labour are prohibited...
- Article 24: No child below the age of fourteen years shall be employed to work in any factory or mine or engaged in any other hazardous employment.

Directive Principles of State Policy

- Article 39: ... (e) ... the tender age of children are not abused... and not forced by economic necessity to enter avocations unsuited to their age or strength; (f) that children are given opportunities and facilities to develop in a healthy manner and in conditions of freedom and dignity and that childhood... protected against exploitation and against moral and material abandonment.
- Article 45: ...provide early childhood care and education for all children until they complete the age of six years.

- Article 46: ...shall promote with special care the educational and economic interests of the weaker sections of the people, and, in particular, of the Scheduled Castes and the Scheduled Tribes,...
- Article 47: ...raising of the level of nutrition and the standard of living of its people and the improvement of public health...
- Article 51: The State shall endeavour to–... (c) foster respect for international law and treaty obligations ...
- Article 51A: ... (k) ... parent or guardian to provide opportunities for education to his child or, as the case may be, ward between the age of six and fourteen years.

Situation of Children in India

In the wake of the 1990 World Summit for Children, the Government of India adopted a National Plan of Action for Children in 1992, with goals for the decade. In the year 1992 itself, it also ratified the CRC and thereafter in its Periodic Country Reports submitted to the UN Committee on the Rights of the Child has dwelled at length about the measures taken for ensuring children's rights. These Reports and the India Report on the World Summit for Children undoubtedly record some positive changes in the situation of children in India. But, there are significant problems and performance gaps too.

Child Sex Ratio

The child sex ratio is calculated as number of girls per 1,000 boys in the 0-6 years age group. In India, the 2001 Census reported a child sex ratio of 927 girls per 1,000 boys, that is definitely adverse to girls. The 1991 Census had reported child sex ratio of 945 girls per 1,000 boys, which signifies that a decade later, the child sex ratio has worsened further by 18 points. Prior to the 1991 Census, this ratio had fallen from 976 in 1961, to 964 in 1971, and 962 in 1981. A stage may soon come when it would become extremely difficult, if not impossible, to make up for the missing girls. The declining child sex ratio has already started showing its ramifications in States like Punjab, Haryana, Gujarat, Delhi, Rajasthan, Maharashtra, Tamil Nadu and Himachal Pradesh. In States like Punjab, Haryana and Gujarat, this ratio has declined to less than 800 girls per 1,000 boys. The Government needs to recognize this discrimination. Girls have a right to live just as boys do. Moreover, missing numbers of either sex, and the resulting imbalance, is bound to destroy the social and human fabric.

Discrimination Against Children

The Government has adopted a policy of affirmative action towards addressing issues of socially backward groups, such as the Scheduled Castes/Tribes and the Other Backward Classes as well as the girl child. Despite these, discrimination–overt and covert–occurs in various forms. The guiding principles underpinning the Constitution of India are equality before law, equal protection to all and non-discrimination. There is affinity between the standards set by the

Constitution and the standards set by Article 2 of the CRC. Equality is a dynamic concept with many aspects and dimensions and therefore cannot be confined within traditional limits. Articles 14, 15, 17, 25-28, 29 and 30 of the Constitution aims to secure social and economic justice to all as well as remove all kinds of biases. Yet, children born in the categories of Scheduled Castes/Tribes and Backward Classes including religious minorities start life with severe handicaps. Considering that these children account for a clear majority of India's child population, it is necessary to look deeply into their problems from all angles.

Education as a Tool for Development of Children

The ability to read and write is an essential element of human capability. Experiences of countries across the world have time and again shown the overall role played by education in national development and in individual and social well-being. It is the first step towards acquiring other tools of learning. Not only this, it equips people to make informed choices, empowers them to resist oppression and enables them to claim their rights. Its usefulness thus has led planners to give high priority to education as it is considered to be 'an investment in human capital'.

This apart, in the measurement of development, literacy and level of education are invariably listed among the key indicators. Female education, in particular, is recognized as a means to a better quality of life for the child and the family, as well as woman's own quest for self-fulfilment. A higher level of education of a woman considerably enhances the child's chances of survival and of entry and continuance in schooling. Elementary education is considered crucial because it lays the foundation for secondary and higher education and training, which is critically important in today's fast-changing technology propelled growth. We have seen above the steps taken by the Government in making right to education a fundamental right. However, if the educational scenario in the country were to be critically reviewed, it would be seen that though there has been some progress towards universalization of elementary education since independence, but for the attainment of this goal completely, there is still a long road ahead.

Official enrolment figures show a massive increase in numbers at primary as well as middle stages in the case of both boys and girls. But, not all children who figure in the enrolment statistics attend school. A positive development, on the whole, has been the consistently higher rate of decadal growth rate of enrolment of girls, both at the primary and middle stages. The gender gap in enrolment also seems to be declining. As of now, the school drop-out rate continues to be very high. The main causes of drop-out are school related, and factors concerning family and home.

Of late, there seems to be some improvement in the physical infrastructure of schools. But, by and large, they are still deficient, particularly in rural areas where poor construction and bad maintenance has often caused fast deterioration of the available structures. Needless to mention, in majority of the schools there is still shortage of space. This leads to several classes being held in the same room by dividing the space or having a class out in the open. The former certainly is not a learner-friendly situation. Drinking water and toilet facilities, particularly for girls, are still poor. Teaching aids and methods used in schools are still far from satisfactory. Primary schools suffer not only from poor physical infrastructure, but also because they do not have enough teachers.

Assessments are not done on a continuing basis. Teacher motivation is low. There is hardly any supervision of teaching. Several malpractices have cropped up. Many villages in rural areas have a negative opinion about the commitment of school teachers and feel that their children do not get a fair deal due to the indifference of teachers, absenteeism, and poor functioning of schools. In addition, there has, unfortunately, come into existence a big caste and class divide coupled with a rural-urban divide in education, in terms of facilities and quality, which has serious social consequences and could lead to social upheaval. Schools in backward rural and tribal areas are the most neglected, and the standard of teaching deplorable. Even in other areas, schools to which children of the underprivileged have access are run by the State or local authorities. By and large, these have a poor record of performance. The low quality of education in schools meant for the masses adversely affects their employment prospects in the long run.

Children from the middle and upper classes attend private schools, which charge exorbitant fees that are not affordable by the poor, but which are far better in terms of providing quality education. It is thus the children of the poor who need most a good public sector school as their families cannot muster financial support for private schools, compensatory teaching, and coaching, and have, further, the disadvantage of little or no academic support at home due to the generally low levels of education of their family members. Though theoretically the State seeks to provide equal opportunities through heavily subsidized education, its poor quality adversely affects the life chances of the socially and economically disadvantaged sections of the society and is likely to further accentuate the divide between the haves and the have not.

Access and quality are, therefore, issues which need to be seriously addressed by the Government along with other stakeholders.

Role of National Human Rights Commission in Protecting and Promoting Children's Rights

National Human Rights Commission (NHRC) has constituted in October 1993. Despite there being major provisions in the Constitution of India for survival, development and protection of children as well as laws to safeguard their interests including the fact that the Government of India had ratified the CRC, children all over the country, especially those belonging to weaker sections of the society, were found to be vulnerable and their dignity and human rights were often trampled. Though, the initial few months of the Commission were spent on making an overall assessment about the range of issues that affected children, but once this task was completed, the Commission concentrated its attention on preventing and eradicating the problems of child labour, child marriage, child trafficking and prostitution, child sexual violence, female foeticide and infanticide, child rape, HIV/AIDS in children and the problem of juveniles.

Child Labour

To end the scourge of child labour from the country, the Commission's efforts have also been directed towards generating greater awareness and sensitivity in the District Administration and Labour Departments of concerned States. In order to create awareness among the masses, it has come out with a '*Know Your Rights*' series, in which one of the booklets deals with the issue of child labour exclusively. Besides, it has issued specific directions to the concerned State

Governments in respect of the detection and withdrawal of children employed in hazardous occupations/processes, the admission of such children into the formal and non-formal system of schooling, particularly the schools established under the National Child Labour Project, the economic rehabilitation of the affected families, and the prosecution of offending employees. (Bhakry, 2006)

Sexual Violence Against Children

Sexual violence against children is another sensitive issue in which the Commission has taken concrete measures. Pained with the plight of child victims, vis-à-vis the manner in which the issue was being reported by the media, the Commission decided to intervene in the matter in the year 1998, when a two-month campaign was launched in New Delhi in collaboration with the Ministry of Women and Child Development, UNICEF and non-governmental organisations. A mid-term appraisal of the campaign revealed that irrespective of the medium, message or location, the campaign effectively raised awareness about sexual violence against children. The respondents were however of the view that in order to further enhance awareness among the people at large, the electronic media too would have to be involved and mobilised. As a result, the NHRC, in partnership with Prasar Bharati and UNICEF held four workshops for radio and television producers. The participants for these workshops were drawn from 20 States. (Bhakry, 2006)

Right to Health

The violation of the rights of children has been considered in the Commission from the angle of health too. In 2000 and 2001, the Commission organised a *Workshop on Human Rights and HIV/AIDS* that was followed by a *Consultation on Public Health and Human Rights*. Both these had direct relevance to the rights of children. Later, in the year 2004, the Chairperson of the Commission addressed letters to the Union Ministers for Human Resource Development, Health and Chief Ministers of all States/Union Territories urging them to take steps to prevent discrimination of children affected by HIV/AIDS with regard to access to education and health care. In particular, the Commission asked them to enact and enforce a legislation to prevent children living with HIV/AIDS from being discriminated against, including being barred from school.

Juvenile Justice

The Commission has been concerned about the plight of juveniles who come in conflict with law and those who are in need of care and protection in the country. Consequently, the Commission in 1996 wrote letters to Chief Secretaries/Administrators of all States/Union Territories on the reporting of deaths/rapes in Juvenile/Children's Homes within 24 hours. On monitoring the situation, it was found that some of the Homes were still not functioning properly. The Commission, in 2002, thus once again directed the Chief Secretaries/Administrators of all States/Union Territories to ensure prompt communication of incidents of custodial deaths/rapes in Juvenile/Children's Homes. This apart, the Law Division of the Commission has been dealing with cases of violations concerning the juveniles and the Research Division has been collating information about the status of implementation of the Juvenile Justice (Care and Protection of Children) Act, 2000 from all States and Union Territories. For the latter purpose, it has devised a format seeking information regarding implementation of the various provisions of the 2000 Act.

Buildinga protective environment for children would require strengthening of Government commitment and capacity to fulfil children's right to protection; promoting the establishment and enforcement of adequate legislation; addressing harmful attitudes, customs and practices; encouraging open discussion of child protection issues with all stakeholders; developing children's life skills, knowledge and participation; building capacity of families and communities who are socially and economically disadvantaged; providing essential services for prevention, recovery and reintegration, including basic health, education and protection; and establishing and implementing continuous and effective monitoring and reporting. It would be meaningful if Millennium Development Goals could also be kept in mind while working towards child protection Right of Children to Free and Compulsory Education Act.

Right to Education Act (RTE)

The Right of Children to Free and Compulsory Education Act or Right to Education Act (RTE), which was passed by the Indian parliament on 4 August 2009, describes the modalities of the importance of free and compulsory education for children between 6 and 14 in India under Article 21A of the Indian Constitution. India became one of 135 countries to make education a fundamental right of every child when the act came into force on 1 April 2010

Present Act has its history in the drafting of the Indian constitution at the time of Independence but are more specifically to the Constitutional

Amendment that included the Article 21A in the Indian constitution making Education a fundamental Right. This amendment, however, specified the need for a legislation to describe the mode of implementation of the same which necessitated the drafting of a separate Education Bill.

A rough draft of the bill was composed in year 2005. It received much opposition due to its mandatory provision to provide 25 per cent reservation for disadvantaged children in private schools. The sub-committee of the Central Advisory Board of Education which prepared the draft Bill held this provision as a significant prerequisite for creating a democratic and egalitarian society. Indian Law commission had initially proposed 50 per cent reservation for disadvantaged students in private schools.

The bill was approved by the cabinet on 2 July 2009. Rajya Sabha passed the bill on 20 July 2009 and the Lok Sabha on 4 August 2009. It received Presidential assent and was notified as law on 26 August 2009 as The Children's Right to Free and Compulsory Education Act. The law came into effect in the whole of India except the state of Jammu and Kashmir from 1 April 2010, the first time in the history of India a law was brought into force by a speech by the Prime Minister. In his speech, Manmohan Singh, Prime Minister of India stated that, "We are committed to ensuring that all children, irrespective of gender and social category, have access to education. An education that enables them to acquire the skills, knowledge, values and attitudes necessary to become responsible and active citizens of India.".

The Act makes education a fundamental right of every child between the ages of 6 and 14 and specifies minimum norms in elementary schools. It requires all private schools to reserve 25 per cent of seats to children from poor families (to be reimbursed by the state as part of the public-private partnership plan). It also prohibits all unrecognized schools from practice, and makes provisions for no donation or capitation fees and no interview of the child or parent for admission. The Act also provides that no child shall be held back, expelled, or required to pass a board examination until the completion of elementary education. There is also a provision for special training of school drop-outs to bring them up to par with students of the same age.

The RTE act requires surveys that will monitor all neighbourhoods, identify children requiring education, and set up facilities for providing it. The World Bank education specialist for India, Sam Carlson, has observed:

> The RTE Act is the first legislation in the world that puts the responsibility of ensuring enrollment, attendance and completion on the Government. It is the parents' responsibility to send the children to schools in the U.S. and other countries.

The Right to Education of persons with disabilities until 18 years of age is laid down under a separate legislation-the Persons with Disabilities Act. A number of other provisions regarding improvement of school infrastructure, teacher-student ratio and faculty are made in the Act.

The Act provides for the National Commission for the Protection of Child Rights, an autonomous body set up in 2007, to monitor the implementation of the act, together with Commissions to be set up by the states.

RTE: Amendment

The Right of Children to Free and Compulsory Education (amendment) Act, 2012 received the assent of the President of India on 19th June, 2012. From then onwards, in the past few weeks there has been a flurry of anxious queries and flutter of illogical answers floating from different parts of the country regarding the Amendment Act. It practically originated from Mumbai on August 4, 2012 through the media under the caption 'Theological schools exempted from RTE Act', after listening to the talk given by Sanjay Deshmukh, project Director of the Sarva Shiksha Abhiyan (SSA) on the amendment. The lack of clarity in understanding the amendment comes from the fact that the amendment was not read together with the 'Principal Act'.

In chapter 1 of the Principal Act, section 1 speaks of 'Short title, extent and commencement'. It has got 3 sub-sections after which sub-sections 4 and 5 were added to elucidate further the extent of its application.

> "(4) Subject to the provisions of articles 29 and 30 of the Constitution, the provisions of this Act shall apply to conferment of rights of children to free and compulsory education. (5) Nothing contained in this Act shall apply to Madrasas, Vedic Pathsalas and educational institutions primarily imparting religious education".

These two sub-sections spell out clearly, without any doubt, the extent of the application of the Act. As a matter of fact sub-section 4 states that the Act is governed by the provisions of Articles 29 and 30 of the Constitutions of India in its implementation. The Act does not take away the rights of the minorities. Sub-section 5 points out that Madrassas, Vedic Pathsalas and educational institutions primarily imparting religious education does not come under the Act.

Section 3 of the Amendment Act speaks about 'child with disability' and its further extension to children suffering from autism, cerebral palsy, mental retardation and multiple disabilities.

Section 4 of the Amendment Act speaks of "child belonging to disadvantaged group" and "child belonging to weaker section".

Section 5 of the Amendment Act is the most important amendment as far as the minority educational institutions are concerned.

> "In section 21 of the principal Act, in sub-section (2), the following proviso shall be inserted namely: "Provided that the School Management committee constituted under sub-section (1) in respect of,(a) a school established and administered by minority whether based on religion or language; and (b) all other aided schools as defined in sub-section (ii) of clause (n) of section 2, shall perform advisory function only."

It is amply clear from here that the amendment as far as the minority educational institutions are concerned whether based on religion or language, the school managing committee performs an **advisory function** only. The administrative powers of the minority school according to this proviso are vested in the School Managing Committee of the school which is not tampered with. However, pressure tactics by the majority community can be had in this scenario. Knowing fully the rights and duties of a minority school is important to ward off unpleasant situations that crop up, time and again, in the educational institutions.

Implementation and Funding

Education in the Indian constitution is a concurrent issue and both centre and states can legislate on the issue. The Act lays down specific responsibilities for the centre, state and local bodies for its implementation. The states have been clamouring that they lack financial capacity to deliver education of appropriate standard in all the schools needed for universal education. Thus it was clear that the central government (which collects most of the revenue) will be required to subsidize the states.

A committee set up to study the funds requirement and funding initially estimated that Rs. 171,000 crores (US$38.2 billion) across five years was required to implement the Act, and in April 2010 the central government agreed to sharing the funding for implementing the law in the ratio of 65 to 35 between the centre and the states, and a ratio of 90 to 10 for the north-eastern states. However, in mid 2010, this figure was upgraded to Rs. 231,000 crores, and the center agreed to raise its share to 68 per cent. There is some confusion on this, with other media reports stating that the centre's share of the implementation expenses would now be 70 per cent. At that rate, most states may not need to increase their education budgets substantially.

A critical development in 2011 has been the decision taken in principle to extend the right to education till Class X (age 16) and into the preschool age range. The CABE committee is in the process of looking into the implications of making these changes.

The RTE Act:

(i) Provides for the Right of children to free and compulsory education till completion of elementary education in a neighbourhood school.

(ii) It clarifies that 'compulsory education' means obligation of the appropriate government to provide free elementary education and ensure compulsory admission, attendance and completion of elementary education to every child in the six to fourteen age group. 'Free' means that no child shall be liable to pay any kind of fee or charges or expenses which may prevent him or her from pursuing and completing elementary education.

(iii) It makes provisions for a non-admitted child to be admitted to an age appropriate class.

(iv) It specifies the duties and responsibilities of appropriate Governments, local authority and parents in providing free and compulsory education, and sharing of financial and other responsibilities between the Central and State Governments.

(v) It lays down the norms and standards relating inter alia to Pupil Teacher Ratios (PTRs), buildings and infrastructure, school-working days, teacher-working hours.

(vi) It provides for rational deployment of teachers by ensuring that the specified pupil teacher ratio is maintained for each school, rather than just as an average for the State or District or Block, thus ensuring that there is no urban-rural imbalance in teacher postings. It also provides for prohibition of deployment of teachers for non-educational work, other than decennial census, elections to local authority, state legislatures and parliament, and disaster relief.

(vii) It provides for appointment of appropriately trained teachers, i.e. teachers with the requisite entry and academic qualifications.

(viii) It prohibits (a) physical punishment and mental harassment; (b) screening procedures for admission of children; (c) capitation fee; (d) private tuition by teachers and (e) running of schools without recognition,

(ix) It provides for development of curriculum in consonance with the values enshrined in the Constitution, and which would ensure the all-round development of the child, building on the child's knowledge, potentiality and talent and making the child free of fear, trauma and anxiety through a system of child friendly and child centred learning.

References

Bhakhry, S. (2006), National Human Rights Commission, New Delhi.

Bose, A.B. (2003), *The State of Children in India*, New Delhi, Manohar Publishers.

Department of Women and Child Development, MHRD, GoI Annual Reports from 1986-87 to 2004-05.

Department of Women and Child Development, Government of India (2005), *National Plan of Action for Children 2005*, New Delhi, DWCD.

14

Child Rights in Asia

According to Quisumbing, 2010, High-Level Meeting on Cooperation for Child Rights in the Asia-Pacific Region Beijing, China in 4-6 November 2010 reported that, Countries in the Asia-Pacific region face the twin challenges of promoting and protecting children's rights as State Parties to the Convention on the Rights of the Child and of meeting the Millennium Development Goals (MDGs) for Sustainable Development by 2015, a scant five years from now. The great diversity in the region, in terms of macro-economic growth, in cultures and in demographics, among others, means that different countries are in different stages of meeting these challenges, with strengths and achievements in some aspects and remaining gaps in others.

Children's rights and the MDGs are not mutually exclusive but highly complementary and often overlapping. Strategies to achieve the MDGs tend to improve compliance with the rights of children, including the rights to life, health, food and non-discrimination. Conversely, initiatives to protect and promote the rights of children can often have a positive impact on MDG achievement, such as programmes seeking to promote children's right to education.

The international community has long been active in assisting countries that are not able to meet these obligations with their existing resources and capacities. Traditionally, such assistance has flowed from an industrialized country to a developing country–the conventional mode of North-South cooperation.

As 2015 draws near, there is a growing international acceptance that traditional North-South donor-recipient aid programmes are unlikely to help developing countries to achieve all of their core development targets and that other forms of cooperation are required,

Similarly, children in the Asia-Pacific region continue to experience serious child protection challenges, varying by country but including sex selection, early marriage, violence and abuse and trafficking. This is despite the efforts of governments to take meaningful steps to ensure a protective environment for children. Developing a comprehensive and effective child protection and child welfare system is not an easy task, strengthening the case for greater exchanges on good practices and lessons learned. It may also be an area in which a supportive transnational commitment and response strategy is warranted, given the transnational impact on children of issues like migration, trafficking and disparities. There are also considerable gains to be made from greater cooperation within Asia and the Pacific in the design and delivery of child-centred disaster risk reduction.

Asian Human Rights Commission (AHRC)

The Asian Human Rights Commission (AHRC) is an independent, non-governmental body, which seeks to promote greater awareness and realization of Human Rights in the Asian region, and to mobilize Asian and international public opinion to obtain relief and redress for the victims of human rights violations. It was founded in 1986 by a prominent group of jurists and human rights activists in Asia and serves to promote civil and political rights as well as economic, social and cultural rights.

The Asian Human Rights Commission (AHRC) was started in 1986 by a group of jurists and human rights activists in Asia. AHRC is a NGO that promotes awareness of human rights in the Asian countries as well as creates worldwide awareness of human rights violations so that they can mobilise action and relief for victims of human rights violations. AHRC upholds civil, political, economic, social and cultural rights. The main purpose of the AHRC is stated in their charter "Many Asian states have guarantees of human rights in their constitutions, and many of them have ratified international instruments on human rights. However, there continues to be a wide gap between rights enshrined in these documents and the abject reality that denies people their rights. Asian states must take urgent action to implement the human rights of their citizens and residents.

The AHRC seeks to achieve the following objectives:

Defend and promote human rights by evaluating, investigating, supporting, and taking legal actions

- Work towards the social inclusion of discriminated groups of people such as women, children and minorities including Dalits.

- Use modern communications techniques to create a large efficient information system to ensure swift and appropriate action against human rights violations
- Create awareness and education about human rights and especially promote the folk school approach;
- Promote countries to undertake legal, judicial and administrative changes that safeguard the rights of people
- Create support of victims and engage their stories and their lives in movements to support human rights hence giving purpose to the fight against violations
- Mediate disputes between countries or parties through peacemaking and conflict resolution techniques.
- Develop culturally relevant programmes for promotion of human rights
- Encourage countries to ratify the UN conventions and modify their laws an system to meet the international commitments as well as help create national human rights commissions
- Support the work of the United Nations, and help people access the programmes and agencies to protect their own human rights
- Aim to develop regional human rights mechanisms that involve people and promote the values of the Asian Human Rights Charter

Allegations of human rights violations can be brought to the AHRC's attention by an individual or organisation. The AHRC will conduct the necessary investigations. AHRC also undertakes preventive work that ensures that countries are prepared to deal with all administrative, legal and judicial matters to avoid human rights violations. The Urgent Appeal Programmes of the AHRC is a network of communications designed to put pressure on governments by creating an aware and active citizenry. The commission runs a number of programmes that do with poverty eradication and human rights training. The commission also runs country specific programmes

According to Asian Human Rights Commission it is agreed

- That, all children have the right to a name and nationality at birth, to care and protection, to emotional, physical, spiritual and intellectual development in conditions of freedom, security and dignity and to participate in decisions affecting them;
- More specifically that, children have the right to a happy and

healthy childhood of nurture and affection including supportive familial relationships with parents or guardians;

- That children have the right to protection from sexual abuse and from abuse of their labour;
- That children have the right to intellectual development through guaranteed access to education;
- That children have the right to survival through protection from all forms of violence and to live in a peaceful environment;
- That children have the right to protection from infanticide;
- That children have the right to adequate health care and to special care if handicapped or abandoned;
- That children have the right to the basic necessities of food, clothing and shelter;
- That the implementation of these rights is a paramount duty of every state and community regardless of economic and security considerations.

Child Rights in Northeast Asia

According to *Yanghee Lee,* Northeast Asian countries share many things in common. Four countries (the Republic of Korea, Democratic Republic of Korea, China, and Japan) in particular currently receive much attention in the international stage. Here the countries focus neither on the political and economic implications surrounding this attention, nor on the many sensitive political issues existing in this sub region. Quite the contrary, they aim to put the "human" aspect back into human rights, especially children's rights.

Human rights have long been understood and accepted as an important concept, but also as "western" concept. And yet even "western" countries find it difficult to fully implement the Convention. This perhaps explains why some of these "western" countries made reservations and declarations to the Convention. Societies that view children as properties of parents seem to have much resistance to compliance with the Convention.

Situation of the Children

Children are considered the future leaders of society. The concern, though not unique to the four countries, about domestic laws not fully reflecting or complying with the principles and provisions of the Convention is another common ground. A major concern is the fact that in practice the

Convention cannot be invoked directly by the Courts. The decentralization process provides greater concern as localities and municipalities adopt different laws or ordinances that do not conform with the Convention, leading to a possible situation where children are "visibly invisible".

Domestic law definition of "child," "juvenile justice," "discrimination," "children with disabilities," "child abuse and neglect," "corporal punishment," "sexual and economic exploitation," among others, is an issue affecting compliance with the Convention. With the legal definition failing to conform with the Convention, *de facto* discrimination against certain groups of children exists alongside *de jure* discrimination (usually against the most vulnerable groups such as children born out-of-wedlock, minority and/or ethnic children, and children with disabilities).

Difference in the age of marriage without parental consent between girls and boys puts the girl-child at a disadvantage. Tradition dictates that girls get married earlier than boys do. This results in States Parties denying the female population of equality between genders. This is a matter the civil society should pay more attention to in countries such as the two Koreas and Japan. Setting a lower age of marriage without parental consent (13 years old) for girls, as is the case of Japan, opens the door wide open for sexual exploitation of young girls. Also, one-child per family birth registration system could put the girl-child at the gravest disadvantage.

Juvenile justice is perhaps the most overlooked part of children's issues. This is most harshly dealt with in all four countries. Extension of pre-trial detention period (adopted by Japan after its initial report and before the second report); continued lack or absence of judicial proceedings (China and DPRK); deprivation of liberty in the absence of on-going criminal procedures, lowering of the age of criminal responsibility, and many of the reforms affecting juveniles do not conform with the principles and provisions of the Convention the Beijing Rules (UN Standard Minimum Rules for the Administration of Juvenile Justice), and the Riyadh Guidelines (UN Guidelines for the Prevention of Juvenile Delinquency). They are often the reality in these four countries.

Corporal punishment, a global issue on violence, led the UN Secretary General (Kofi Annan) to call for a study on all forms of violence against children (UN Study on the Violence Against Children). The common saying in the West "spare the rod and spoil the child" has a Northeast Asian equivalent: "rod of love" (ROL). If you love your children, then you will not hesitate to discipline them using the rod. What has been overlooked in our societies is the fact that this is a definite form of violence against children. It serves no purpose but to punish them (even so, this form of punishment has no positive effects, and is morally wrong!). If we are concerned with the betterment, and the learning process, of the children, and not simply to punish them, alternate forms of disciplining must be considered and carried out. In compliance with the Convention, the four countries banned corporal punishment in schools, institutions, and homes.

Basic Principles

Perhaps the three principles of the CRC that are least understood and even ignored are the "best interest of the child" (Article 3); "evolving capacities of the child" (Article 5); and "respect for the views of the child" (Article 12). Often, these principles are treated as mere rhetoric.

In a culture where children are viewed as important leaders of the future, this principle probably requires no further explanation. And yet, this is exactly the reason why the principle of the best of interest of the child deserves more attention than it had in the past. Article 3 of the Convention stipulates, "that all actions concerning children, whether undertaken by public or private social welfare institutions, courts of law, administrative authorities or legislative bodies, the best interests of the child shall be a primary consideration." It goes on to state that it is the responsibility of the State to ensure the child such protection and care and to take "all appropriate legislative and administrative measures", while taking into account the rights and duties of all persons legally responsible for the child.

This article puts the child to the forefront as an entity with rights that need to be protected and respected. Traditions in Northeast Asia such as respect for the elderly, filial piety, father before self, and country before self have left little room for children to be viewed as primary concern. To use a modern terminology, a "top-down" approach has been more of the norm in this part of the world. It even goes beyond the concept of "father knows best". The country comes first, then the father, followed by the son, the mother, and finally the daughter-in this strict order. This type of social structure has in the past supported authoritarian decision-making and the adoption of certain special interests other than those of children as primary concern.

Article 5 further emphasizes that the State should respect the "responsibilities, rights, and duties of parents or, where applicable, the members of the extended family or community as provided for by local custom, legal guardians or other persons legally responsible for the child, to provide, in a manner consistent with the evolving capacities of the child, appropriate direction and guidance in the exercise by the child of the rights." This article, again, emphasizes the role of the State in ensuring full realization of the rights of the child. It again highlights the duties and responsibilities of the parents and all persons responsible for the child. The Convention has already stipulated that the best interest of the child shall be the foremost concern.

The Convention is often misunderstood as relinquishing the rights of parents or those who are responsible for the child. Quite the contrary, it should be understood to mean that the State should be responsible in providing the means to ensure that the family, etc., can assist the child in exercising her/his rights. Childhood is a period of constant change. This means that the child is in a state of change, or development, with capacities commensurate to the different developmental stages. Recognizing the capacities of the child in different periods of life is imperative in decisions that are made for the child.

Article 12 emphasizes that the State "shall assure to the child who is capable of forming his or her own views the right to express those views freely in all matters affecting the child, the views of the child being given due weight in accordance with the age and maturity of the child." This article should be understood together with the aforementioned two articles. The best interest of the child shall be of utmost priority and that the child, recognizing the nature of the evolving capacities shall be given the right to participate in all matters concerning her/him. This translates into all matters, small or large, family or school, community or national, and legal or non-legal.

Challenges

The challenge for the countries in Northeast Asia is in the creation of a culture that regards children as rights-bearing, important members of society. In considering low birth-rate in the Republic of Korea and Japan, or the opposite situation in China, the needs-based approach addresses only the aging society issue or the enforcement of strict population control policy. The real challenge in these countries is the resolution of this issue in a child-sensitive, rights-based fashion.

Regardless of the political, economic, or social structures, children must be the utmost priority. If children are indeed viewed as the leaders of the future, their situation at present, here and now, should not be forgotten in order that they are prepared for this expected role.

15

Child Rights in Africa

African children can have difficult lives. They may have to walk for miles to school or maybe they live in a conflict zone The section deals with some of the common challenges and the basic rights of young Africans.

While European kids are still playing with toys, African children usually have to work. In the country, hundreds of thousands go to school in the morning and in the afternoon they help their parents in the fields. And many have to look after themselves at a pretty tender age, because their parents can't feed them. African children often have a tough life. They are more likely to die before the age of five than children on any other continent. They sometimes live in areas afflicted by violence and insecurity. Besides, they are less likely to get a good education than their contemporaries in Asia, America or Europe.

Learning by Ear tells the stories of some of these small African heroes. But it isn't all about the struggles they face. It's also about people fighting for children's' rights and trying to make a difference. For instance, there's a children's parliament that is fighting for children's rights in Nigeria. Children in Africa are affected by many different types of abuse, including economic and sexual exploitation, gender discrimination in education and access to health, and their involvement in armed conflict. Other factors affecting African children include migration, early marriage, differences between urban and rural areas, child-headed households, street children and poverty. Furthermore, child workers in Sub-Saharan Africa account for about 80 million children or 4 out of every 10 children under 14 years old which is the highest child labour rate in the world.

Ratification of the African Charter on the Rights and Welfare of the Child

As at February 2009, the ACRWC (African Charter on the Rights and

Welfare of the Child) has been ratified by 45 of the 53 countries in the continent. The Democratic Republic of the Congo (DRC) and the islands of São Tomé and Príncipe have not signed or ratified the charter and 8 countries have not ratified it.

The ACRWC defines a "child" as a human being below the age of 18 years. It recognises the child's unique and privileged place in African society and that African children need protection and special care. It also acknowledges that children are entitled to the enjoyment of freedom of expression, association, peaceful assembly, thought, religion, and conscience. It aims to protect the private life of the child and safeguard the child against all forms of economic exploitation and against work that is hazardous, interferes with the child's education, or compromises his or her health or physical, social, mental, spiritual, and moral development. It calls for protection against abuse and bad treatment, negative social and cultural practices, all forms of exploitation or sexual abuse, including commercial sexual exploitation, and illegal drug use. It aims to prevent the sale and trafficking of children, kidnapping, and begging of children.

Some of the states which are non-signatories are also gross violators of human rights. Examples include the DRC, Sahrawi Arab Democratic Republic, Somalia and the Sudan. These violations range from recruitment of child soldiers, early child marriages, and child trafficking to enslavement, drug abuse, sexual exploitation, child labour and harmful cultural practices like female genital mutilation and male child preference.

While many children in Africa are able to grow, learn and thrive as part of loving families and communities, others suffer due to issues like poverty, conflict, natural disasters, and harmful practices such as early marriage. Many children in Africa are affected by different types of abuse, including economic and sexual exploitation, gender discrimination in education, and their involvement in armed conflict. Worldwide, UNICEF estimates that 150 million children aged 5-14 years work. The problem is most common in sub-Saharan Africa, where more than a third of children are engaged in child labour.

Like the Convention on the Rights of the Child (CRC), the African Charter on the Rights and Welfare of the Child (ACRWC) was created to protect children. The Charter spells out the rights that African countries must ensure for their children, and it is the main instrument of the African human rights system for promoting and protecting child rights.

The Charter, which was adopted by the Organisation of African Unity (now the African Union) in July 1990, was entered into force in November

1999. It was the first regional treaty to address child rights, and was created partly to complement the CRC, but also because African countries were under-represented in the drafting process of the CRC, and many felt another treaty was needed to address the specific realities of children in Africa.

The ACRWC and the CRC are the only international and regional human rights treaties that cover the whole spectrum of civil, political, economic, social and cultural rights. Like the CRC, the ACRWC talks about the same principles of non-discrimination and participation. Some of the other issues that African States wanted the Charter to address were: children living under apartheid, harmful practices against the girl child, such as female genital mutilation (FGM), internal conflicts and displacement, the definition of a child, the rights of children of imprisoned mothers, poor and unsanitary living conditions, the African conception of communities' responsibilities and duties, weak enforcement and monitoring mechanisms, role of the family in adoption and fostering, and the duties and responsibilities of the child towards the family and community.

In the Eastern and Southern Africa region, almost all countries have ratified the African Charter, with the exception of Somalia and Zambia, both have signed but not yet ratified it.

The ACRWC is divided into two parts. Part one deals with the rights, freedoms and duties of the child and has 31 articles. Part two deals with States' obligations to adopt laws to enforce the provisions of the Charter, and has 18 articles.

Children's Charter and C R C

The Children's Charter originated because the member states of the African Union believed that the CRC missed important socio-cultural and economic realities particular to Africa. It emphasizes the need to include African cultural values and experiences when dealing with the rights of the child in such as:

- Challenging traditional African views which often conflict with children's rights such as child marriage, parental rights and obligations towards their children, and children born out of wedlock;
- Expressly saying that the Children's Charter is higher than any custom, tradition, cultural or religious practice that doesn't fit with the rights, duties and obligations in the Charter;

- The Children's Charter has a clearer definition of the child as a person aged under 18 years old;
- Outright prohibition on the recruitment of children (i.e. under 18 years old) in armed conflict and deals with conscription of children into the armed forces;
- Prohibiting marriages or betrothals involving children;
- Prohibiting the use of children as beggars;
- Granting girls the right to return to school after pregnancy;
- Promoting affirmative action for girls' education;
- Tackling specific African issues that affect children. For example it called for the confrontation and abolishment of apartheid and similar systems; and although, apartheid is now over, this provision is still applicable to children living under regimes practicing ethnic, religious or other forms of discrimination;
- Protecting internally displaced and refugee children;
- Protecting imprisoned expectant mothers and mothers of infants and young children;
- Providing a way for children themselves to petition the Children's Charter's Committee of Experts regarding infringements of their rights;
- Including special reference to care of the child by extended families;
- Encouraging the state to provide support for parents "in times of need";
- Protecting handicapped children.

The Fundamental Principles Guiding Implementation of These Rights Include:

- Non-discrimination;
- The best interests of the child;
- The life, survival and development of the child;
- Child participation;
- Providing for the responsibilities that every child has with regard to their and society, the state and the international community.

Shortcoming and Criticism

- It doesn't protect children from life imprisonment without the possibility of release;
- When dealing with criminal activities, there is no provision for alternative measures such as community rehabilitation;

- No mention of the rights such as to remain silent, to be protected from retroactive legislation, to challenge detention, or to be compensated for miscarriages of justice;
- Article 20 can be construed as supporting physical punishment by parents as it is unclear regarding the meaning of "domestic discipline;"
- There is some confusion regarding Article 31 that deals with children's responsibilities. Children are required to respect parents, superiors and elders at all times which could conflict with the child's right to participate in decisions that affect them;
- The omission of a provision which requires countries to fully commit and use their resources means that the Children's Charter has no way to ensure or force states to provide resources to ensure the realisation of children's rights;
- Although the Children's Charter makes provision for special protection measures for the disabled, it fails to expressly include disability as a prohibited ground of discrimination;
- Unlike the CRC, which specifically ascribes rights to children of minorities, there is no similar provision in the African Charter, despite many countries in the region having significant populations of minority and indigenous groups.

African Committee of Experts on the Rights and Welfare of the Child

The Committee was formed in July 2001, one and half years after the Children's Charter came into force. The members are elected by the Assembly of Heads of State and Government of the African Union. The criteria for the selection of members are:

- Members must be nationals of a State Party to the Children's Charter;
- They must be individuals of high moral standing, integrity, impartiality and competence in matters of the rights and welfare of the child;
- Members are nominated by signatory countries and elected by the Assembly of Heads of State of the African Union;
- Members are elected for a term of five years and serve voluntarily in their individual capacity. They may not be re-elected.

The Committee of Experts meets twice each year, usually in May and November in Adis Ababa, Ethiopia. The exact dates depend on other items on the AU agenda around these times. They are empowered to receive and examine the country ("state") reports on the measures they have adopted to implement the provisions of the Children's Charter as well as the progress achieved regarding how the rights are being protected. The final protective function of the Committee of Experts is related to the investigations procedure. They are empowered to resort to any appropriate method of investigation in respect of any issue covered in the Children's Charter.

Protecting Child Rights in Africa

The African Committee of Experts on the Rights and Welfare of the Child urges action by all partners and governments to address the growing epidemic of street children. Street children are any girl or boy who has yet to reach adulthood who seeks a livelihood or residence in the street. The demographic is growing globally, with an estimated 120 million or 1 in 5 children turning to the street. One quarter of the total-45 million-are in Africa; the majority of those boys.

> "If I had a choice, I would go to school like other kids my age, but then what would my brothers and sisters eat," 15-year old Senegalese boy who drives a cart to support his family.

This boy's story is too often heard, he is a member of a lost African generation without education or vocational training. Both a symptom and a cause of poverty, street children put a face to massive human rights violations daily.

For more than 70 years, Plan International has been working to improve the lives of children so they do not have to seek refuge in the street. Plan raises awareness of child rights by working with communities to improve education and health while creating an environment free from violence and exploitation in which children can participate. The end result is a community where children feel safe and go to school; there is no need to seek refuge in the street.

Children leave their homes and communities and turn to the streets for many reasons. Plan commissioned a study on street children in Africa. The study was designed to inform programmes to increase outreach to street children. The findings and recommendations include:

- Develop children as the main actors in realising the rights of street involved children through their active participation and building their resilience and capacity to protect themselves.

- Build the sense of responsibility and capacity of families and communities to care and protect all children, including those that are street involved.
- The prevention of family separation and street involvement by children at specific risk may require intensive support to individual families.
- National child protection and child welfare systems that are sensitive to the rights of street children to care and protection are needed, and should be adequately funded to operate effectively.
- Organisations working in rural areas on issues of childhood migration need to link with those working in urban areas on childhood safety, to reduce the levels of vulnerability that arise with mobility.
- Specialist agencies working with a particular focus on street involved children, or children without parental care, need to collaborate with generalist child focused organisations to ensure that their issues are included in broader agendas.

The Day of the African Child commemorates the bravery of children who took to the streets to ask for quality education in Soweto (1976) only to be massacred. While today's children in the streets may not have the combined focus on one issue as those in Soweto, they do have voices and deserve access to their rights. We in the international community need only listen to understand the issues and follow the lead of the children to finding the solutions.

16

Child Rights in Europe

Challenges Children Facing in Europe

Key challenges facing children in the EU today include demographic change, poverty and social exclusion, EU enlargement, violence to children, migration, discrimination, and environmental degradation. Within the EU, issues such as these are likely to have a huge direct and indirect impact on children's lives-mediated by factors such as age, race, gender, disability, and sexual orientation-both now and into the future:

i) *Demographic change* on an unprecedented scale is facing the Union, as a result of common EU-wide trends such as increasing life expectancy, a declining population of working age, and falling birth rates. Overall, the proportion of the EU population aged between 0 and 14 is expected to decrease from 16.4 per cent in 2004 to 13.4 per cent in 2050 These shifts, together with factors such as political and economic constraints on levels of taxation and public borrowing, falling support for state services, and changes in family structure, are putting increasing strain on the European Social Model-and bringing risks of a decline in children's services.

The European Commission has suggested that Member States should develop further measures to assist parents to reconcile work and family commitments, and that this may help to reverse declining fertility rates-and ultimately foster economic growth and prosperity within the Union Whilst this perspective can help to focus attention on issues facing children, it tends to over emphasize children purely as "investments" for the future. It also underplays the importance of children's daily lives in the present, their human rights as citizens, and the impact of demographic ageing on childhood. A focus on the latter would highlight, for instance, the consequences for children of growing up with fewer siblings and the increasing separation between generations as fewer adults live with children, which may make it "increasingly difficult to articulate the interests, wants and needs of children".

ii) *Child poverty and social exclusion* have increased significantly in some EU countries during the past 20 years or more, with younger children facing a higher risk of relative poverty than any other group This is connected to parental unemployment, family structure (and especially lone parenthood), and to the number of children in the family (large families tend to be poorer). In practice, many children may be going hungry (or their parents may be foregoing meals themselves in order to feed them); children may have insufficient clothing, or be living in overcrowded or temporary accommodation in run-down areas; and children may have no access to their own money, toys, books, school trips and holidays. For those whose parents are on their own, or ill or disabled, or from an ethnic minority-or a combination of all of these factors-the difficulties may be particularly severe. And although economic growth can create new job opportunities and help families out of poverty, for some parents it may mean insecure, temporary and low-paid employment, with negative consequences for family life.

iii) *EU enlargement* has also focused attention on child poverty and social exclusion. Ten countries joined the Union in May 2004, and other states, such as Romania and Bulgaria, did so from 2007. During the 1990s people in the former Soviet Union experienced a turbulent and difficult transition to market economies. While some have subsequently seen a radical improvement in their living conditions, many have experienced only moderate advances, and for a minority living conditions have became worse. Although EU entry has provided significant new opportunities, many children have experienced-and continue to experience-high levels of poverty, discrimination and exploitation. NGO participants at a series of Euronet seminars in Warsaw, Prague and Ljubljana in 2005. highlighted a range of specific concerns, such as: the conditions facing children in residential institutions. Lack of child participation; failure to address the rights of young offenders, school drop-outs, Roma children, and disabled children; abuse and violence against children; children's poor health (especially HIV/AIDS); the closure of childcare facilities; and funding problems.

iv) *Violence against children* has been an increasing source of concern within the EU in recent years. It takes a range of forms, from violence in the family, in schools, or in the community, to issues with a transnational dimension, including child trafficking, child sex tourism, and child pornography and sexual exploitation via the internet. The latter have become more prominent since the late 1980s, fuelled by factors such as: cheaper air travel; increasing demand for children for the purpose of sexual exploitation (linked to the emergence of HIV/AIDS and other sexually transmitted diseases; the rise of new technology; the emergence of humanitarian crises and wars; and the global growth of poverty and inequality. There has been strong political and public support for the EU to respond to forms of violence that have a cross-border dimension, which has resulted in a significant child protection focus within the Union's justice and home affairs agenda.

v) *Migration* is another outcome of factors such as those described under "Violence to children" above. Conflict, war and instability, together with serious violations of human rights, continue to have a catastrophic impact on children and their families, affecting millions worldwide; whilst most of the population movement that results is between or within developing countries, since the early 1990s increasing numbers-among them many children separated from their parents or caregivers-have been seeking asylum in EU countries. Other children flee because of extreme poverty and lack of opportunity in their home countries, prompted by the (often unrealistic) hopes of their parents. Some are duped by tales of secure wages abroad, or even abducted by traffickers for the purpose of exploitation. Children in all these groups often face gruelling journeys in order to reach EU territory.

Most endure severe hardship on arrival too, facing unsympathetic officials and harsh procedures, and end up working illegally in unregulated sectors as domestic slaves, or in sweatshops or brothels. In addition, in recent years issues of identity have also come to the fore across Europe. Fuelled by new insecurities and tensions, racism and discrimination have surged, including, for instance, gang violence on the streets, negative imagery in the media, and entrenched discrimination within institutions. Alongside these aspects, hostility towards and fear of "outsiders", and in particular to people from different religions, to migrants and asylum-seekers, has become increasingly commonplace-and children are easy targets for such racism. This is providing the backdrop to tougher policy responses, threatening the basic rights of some of the most vulnerable people in society.

vi) *Environmental degradation* has a disproportionate effect on children and their health. The World Health Organisation (WHO) estimates that over 40 per cent of the global burden of disease attributed to environmental factors falls on children under the age of five.

Within the EU, children are especially vulnerable to damaging risks, including unsafe water, poor sanitation, poor air quality, pollution, chemicals in food, and emerging global threats such as climate change and contagious diseases. Children are less able to resist these risks, owing to their less developed immune, respiratory and nervous systems, and in the early years in particular, are dependent on adults to protect them. Access to outside space is also limited by heavier traffic and increasing urbanization, an important reason behind the dramatic increase in children's indoor pursuits (TV, Computers). The issues vary between countries, however; in some, outdoor spaces are increasingly "troubled" and parents worry about their children's safety; in others, children still play in the streets under the supervision of older children or adults. In general, however, it appears that children's independent mobility has declined, with many being driven to school where ten or twenty years ago they would have cycled or walked

Children's Rights and the EU Treaties

Unlike the CRC, which recognizes children as the holders of civil, cultural, political, social and economic rights, the predominant focus within the European Union (EU) Treaties on the "citizen-as-worker" means that children's interests are excluded from consideration across the majority of policy areas. Where children have been addressed at European Union level, they have been viewed through a narrow lens as the objects rather than the subjects of human rights, and the values underpinning the EU's approach have been correspondingly limited.

Children are considered primarily as "victims" in need of protection from violence; important though this perspective is, it ignores the importance of children's active participation in shaping their futures (as in Article 12, UNCRC). Similarly, the EU's long-standing concern with freedom of movement and with reconciling work and family issues has also placed insufficient emphasis on children's perspectives. For instance, policy initiatives to meet the childcare needs of parents (and in particular women) as workers in the single market have tended to regard children as "barriers to work" or "dependants"-as burdens on families and society, rather than as actual and potential contributors.

It is possible too to discern the emergence at EU level of a social investment perspective over a social protection agenda-particularly in relation to demography, employment, education, and childcare-which has implications for children. Such a perspective places a strong emphasis on the future needs of the economy rather than the present needs of citizens. On the one hand, this can have the positive effect of moving children and families higher up the policy agenda as improving their circumstances is seen to be an investment in society's future. On the other, it can simultaneously deflect attention from children's rights and well-being in the present, and prioritize the interests of children who are likely to become productive workers in the future over the interests of those who are less likely to do so (e.g. disabled children).

This incoherence in the EU's current approach is, at least in part, due to the lack of a clear legal base in the Treaties to enable the EU to address children's issues. The insertion of a legal base would ensure that children's rights were much more visible in EU policy-making, and would have several advantages:

- there would be a duty to consider the "best interests of the child" (Article 3, UNCRC) in all relevant legislative initiatives, so legislation would, in effect be "child proofed";
- political actions in favour of children would be given additional weight. At present, only the most extreme cases-for instance, children affected by armed conflict (external policy), and sexual exploitation and trafficking (internal policy)-have resulted in significant EU action;
- there would be stronger justification for increasing expenditure on children beyond the narrow limits of existing EU budget lines;
- EU institutions would no longer be able to justify failure to address children's rights on the lack of a legal base, and would be able to take action on children's rights in areas that fall within community competence;
- politically, it would provide a clear signal from the Member States that they understand that EU policy affects children, and their interests must be addressed.

Below we chart the gradual shift recently towards the development of a legal base in the EU Treaties. A legal base would not in itself be a panacea for the weaknesses in the EU's approach. Effective implementation of policy initiatives remains essential. Nevertheless it would provide the bedrock for sustained and coherent action at EU level.

Charter of Fundamental Rights

Emerging from growing support for the inclusion of a minimum core of fundamental rights in the EU Treaties, the Charter of Fundamental Rights was adopted by the European Council, European Parliament, and European Commission on 7 December 2000. The Charter governs the EU institutions, which must conform to the rights and observe the principles enshrined within it; it also applies to all EU Member States, but only when they are implementing EU law.

In contrast to the existing Treaties, the Charter includes a statement of children's basic rights. It goes well beyond the rights for children set out in the 1950 European Convention on Human Rights (ECHR), which only refers directly to education. In addition to a general equality provision which states that "everyone is equal before the law" (Article 20), the most relevant generic provisions of the Charter that could be applied to children are:

- the right to the integrity of the person (Article 3(2);
- the prohibition against torture and inhuman and degrading treatment or punishment (Article 4);
- the prohibition against slavery and forced labour, specifically in the context of human
- trafficking (Article 5(1) and (3);
- the right to respect for private and family life (Article 7);
- and measures to reconcile professional and family life (Article 33).

These provisions are complemented by other child-specific measures:

- Article 14 provides a right to education;
- Article 32 prohibits exploitation and safeguards the health and welfare of children in the labour market;
- Article 21 restates and extends the anti-discrimination provision of Article 13 EC.

Most importantly, Article 24 is dedicated to children's rights. The Article does refer specifically to the UNCRC 30, however the text includes references to "the best interests of the child", and to the child's right to participate, incorporating key principles of the UNCRC. Although Article 24 clause 1 only states that children "may express their views freely"- rather than providing this as a right (as in the UNCRC), the Article still represents an advance towards seeing children not just as in need of protection, but also as independent and autonomous rights holders.

Although less comprehensive than the UNCRC, the Charter is

significant in the development of children's rights at EU level, ensuring greater visibility for children's issues within the Union. The proposed incorporation of the Charter into Part II of the EU Constitutional Treaty would have made it legally binding, but it now appears unlikely that the Constitution in its current form will be fully ratified by the Member States.

European Union Initiatives on the Right of the Child

Reflecting the increasing momentum at international level to promote children's rights, in recent years signs have emerged that the EU is also taking a more proactive approach, especially in relation to external policy (EP).

For example:

- In December 2003 the Council of Ministers adopted "EU Guidelines on Children and Armed Conflict", setting out commitments in relation to: monitoring and reporting by Heads of Missions, EU Military Commanders and Special Representatives of the effects of conflict on children; providing assessments and developing recommendations; and implementing EU action in relation to third countries (e.g. political dialogue, multilateral co-operation, crisis management operations, and training).
- In 2003, the European Parliament's Annual Report called upon the Council to adopt a strategy on children and armed conflict, and the EU-ACP Joint Parliamentary Assembly adopted a resolution on children and armed conflict. Other EP resolutions have addressed trafficking of children, and human rights in the world.
- The promotion of children's rights was one of the priorities for funding under the "European Initiative for Human Rights and Democracy" in 2001 and was mainstreamed in funding for the period 2002-2004. Through the campaign "Promoting a culture of human rights" in 2005-2006, it provides support for training and awareness-raising on children's rights in third countries.
- The European Community Humanitarian Office (ECHO) has in the past supported specific humanitarian operations relating to children (e.g. feeding, vaccination, primary education, reintegration of child soldiers), and has funded relevant NGO research and advocacy activities. Children have also been identified as a priority in ECHO's last two annual strategic plans, and in ECHO guidelines.

Child Rights in Scandinavia

Whenever measures of social progress or human development are published, it is usual to find Sweden–along with its Nordic neighbours, Denmark, Finland, Iceland and Norway–close to the top. All five nations rank among the top 5 in the United Nations Development Programme's *Human Development Index 2008* (based on 2006 data), with Sweden in seventh place. The country ranked first in the Economist Intelligence Unit's *Democracy Index 2008* and third best in Transparency International's *Corruption Perceptions Index* for the same year. Sweden's high level of social development reflects a democratic and stable political system and high standards of living. In 2006, GDP per capita, in purchasing power parity terms, stood at US$34,000. A sound health-care system has reduced mortality rates at all levels to low rates. The latest UN inter-agency estimates show the under-five mortality rate for 2007 at 3 deaths per 1,000 live births and the lifetime risk of maternal mortality at 1 in 17,400. Education is universal at both the primary and secondary levels.

A strong supporter of the Convention while it was being drafted, Sweden was one of the first countries to ratify the treaty, on 29 June 1990, and has also ratified its two Optional Protocols. The country's focus on meeting children's needs and fulfilling their rights predates the Convention, however. Since the early 1970s, it has been actively committed to providing children with necessary care and support, especially in health and education, through innovative, well resourced government policies and programmes. Abroad, the Swedish International Development Cooperation Agency has a long history of engagement and investment in child rights across the developing world. Among the 30 member states of the Organisation for Economic Co-operation and development, Sweden spends the most on the preschool child. And it was the only country of 25 with comparable data to achieve all 10 benchmarks for early childhood care and education in a 2008 study by UNICEF's Innocent Research Centre.

One example of this attentiveness to child rights is the Swedish Government's Early Childhood Education and Care programme, which has been given high priority during recent decades and forms a cornerstone of family policy. Research has consistently shown the benefits of early childhood care, which is strongly advocated in General Comment No. 7 to the Convention. Pedagogic activities and stimulation form a strong foundation for development and learning and contribute to better educational outcomes in primary, secondary and tertiary levels–which in turn support higher average earnings and better living standards.

To encourage such early childhood development, parents in Sweden have a right to take more than two years of temporary leave to care for infants and young children. In addition, the Early Childhood Education and Care programme helps working parents balance parenthood with work and studies. This programme and other child friendly initiatives are the responsibility of the Ministry of Health and Social Affairs, one of whose functions is to ensure that child rights are considered in all areas of government policy and public affairs affecting children and young people. To this end, in 1999 the Swedish Parliament adopted a national strategy for the implementation of the Convention. The objective of this approach is to foster respect for the principles that underpin the Convention; provide essential services, protection and opportunities for development; protect children against harm and neglect; and encourage their participation in the community and throughout society.

To further protect child rights, the Government of Sweden has appointed a children's ombudsperson to represent the interests of children and young people and monitor compliance with the Convention at all levels of society. Each year, the ombudsperson submits a report to the Government on the situation of the country's children and young people, highlighting the opportunities and obstacles encountered in fulfilling their rights. This firm framework for child rights is not without its challenges. Like other industrialized countries, Sweden is experiencing an increase in the number of children and young people who suffer from psychological distress and obesity. In its concluding observations to the country's fourth periodic report, presented in 2007, the Committee on the Rights of the Child expressed concern at the broad disparities among municipalities, counties and regions in the implementation of the Convention, and recommended that the Government strengthen measures to guarantee equal access and availability of services for all children, regardless of where they live.

Sweden has also experienced significant immigration during recent decades and faces the task of ensuring that the rights of immigrant children are met. Strengthening mechanisms to address the rights of children belonging to vulnerable groups–including unaccompanied, refugee and asylum-seeking children–is a relatively new challenge, one that Sweden is well placed to confront, given its legacy of respect for and commitment to child rights.

Since *A Children's Policy for 21st Century Europe: First steps* was published by the European Children's Network (EURONET) in 1999, the EU has experienced dramatic economic and political change, including the introduction of the single currency, enlargement to 25 Member States, and the rejection of the EU Constitutional Treaty by voters in France and the Netherlands. Social changes are also accelerating. For instance, the EU is facing demographic shifts on an unprecedented scale as a result of common trends such as increasing life expectancy, a declining population of working age, and falling birth rates. Factors such as these are likely to have a huge direct and indirect impact on children living in the EU. For example, although enlargement has provided significant new opportunities, many children in the new Member States will still experience high levels of poverty, discrimination and exploitation. The uncertain political climate may also undermine efforts to strengthen the response of the EU institutions to children's rights. And demographic change brings risks of a steady decline in children's services within Member States.

The Millennium Development Goals and World Fit for Children

In May 2002, governments emphasized their global commitment to children's rights at the landmark Special Session of the UN General Assembly on Children. The Session was attended by more than 7,000 people, including not only Heads of State, prime ministers and high-ranking delegations but also NGOs and-for the first time-children themselves. Whilst mirroring and reaffirming commitment to the Millennium Development Goals, the outcome document 36 adds new elements, highlighting ten broad principles and objectives:

- primary consideration of the "best interests" of the child in all actions related to them;
- the eradication of poverty, and investment in children;
- freedom from discrimination;
- children's survival, protection, growth and development in good health and with proper nutrition;
- education for all, and elimination of gender disparities;
- protection of children from harm and exploitation;
- protection of children from war;
- combating HIV/AIDS;
- respect for children's right to participate in all matters affecting them, in accordance with their age and maturity;
- protection of the Earth for children, minimizing the impact of natural disasters and environmental degradation on them.

These processes provide the underpinning for a global strategy to advance children's rights and build a "World Fit for Children". This is an agenda to which the EU has also signed up.

Children's Rights Today

As was mentioned by way of introduction, children's rights have been successively strengthened during the 20th century, as far as concerns "family law children's rights", to which can be counted such questions as the confirmation of paternity, custody, visitation rights, adoption and alimony. According to Sandy Ruxton the very important improvement that has taken place regarding the legal standing of children who were previously, in Swedish law, termed "children out of wedlock".

In 1976 the terms "children born within marriage" and "children out of wedlock" were completely eliminated from Swedish legislation. Instead Swedish law today makes a distinction between children born from a wed or an unwed mother. The situation is nowadays the same in Norwegian law. On Island, where all differences, from a legal perspective, between "children born within marriage" and "children born out of wedlock" were abolished in 1981, these terms were first eliminated through a 1992 statute. Also within Swiss law these terms have been eliminated from the statutory legislation. In certain other countries in Europe, as for example Greece, the terminological renewal within this area has only signified that one has abolished the terms "legitimate" and "illegitimate children" and instead incorporated the terms "born within marriage" and "born out of wedlock".

Through legislation from 1969 Sweden acknowledged for "children born out of wedlock" the same right to inheritance after the father and father's parents as for "children born within marriage". A presidential nation in Europe regarding equality of children's inheritance rights was, however, another northern country, namely Norway, which enacted such legislation as early as 1915. Only much later have other countries in Europe followed suit regarding this issue, besides the other northern countries, also France, Belgium, Switzerland and Germany.

However, as will be shown in the following presentation there still remain, in Swedish law, certain distinctions within other areas of family law between children born from a married and children born from unwed mothers, namely regarding questions dealing with the confirmation of fatherhood and child custody.

Confirmation of Parentage

According to Article 7 of the UN's Convention on Children's Rights, children shall be immediately registered after birth and shall as far as possible, have a right to knowledge about their parents. Furthermore a convention state shall guarantee the carrying out of these rights in accordance with its national legislation and its undertakings with regard to applicable international instruments within the area in question.

Swedish law, going back a long time has stated that a child's birth shall be reported to the national registration authority. Such a report shall, among other hinges, clarify the identity of the child's mother. In Sweden, as in most other countries, other rules regarding the confirmation of motherhood have been considered unnecessary according to the clause "mater semper certa est", since the delivery usually shows who the mother of the child is.

In the Swedish legal system this paternity presumption signifies that if the mother is married at the child's birth or if the child is born at such time after the husbands death that it can have been conceived before the date of death, then the now deceased husband is presumed to be the child's father (FB 1:1). Before 1977, the paternity presumption also applied in cases where the woman gave birth at such a time after a divorce that it could have been conceived prior to the divorce.

Concerning the confirmation of paternity of children born from unmarried mothers, the rule in Sweden has been, since the creation of the 1917 statute regarding children born out of wedlock, that it is a matter for the public authorities (currently the Social Welfare Board) to act in the child's best interests in order to determine paternity. In principle this should be done regardless of the mother's view on its necessity. In Norway, similar rules have been in effect since the creation of a statute in 1915, while in Finland an applicable law states that the mother has the right to oppose the carrying out of an investigation into the paternity question.

The adopted point of view in Swedish law regarding the public authority's task in this area was at first motivated by the child's, but also the mother's and society's economic interest in making a man, through determined paternity, become obliged to contribute child support, a position that was reflected in older rules about determining paternity through acknowledgment or judgment, rules which were designed in such a way that they gave small guarantees that the confirmation of paternity in reality coincided with the true genetic relationship. In 1969, as has previously been mentioned, Sweden carried out an inheritance reform that implied the incorporation of full inheritance rights for illegitimate children even in relation to the father and the father's relatives. This reform was the result of a number of factors: the successively improved economic and social status of illegitimate children in society; through various social reforms; the changed perception on non-marital relations and the fruits thereof; the successively strengthened and improved ability to determine paternity issues through medical evaluation; a man's legal rights if alleged to be the father; and also children's interest in a correct agreement between legal and genetic paternity.

All of these factors resulted, through legislation in 1969, in the implementation of new rules regarding the confirmation of paternity through admission and judgment. This legislation aims at creating more precise decisions in paternity questions than was previously possible. After this reform, the task of the state, was delegated to the social services authority, to act in public interest to determine the paternity of children born of unmarried mothers. This can now can be motivated by the child's right to knowledge about its origins.

Child Abuse

The number of cases of child abuse has increased dramatically during the last several years. This tragic development when parents exercise child abuse, can in part be explained by the helplessness that many parents feel, for instance, as a result of unemployment and the economically strained situation that this creates. Children of immigrant families are said to constitute an especially vulnerable group when it comes to assaults by parents. There can be several reasons for this, among others, the view of corporal punishment in bringing up children in the immigrant parent's homeland. The view on corporal punishment can to a certain extent can explain the situation of child abuse in Great Britain.

It is said that-aside from sexual abuse-physical and psychological child abuse occurs very frequently. At least four children per week, or grossly 200 children per year, are supposedly abused to death in Great Britain, compared to five to six children per year in Sweden. In Great Britain corporal punishment is thought to be a traditional parental right, a right that parents in Sweden lost through legislation already some thirty years ago. In Sweden, which in 1979 became the first nation in the world to incorporate in legislation an explicit prohibition against corporal punishment, the attitude towards corporal punishment has become increasingly negative since the mentioned legislation was adopted.

An express statutory prohibition against corporal punishment now exists also in some other European countries, at any rate Norway, Denmark, Finland and Austria. However, since conditions supporting this were non-existent, the UN Children's Convention did not include any article with an express prohibition against corporal punishment. According to Article 19, which is directed towards all forms of physical and mental abuse of children, the member states shall however "take all appropriate legislative, administrative and social measures as well as measures in an educational purpose to protect the child against all forms of physical and mental violence, injury or assault,. abuse or exploitation, including sexual assaults, while the child is in the parent's or a parent's, guardian's or other person's care".

Through education, social mobilization and development, a climate is to be created, guaranteeing that parents and others with a legal responsibility towards children can realize their rights and obligations, as well as their responsibilities to protect children from sexual exploitation. National plans of action within this current area shall be determined no later than the year 2000. Finally, it should be mentioned that, during a meeting at the end of November 1996, the EU Council for Justice and Home Affairs, also agreed upon cooperation between the member states in order to attempt to come to terms with this problem. Sweden has played a leading role, not the least in the creation of the UN Convention on Children's Rights.

Hopefully the current legislative work in Sweden in this area, as well as the work accomplished during the recent 1996 world congress in Sweden against child pornography, child prostitution and the sexual exploitation of children, both globally and even within the EU, will lead to cooperation between different states and to a greatly improved protection for children.

Rights of the Child in Sweden—A Special Case

> "It is the children who pay the highest price of our shortsighted politics, our political mistakes, our wars."
>
> —Eglantyne Jebb, founder of Save the Children, 1919

Every child up to the age of 18 has special rights. Children are competent individuals who must be respected and allowed to participate in decisions that concern them. They have the right to a secure upbringing and opportunities to develop. The Government's child rights policy aim to apply and strengthen the rights and interests of the child in society, based on the UN Convention on the Rights of the Child.

The Government's child rights policy support the rights of the child. Children must be able to grow up in a secure environment and to develop at their own pace and on the basis of their own abilities and needs. A child perspective and a child rights perspective are to be mainstreamed into all areas and activities involving children, such as educational policy, migration policy, cultural policy and social services policy. For decision-makers and others, applying a child perspective means that before taking decisions or measures they must consider whether these affect the child or children and, if so, in what way.

Adopting a child perspective is a matter of attitudes, knowledge and working methods. It reflects a view of children as fully fledged citizens and competent individuals who should be met with respect in all circumstances. If the measures or decisions are considered to affect the child or children, consideration must be taken of the human rights that children have, for example, under the Convention on the Rights of the Child.

The Convention on the Rights of the Child guides Sweden's child rights work

The Convention on the Rights of the Child was adopted by the UN General Assembly in 1989. Sweden ratified the Convention following a decision by the Riksdag in 1990. Almost every country in the world has ratified the Convention on the Rights of the Child.

The Convention must be viewed as a single unified document and the various rights it sets out are equally important. It focuses on the individual and the right of the child to have his or her fundamental rights and needs met. In summary, the Convention recognises the right of the child to respect, and that childhood is valuable and must therefore be protected.

Optional Protocols to the CRC to Which Sweden has Acceded

To strengthen and deepen the commitments in the Convention on the Rights of the Child, there are two facultative-i.e. optional-protocols to the Convention to which Sweden has acceded:

- Optional Protocol to the Convention on the Rights of the Child on the involvement of children in armed conflict
- Optional Protocol to the Convention on the Rights of the Child on the sale of children, child prostitution and child pornography.

Sweden Reports to UN Committee on the Rights of the Child

Under the Convention on the Rights of the Child, Sweden is to report every five years to the UN Committee on the Rights of the Child on how it is implementing the Convention and living up to its commitments in the protocols mentioned above.

Strategy to Strengthen the Rights of the Child in Sweden

In 2010 the Riksdag approved the Government's strategy to strengthen the rights of the child. This strategy replaces the strategy adopted by the Riksdag in 1999.

The strategy consists of nine principles expressing the fundamental conditions for strengthening the rights of the child in Sweden. It is based on the human rights that every child up to the age of 18 has under the international agreements, in particular the Convention on the Rights of the Child.

To strengthen the rights of the child, the following strategies are to apply:

1. All legislation concerning children must be designed in accordance with the Convention on the Rights of the Child.
2. The child's physical and mental integrity must be respected in all circumstances.
3. Children must have the right to express their views in all matters that concern them.
4. Children must receive information about their rights and what they mean in practice.
5. Parents must receive information about the rights of the child and be offered parenting support.
6. Decision-makers and relevant professional groups must have knowledge of child rights and put this knowledge into practice in their relevant professional activities.
7. Actors involved in activities concerning children must strengthen child rights by working in partnership.
8. Current knowledge of children's living conditions must form the basis of decisions and priorities affecting children.
9. Decisions and measures affecting children must be monitored and evaluated based on a child rights perspective.

The Ombudsman for Children in Sweden

The Ombudsman for Children (Barnombudsmannen, BO) is a government agency whose task is to represent the rights and interests of children and young people, based on the Convention of the Rights of the Child, and to monitor compliance with the Convention.

Its main responsibilities include participating in efforts to implement the Convention in Sweden by pushing for its implementation in municipalities, county councils, regions and government agencies. Another important task involves putting forward proposals to the Government for amendments to Swedish legislation or other measures needed to ensure that the rights and interests of children and young people are met, and also to inform about the rights and interests of children and young people.

The Ombudsman for Children is not a supervisory authority but has legal powers to summon parties for deliberations. By law, the Ombudsman for Children is not permitted to intervene in individual cases but is obliged to report cases of child maltreatment.

The Academy for the Rights of the Child

Background

Sweden ratified the UN Convention on the Rights of the Child (UNCRC) in 1990. The first national strategy for the implementation of the CRC was approved by the Swedish parliament (Riksdag) in 1999, followed by a second, revised, strategy approved in November 2010. The national strategy stresses the importance of training and capacity building of professional groups in charge of issues affecting children's lives, including policy and decision makers at local, regional and national levels. This work is extremely important for Sweden to be successful in turning the principles of the UNCRC into practice.

The Academy on the Rights of the Child was initiated by Örebro University (with financial support from the Ministry of Social Affairs during the start up years 2007-2009) with a mission to offer academic courses and in-service training on children's rights and the implementation and monitoring of the UNCRC.

Vision and Objectives

Policy makers, decision makers and professional groups working with children at different levels in society work in accordance with the basic principles of the UNCRC, i.e. the right to life, survival and development (article 6), the right to non-discrimination (article 2) the right to be heard (article 12) and the principle of the best interest of the child.

The vision shall be realized through the following objectives:

1) Training (academic courses and tailor made in-service training).
2) Interdisciplinary research on children's rights.
3) International collaboration in research and academic education programs.

The Academy for the Rights of the Child is a member of the European Network of Masters in Children's Rights (ENMCR) and Child Rights Information Network (CRIN).

Reference

Ruxton, S. (2008), Report on The European Children's Network. (EURONET). Jointly financed by The NSPCC, Save the Children (UK).

17

Child Rights and United States

Recently the U.N. special representative on violence against children called on member countries to ratify two optional protocols to the U.N. Convention on the Rights of the Child which would help prevent the sale of children, child prostitution, child pornography and the involvement of children in armed conflict around the world. The Convention was adopted in 1989 to promote basic human rights for children everywhere, but the latest effort to extend those protections underscores a disturbing truth: the United States is one of only two U.N. member countries not to have ratified the original Convention (the other country is Somalia — which doesn't have a functioning government.) The Convention was drafted during the Reagan and Clinton administrations — with a great deal of influence from the United States — but has never been presented to the Senate for consent, which is the final step to ratification.

The opposition is primarily based on fears of U.N. interference in U.S. laws and families. The biggest worry appears to be that the treaty will undermine parental rights even though the Convention explicitly grants responsibilities and protections to parents and guardians. One of the alarms raised by Parental Rights.org, an organization that supports a parental-rights amendment to the U.S. Constitution, is that the Convention will prevent parents from spanking their children or opting them out of sex education. But the Convention does not require us to choose between the rights of children and the rights of parents-it protects both.

Some of the key provisions of the Convention are that children should be raised in an atmosphere of happiness, love and understanding; governments should respect the rights and duties of parents and families; courts should take into account the best interest of children when making decisions; institutions that care for children should be safe and properly staffed; and children should be protected from trafficking, illicit transfer across borders, torture, physical abuse, sexual exploitation, sexual abuse, and conscription into armed conflicts.

The benefits of international cooperation in these areas and American implementation of these principles seem obvious to us, but there are still enough objections to ratification within the U.S. to make approval by a two-thirds majority in the Senate unlikely at this time. Parental rights.org also objects to the idea that children should have the right to choose their own religion, as well as freedom of thought and expression. But isn't religion always a matter of one's own conscience, no matter what age? With or without a treaty, effective parenting means not forcing anything onto children—be it religion, sexual orientation or green beans. Authoritarian parenting erodes the internal decision-making capacity of a child and erodes closeness between parent and child.

The supposed danger of loss of national sovereignty is also a false alarm. In fact, no international treaty has the power to override the U.S. Constitution, as put forth in the landmark Supreme Court ruling in Reid v. Covert (1957). What is required by the Convention is simply a periodic report to the Committee on the Rights of the Child outlining the situation of children in the country and explanation of the measures taken to realize children's rights. The Committee then urges all levels of government to use the Convention as a guide in policymaking and implementation.

Sharon Smith, the author of Women and Socialism and Subterranean Fire: a History of Working-Class Radicalism in the United States, reported as follows:

The U.S. is the only United Nations member-state except Somalia that has neglected to ratify the UN's 1989 Convention on the Rights of the Child. In February 2001, George W. Bush explicitly objected to its "human rights-based approach"-which, among other things, prohibits prosecuting and incarcerating children as adults because their minds are too immature to form "criminal intent."

Indeed, the U.S. stands alone in its rush to sentence children to a lifetime in prison without the possibility of parole, and is home to more than 99 per cent of youths serving this sentence worldwide. According to a joint 2005 study by Human Rights Watch and Amnesty International, the U.S. had 9,400 prisoners serving life prison terms for crimes committed before the age of 18, of which 2,225 were serving life without parole. Of those, 16 per cent were between 13 and 15 years old at the time they committed the crimes for which they were convicted.

More than 100,000 children are currently incarcerated in local detention and state correctional institutions across the country. "Zero tolerance" advocates would have us believe that the number has skyrocketed because our nation is overrun with teenage predators committing an unprecedented number of heinous crimes.

Over the last decade, scores of young children have been handcuffed, arrested, shoved into patrol cars, fingerprinted, jailed and convicted of crimes stemming from incidents as trivial as temper tantrums in kindergarten, schoolyard fights or setting off a fire alarm-which once would have warranted a trip to the principal's office at worst. Now a six-year-old's temper tantrum can bring felony charges. Oftentimes, the children's two wrists are small enough to fit into a single handcuff.

In December 2001, after arresting a 10-year-old autistic fourth grader who disrupted a special education class, the Okaloosa, Florida Sheriff's Department's Rick Hord defended his actions, arguing, "[T]here's no question but that we had all the elements of a felony crime present."

Not all children are treated equally. Race and class loom large. As the Times noted, "there is a stark difference among arrests of children by race — one that gets sharper as the children get younger." The young targets of "zero tolerance" arrests nationwide are overwhelmingly Black, Latino and Native American. In 2000, according to the Suffolk University Law School Juvenile Justice Center (JJC), African-American children-who made up just 15 per cent of the U.S. juvenile population-were 46 per cent of those incarcerated and 52 per cent of those whose cases ended up in adult criminal court. Black children are imprisoned at five times the rate of whites, while Latino and Native American children are placed in correctional institutions at two and a half times that of whites.

In April 2005, 11-year-old Maribel Cuevas was involved in a neighborhood squabble and returned a rock that a group of boys threw at her outside her Fresno, California home-hitting 8-year-old Elijah Vang in the forehead. Although Vang's parents pressed no charges, police arrested the 11-year old and took her to a juvenile detention center for felony assault–holding her for five days before she was released on the condition that she wear an electronic ankle bracelet to monitor her location.

Children are generally afforded the basic rights embodied by the Constitution, as enshrined by the Fourteenth Amendment to the United States Constitution. The Equal Protection Clause of that amendment is to apply to children, born within a marriage or not, but excludes children not yet born. This was reinforced by the landmark US Supreme Court decision of In re Gault. In this trial 15-year-old Gerald Gault of Arizona was taken into custody by local police after being accused of making an obscene telephone call. He was detained and committed to the Arizona State Industrial School until he reached the age of 21 for making an obscene phone call to an adult neighbour. In an 8–1 decision, the Court ruled that in hearings which could result in commitment to an institution, people under the age of 18 have the right to notice and counsel, to question witnesses, and to protection against self-incrimination. The Court found that the procedures used in Gault's hearing met none of these requirements.

There are other concerns in the United States regarding children's rights. The American Academy of Adoption Attorneys is concerned with children's rights to a safe, supportive and stable family structure. Their position on children's rights in adoption cases states that, "children have a constitutionally based liberty interest in the protection of their established families, rights which are at least equal to, and we believe outweigh, the rights of others who would claim a 'possessory' interest in these children." Other issues raised in American children's rights advocacy include children's rights to inheritance in same-sex marriages and particular rights for youth.

In the view of Howard Davidson, J.D. is Director of the American Bar Association Center on Children and the Law, CRC is important to United States. He expressed that, American critics of the Convention on the Rights of the Child (CRC) have galvanized opposition by mislabeling it as a potential threat to the American family and by making unsubstantiated claims that it would, if ratified by the United States, undermine national sovereignty and interfere with American parent-child relationships. Let us put those untruths aside and refocus the argument on why it is important for Àmerica to ratify the CRC.

One good reason for ratification is that the United States can become an unencumbered world leader in promoting national laws and government policies across the globe that can help protect children from violence and neglect. This is something in which America has a great deal of expertise.

While recently reconsidering the CRC's potential impact in the United States and the status of children's rights within the country, Davidson was asked by an American Bar Association (ABA) international programme to review and comment on a draft children's rights code for the nation of Kyrgyzstan. He was impressed with the breadth of that draft law and with its sweeping articulation of the rights of their children in accordance with the principles of the CRC. He could not help but think that in his thirty-plus years in the field of child protection law he had—despite the draft's many flaws—never seen any U.S. federal or state law remotely like that !.

Few American laws have "children's rights" in their title. This is in part because many believe that if children are afforded "rights" that they will come at the expense of parental rights. The relationship between the rights of American parents and those independently possessed by American children is the subject of a recent book titled What's Wrong with Children's Rights, written by Martin Guggenheim, a distinguished American law professor at New York University. Notice that there is no question mark at the end of the title.

Despite concerns of many American parents about children possessing independent rights, if the CRC was ratified it would likely result in new legal protections for children that would—as with many U.S. child protection law reforms—have broad bipartisan support. Americans who may be fearful of children's "rights" are unlikely to have reservations about enhancing protections for children. Over fifty years of judicial decisions address children's constitutional protections applied to a variety of factual situations. The cases range from those considering juvenile incarceration without access to legal counsel to those dealing with the ability of students to express political views in non disruptive ways. Court decisions also address the protection of children in foster care and, more recently, curtailment of the juvenile death penalty. In the legislative arena, there are model federal and state special education laws and other laws to protect children from being deprived of educational opportunities such as universal free elementary and secondary education.

The United States has a vast body of American children's "rights" law that the CRC encourages. One of the most important reforms in U.S. law as it relates to children has been a focus on the "protection rights" of children, both at home and in the foster care system. One reason that the Bush administration was comfortable quickly ratifying the Optional Protocol to the CRC on the sexual exploitation of children was past U.S. legal achievements in child protection.

References

Howard Davidson, J.D. (1990), Children's Rights in America: U.N. Convention on the rights of the child compared with United States Law. Cynthia Price Cohen and Howard Davidson eds.

Smith, S. (2001), Women and Socialism and Subterranean Fire: A History of Working class Radication in the United States. http://www.amazon.com

Appendix I
UN Convention on the Rights of the Child (CRC)

The Convention on the Rights of Children was adopted in 1989, in recognition of the fact that in all countries, there are children living in exceptionally difficult conditions, who need special protection. The Convention seeks to assure to all children most of the rights and freedoms guaranteed in the International Bill of Rights, like life, liberty, the freedom of expression and conscience, non discrimination, and privacy.

Fundamental Principles

Respect for the Child's Opinion: The corollary to children as subjects of rights is the principle that their opinion should be respected. It means that the child has the right to freedom of expression, freedom of thought, freedom of conscience and freedom of assembly.

Each Child has Rights: The recognition that children have equal value as adults implies that each child has rights. The principle that all children should enjoy rights is fundamental to the Convention. The principle is based on the notion that children are subjects and not objects of the rights. Moreover, children should enjoy their rights without discrimination. It means that girls should be given the same opportunities as the boys. Similarly, disabled children and children of disadvantageous groups should enjoy the same rights as others.

Equal Value as Human Beings: An underlying principle of the Convention is that of according children the same value as adults. This principle stresses that childhood has value in itself. It is not merely a preparatory stage for adulthood. The implication of this principle is that the society has an obligation to create conditions for the child to enjoy his or her childhood.

Best Interests of the Child: While children have equal value as grownups they also need the protection and support from the society for enjoying their childhood. The principle of best interests of the child balances the need for providing protection to children while respecting.

This principle is most clearly stated in article 3 (1) of the Convention.

'In all actions concerning children, whether undertaken by public or private social welfare institutions, courts of law, administrative authorities or legislative bodies, the best interests of the child shall be a primary consideration'.

The interests of the child take precedent over the interests of parents or the state. The principle as stated in article 3 (1) applies to ' all actions concerning children' and not restricted to legal or administrative proceedings.

The following section provides the details of the articles of the convention.

PART 1

Article 1: ***Definition of a Child***: For the purposes of the present Convention, a child means every human being below the age of eighteen years unless, under the law applicable to the child, majority is attained earlier.

Article 2: ***Non-Discrimination***

1. States Parties shall respect and ensure the rights set forth in the present Convention to each child within their jurisdiction without discrimination of any kind, irrespective of the child's or his or her parent's or legal guardian's race, colour, sex, language, religion, political or other opinion, national, ethnic or social origin, property, disability, birth or other status.
2. States Parties shall take all appropriate measures to ensure that the child is protected against all forms of discrimination or punishment on the basis of the status, activities, expressed opinions, or beliefs of the child's parents, legal guardians, or family members.

Best Interests of the Child

1. In all actions concerning children, whether undertaken by public or private social welfare institutions, courts of law. Administrative authorities or legislative bodies, the best interests of the child shall be a primary consideration.
2. States Parties undertake to ensure the child such protection and care as is necessary for his or her well-being, taking into account the rights and duties of his or her parents, legal guardians, or other individuals legally responsible for him or her, and to this end, shall take all appropriate legislative and administrative measures.
3. States Parties shall ensure that the institutions, services and facilities responsible for the care or protection of children shall conform with the standards established by competent authorities, particularly in the areas of safety, health, in the number and suitability of their staff as well as competent supervision.

Article 4: ***Implementation of Rights:*** States Parties shall undertake all appropriate legislative. Administrative, and other measure for the implementation of the rights recognized in the present Convention. With regard to economic, social and cultural rights, States Parties shall undertake such measures to the maximum extent of their available resources and, where needed, within the framework of international co-operation.

Article 5: ***Parental Guidance and the Child's Evolving Capacities:*** States Parties shall respect the responsibilities, rights and duties of parents or, where applicable, the members of theustom, legal guardians or other persons legally responsible for the child, to provide, in a manner consistent with the evolving capacities of the child, appropriate direction and guidance in the exercise by the child of the rights recognised in the present Convention.

Article 6: *Survival and Development*

1. States Parties recognize that every child has the inherent right to life.
2. States Parties shall ensure to the maximum extent possible the survival and development of the child.

Article 7: *Name and Nationality*

1. The child shall be registered immediately after birth and shall have the right from birth to name, the right to acquire a nationality and, as far as possible, the right to know and be cared for by his or her parents.
2. States Parties shall ensure the implementation of these rights in accordance with their national law and their obligations under the relevant international instruments in this field, in particular where the child would other-wise be stateless.

Article 8: *Preservation of Identity*

1. States Parties undertake to respect the right of the child to reserve his/her identity, including nationality, name and family relations as recognized by law without unlawful interference.
2. Where a child is illegally deprived of some or all of the elements of his or her identity. States Parties shall provide appropriate assistance and protection as a view to speedily re-establishing his or her identity.

Article 9: *Separation from Parents*: This article provides that ordinarily a child shall not be separated from his or her parents. Articles 9 permits separation of a child from his or her parents if it is required for the best interests of the child. However, competent authorities under relevant laws should decide it and such decisions should be subject to judicial review. The child who is separated from one or both parents has a right to maintain personal relations and direct contact with both parents, except if it is contrary to the child's best interests.

Article 10: *Family Reunification*: This article stipulates that States should facilitate reunification of families by permitting travel into, or out of their territories. This right is subject to limitations when necessary to protect the national security, public order (ordre public), public health or morals or the rights and freedoms of others. The limitations imposed should be based on law and consistent with the rights recognized in the present Convention.

Article 11: ***Illicit Transfer and Non-Return***

1. States Parties shall take measures to combat the illicit transfer stands non-return of children abroad.
2. To this end, States Parties shall promote the conclusion of bilateral or multilateral agreements or accession to existing agreements.

Article 12: *The Child's Opinion*

1. States Parties shall assure to the child who is capable of forming his or her own views the right to express those views freely in all matters affecting the child, the views of the child being giving due weight in accordance with the age and maturity of the child.
2. For this purpose, the child shall in particular be provided the opportunity to be heard in any judicial and administrative proceedings affecting the child, either directly, or through a representative or an appropriate body, in a manner consistent with the procedural rules of national law.

Article 13: ***Freedom of Expression***

1. The child shall have the right to freedom of expression; this right shall include freedom to seek, receive and impart information and ideas of all kinds, regardless of frontiers, either orally, in writing or in print, in the form of art, or through any other media of the child's choice.
2. The exercise of this right may be subject to certain restrictions, but these shall only be such as are provided by law and are necessary;
   (a) For respect of the rights or reputations of others; or
   (b) For the protection of national security or of public order (ordre public), or of public health or morals.

Article 14: ***Freedom of Thought, Conscience and Religion:*** This article guarantees the right of the child to freedom of thought, conscience and religion. The State should also respect the rights and duties of parents to provide direction to the child in a manner consistent with the evolving capacities of the child. This right is subject to limitations when necessary to protect public safety, order, health or morals or the fundamental rights and freedoms of others.

Article 15: ***Freedom of Association***

1. States Parties recognize the rights of the child to freedom of association and to freedom of peaceful assembly.
2. No restrictions may be placed on the exercise of these rights other than those imposed in conformity with the law and which are necessary

in a democratic society in the interests of national security or public safety, public order (ordre public), the protection of public health or morals or the protection of the rights and freedoms of others.

Article 16: ***Protection of Privacy***

1. No child shall be subjected to arbitrary or unlawful interference with his or her privacy, family home or correspondence, nor to unlawful attacks on his or her honour and reputation.
2. The child has the right to the protection of the law against such interference or attacks.

Article 17: ***Access to Appropriate Information*****:** Article 17 recognizes the importance of mass media and requires that State parties ensure that the child has access to information and material from a diversity of sources. State parties are also required to encourage mass media to disseminate information and material of benefit to children., In addition, State parties should develop appropriate guidelines for protecting the child from material harmful to his well-being.

Article 18: ***Parental Responsibilities:*** This article acknowledges the principle that the primary responsibility for the upbringing and the development of the child rests with both parents or legal guardians. The best interests of the child will be their primary concern. The State should develop institutions, facilities and services for the care of children o assist parents or legal guardians to perform their child-rearing responsibilities. States parties should also take measures to ensure that children of working parents benefit from child-care services and facilities.

Article 19: ***Protection from Abuse and Neglect:*** Article 19 obligates State parties to take legislative, administrative, social and educational measures to protect the child from physical or mental abuse, neglect, exploitation including sexual abuse by parents or others responsible for the care of the child. The State parties should also take measures to develop social programmes for prevention of abuse and treatment of victims.

Article 20: ***Protection of Children Without Families:*** This article requires that State Parties provide special protection and assistance to a child deprived of his or her family environment. State parties should provide alternative care for such a child including adoption or institutional placement. In providing such alternative, care, the State should take into account the child's ethnic, religious, cultural and linguistic background.

Article 21: ***Adoption:*** This article stipulates that those States Parties that recognize or permit adoption should ensure that it is carried out in the best interests of the child. Competent authorities according to the relevant law should authorize all adoption.

Recognizes inter country adoption. However, they should enjoy safeguards and standards similar to national adoption.

Article 22: ***Refugee Children:*** Article 22 provides that State Parties take measures to provide protection and humanitarian assistance to a refugee child or a child seeking refugee status.

Article 23: ***Disabled Children:*** The article requires that State Parties recognize that a mentally or physically disabled child should enjoy a full and decent life in dignity and promote their self-reliance and active participation in the community. Disabled children shall have the right to special treatment, education and care.

Article 24: ***Health and Health Services:***Article 24 stipulates that State Parties recognize the right of the child to the enjoyment of the highest attainable standard of health and to treatment of illness and rehabilitation of health, 'State parties shall strive to ensure that no child is deprived of his or her right of access to such health care services'.

In implementing this right, State Parties should take measures to diminish infant and child mortality, development of primary health care, to combat disease and malnutrition, ensure pre-natal and post-natal health care for mothers and abolish traditional practices that harm the health of the children.

Article 25: ***Periodic Review of Placement:*** States Parties recognize the right of a child who has been placed by the competent authorities for the purposes of care, protection, or treatment of his or her physical or mental health, to a periodic review of the treatment provided to the child and all other circumstances relevant to his or her placement.

Article 26: ***Social Security***

1. States Parties shall recognize for every child the right to benefit from social security, including social insurance, and shall take the necessary measures to achieve the full realization of this right in accordance with their national law.
2. The benefits should, where appropriate, be granted, taking into account the resources and the circumstances of the child and persons having responsibility for the maintenance of the child, as well as any other consideration relevant to an application for benefits made by or on behalf of the child.

Article 27: ***Standard of Living:*** This article recognizes the right of every child to a standard of living adequate for the child's physical, mental, spiritual, moral and social development. The parents have the primary responsibility to ensure the standard of living adequate for the child's development. The State parties should provide assistance including where necessary material assistance to enable parents to implement this right.

Article 28: ***Education:*** Article 28 provides that State parties recognize the right of the child to education. To realize this right, they shall make primary education free and compulsory. They will also encourage different forms of secondary education and make them accessible to every child by providing it free or offering financial assistance. States parties shall take measures to ensure that school discipline is administered in conformity with a child's dignity and rights.

Article 29: ***Aims of Education:*** This article requires that the education of the child shall be directed to the development of the child's personality, talents and mental and physical abilities. It should prepare the child for leading a responsible life in a free society. It should also foster respect for his or her parents, his or her own cultural identity, other cultures and for human rights and fundamental freedoms.

Article 30: ***Children of Minorities or Indigenous Peoples:*** In those States in which ethnic, religious or linguistic minorities or persons of indigenous origin exist, a child belonging to such a minority or who is indigenous shall not be denied the right, in community with other members of his or her group, to enjoy his or her own culture, to profess and practice his or her own religion, or to use his or her own language.

Article 31: ***Leisure, Recreation and Cultural Activities***

1. States parties recognize the right of the child to rest and leisure, to engage in play and recreational activities appropriate to the age of the child and to participate freely in cultural life and the arts.
2. States Parties shall respect and promote the right of the child to participate fully in cultural an artistic life and shall encourage the provision of appropriate and equal opportunities for cultural, artistic, recreational and leisure activity.

Article 32: ***Child Labour***

1. States Parties recognize the right of the child to be protected from economic exploitation and from performing any work that is likely to be hazardous or to interfere with the child's education, or to be harmful to the child's health or physical, mental, spiritual, moral or social development.
2. States Parties shall take legislative, administrative, social and educational measures to ensure the implementation of the present article. To this end, and having regard to the relevant provisions of the international instruments.

States Parties shall in particular:

(a) Provide for a minimum age or minimum ages for admission to employment;

(b) Provide for appropriate regulation of the hours and conditions of employment;

(c) Provide for appropriate penalties or other sanctions to ensure the effective enforcement of the present article.

Article 33: ***Drug Abuse:*** States Parties shall take all appropriate measures, including legislative, administrative, social and educational measures, to protect children from the illicit use of narcotic drugs and psychotropic substances as defined in the relevant international treaties, and to prevent the use of children in the illicit production and trafficking of such substances.

Article 34: ***Sexual Exploitation:*** States Parties undertake to protect the child from all forms of sexual exploitation and sexual abuse. For these purposes, States Parties shall in particular take all appropriate national, bilateral and multilateral measures to prevent:

(a) The inducement or coercion of a child to engage in any unlawful sexual activity;
(b) The exploitative use of children in prostitution or other unlawful sexual practices;
(c) The exploitative use of children in pornographic performances and materials.

Article 35: ***Sale, Trafficking and Abduction:*** States Parties shall take all appropriate national, bilateral and multilateral measures to prevent the abduction of, the sale of or traffic in children for any purpose or in any form.

Article 36: ***Other Forms of Exploitation:*** States Parties shall protect the child against all other forms of exploitation prejudicial to any aspects of the child's welfare.

Article 37: ***Torture and Deprivation of Liberty:*** This article provides that no child shall be subjected to torture or other cruel, inhuman or degrading treatment or punishment. No capital punishment or life imprisonment with-out the possibility of release shall be imposed on persons below 18 years.

This article also prohibits unlawful or arbitrary deprivation of the liberty of any child. The Convention does not ban the imprisonment of minors. But the arrest, detention and imprisonment of young offenders should be used as a last measure and for the shortest possible time. Every child deprived of his or her liberty should be treated with humanity and in particular separated from adults unless it is done in the child's best interest. Every child deprived of his or her berty shall have legal and other assistance and the reason to challenge the legality of the deprivation of his or her liberty before a court or other authority.

Article 38: ***Armed Conflict***

1. States Parties undertake to respect and to ensure respect for rules of international humanitarian law applicable to them in armed conflicts which are relevant to the child.
2. States Parties shall take all feasible measures to ensure that persons who have not attained the age of fifteen years do not take a direct part in hostilities.
3. States Parties shall refrain from recruiting any person who has not

attained the age of fifteen years into their armed forces. In recruiting among those persons who have attained the age of fifteen years but who have not attained the age of eighteen years, States Parties shall endeavour to give priority to those who are oldest.

4. In accordance with their obligations under international humanitarian law to protect the civilian population in armed conflicts, States Parties shall take all feasible measures to ensure protection and care of children who are affected by an armed conflict.

Article 39: ***Rehabilitative Care:*** States Parties shall take all appropriate measures to promote physical and psychological recovery and social reintegration of a child victim of any form of neglect exploitation or abuse. Torture or any other form of cruel, inhuman or degrading treatment or punishment; or armed conflicts. Such recovery and reintegration shall take place in an environment which fosters the health, self-respect and dignity of the child.

Article 40: ***Administration of Juvenile Justice:*** This article provides for safeguards in the administration of juvenile justice. Every child alleged as, or accused of infringing the penal law has the right to treatment consistent with the promotion of the child's sense of dignity and worth.

In the administration of juvenile justice, State parties shall ensure the respect for the principle that no one shall be held guiltily of any criminal offence on account of any act or omission which did not constitute a criminal offence, under national or international law, at that time when it was committed. State parties should also ensure the following guarantees:

1. Presumption of innocence;
2. Inform promptly and directly of the charges against him or her;
3. To determine the matter by a competent, independent and impartial authority or judicial body;
4. Not to compel to give testimony or confess guilt;
5. The right to review and appeal to a higher authority or judicial body;
6. To have free access to an interpreter if the child cannot understand or speak the language; and
7. To respect his or her privacy at all stages of the proceedings.

Article 41: ***Respect for Existing Standards:*** Nothing in the present Convention shall affect any provisions which are more conducive to the realization of the rights of the child and which may be contained in;

(a) The law of a State Party; or
(a) International law in force for that State.

PART II
IMPLEMENTATION AND ENTRY INTO FORCE

Article 42: It obligates State parties to make the principles and provisions of the Convention widely known by both adults and children alike.

Article 43

1. For the purpose of examining the progress made by States Parties in achieving the realization of the obligations undertaken in the present Convention, there shall be established a Committee on the Rights of the Child, which shall carry out the functions hereinafter provided.
2. The Committee shall consist of eighteen experts of high moral standing and recognized competence in the field covered by this Convention.1/ The members of the Committee shall be elected by States Parties from among their nationals and shall serve in their personal capacity, consideration being given to equitable geographical distribution, as well as to the principal legal systems.
3. The members of the Committee shall be elected by secret ballot from a list of persons nominated by States Parties. Each State Party may nominate one person from among its own nationals.
4. The initial election to the Committee shall be held no later than six months after the date of the entry into force of the present Convention and thereafter every second year. At least four months before the date of each election, the Secretary-General of the United Nations shall address a letter to States Parties inviting them to submit their nominations within two months. The Secretary-General shall subsequently prepare a list in alphabetical order of all persons thus nominated, indicating States Parties which have nominated them, and shall submit it to the States Parties to the present Convention.
5. The elections shall be held at meetings of States Parties convened by the Secretary-General at United Nations Headquarters. At those meetings, for which two thirds of States Parties shall constitute a quorum, the persons elected to the Committee shall be those who obtain the largest number of votes and an absolute majority of the votes of the representatives of States Parties present and voting.
6. The members of the Committee shall be elected for a term of four years. They shall be eligible for re-election if renominated. The term of five of the members elected at the first election shall expire at the end of two years; immediately after the first election, the names of these five members shall be chosen by lot by the Chairman of the meeting.
7. If a member of the Committee dies or resigns or declares that for any other cause he or she can no longer perform the duties of the Committee, the State Party which nominated the member shall appoint another expert from among its nationals to serve for the remainder of the term, subject to the approval of the Committee.

8. The Committee shall establish its own rules of procedure.
9. The Committee shall elect its officers for a period of two years.
10. The meetings of the Committee shall normally be held at United Nations Headquarters or at any other convenient place as determined by the Committee. The Committee shall normally meet annually. The duration of the meetings of the Committee shall be determined, and reviewed, if necessary, by a meeting of the States Parties to the present Convention, subject to the approval of the General Assembly.
11. The Secretary-General of the United Nations shall provide the necessary staff and facilities for the effective performance of the functions of the Committee under the present Convention.
12. With the approval of the General Assembly, the members of the Committee established under the present Convention shall receive emoluments from United Nations resources on such terms and conditions as the Assembly may decide.

Article 44

1. States Parties undertake to submit to the Committee, through the Secretary-General of the United Nations, reports on the measures they have adopted which give effect to the rights recognized herein and on the progress made on the enjoyment of those rights
   (a) Within two years of the entry into force of the Convention for the State Party concerned;
   (b) Thereafter every five years.
2. Reports made under the present article shall indicate factors and difficulties, if any, affecting the degree of fulfilment of the obligations under the present Convention. Reports shall also contain sufficient information to provide the Committee with a comprehensive understanding of the implementation of the Convention in the country concerned.
3. A State Party which has submitted a comprehensive initial report to the Committee need not, in its subsequent reports submitted in accordance with paragraph 1 (b) of the present article, repeat basic information previously provided.
4. The Committee may request from States Parties further information relevant to the implementation of the Convention.
5. The Committee shall submit to the General Assembly, through the Economic and Social Council, every two years, reports on its activities.
6. States Parties shall make their reports widely available to the public in their own countries.

Article 45: In order to foster the effective implementation of the Convention and to encourage international co-operation in the field covered by the Convention:

a. The specialized agencies, the United Nations Children's Fund, and other United Nations organs shall be entitled to be represented at the consideration of the implementation of such provisions of the present Convention as fall within the scope of their mandate. The Committee may invite the specialized agencies, the United Nations Children's Fund and other competent bodies as it may consider appropriate to provide expert advice on the implementation of the Convention in areas falling within the scope of their respective mandates. The Committee may invite the specialized agencies, the United Nations Children's Fund, and other United Nations organs to submit reports on the implementation of the Convention in areas falling within the scope of their activities;

b. The Committee shall transmit, as it may consider appropriate, to the specialized agencies, the United Nations Children's Fund and other competent bodies, any reports from States Parties that contain a request, or indicate a need, for technical advice or assistance, along with the Committee's observations and suggestions, if any, on these requests or indications;

c. The Committee may recommend to the General Assembly to request the Secretary-General to undertake on its behalf studies on specific issues relating to the rights of the child;

d. The Committee may make suggestions and general recommendations based on information received pursuant to articles 44 and 45 of the present Convention. Such suggestions and general recommendations shall be transmitted to any State Party concerned and reported to the General Assembly, together with comments, if any, from States Parties.

PART III

Article 46: The present Convention shall be open for signature by all States.

Article 47: The present Convention is subject to ratification. Instruments of ratification shall be deposited with the Secretary-General of the United Nations.

Article 48: The present Convention shall remain open for accession by any State. The instruments of accession shall be deposited with the Secretary-General of the United Nations.

Article 49

1. The present Convention shall enter into force on the thirtieth day following the date of deposit with the Secretary-General of the United Nations of the twentieth instrument of ratification or accession.
2. For each State ratifying or acceding to the Convention after the deposit of the twentieth instrument of ratification or accession, the Convention shall enter into force on the thirtieth day after the deposit by such State of its instrument of ratification or accession.

Article 50

1. Any State Party may propose an amendment and file it with the Secretary-General of the United Nations. The Secretary-General shall thereupon communicate the proposed amendment to States Parties, with a request that they indicate whether they favour a conference of States Parties for the purpose of considering and voting upon the proposals. In the event that, within four months from the date of such communication, at least one third of the States Parties favour such a conference, the Secretary-General shall convene the conference under the auspices of the United Nations. Any amendment adopted by a majority of States Parties present and voting at the conference shall be submitted to the General Assembly for approval.
2. An amendment adopted in accordance with paragraph 1 of the present article shall enter into force when it has been approved by the General Assembly of the United Nations and accepted by a two-thirds majority of States Parties.
3. When an amendment enters into force, it shall be binding on those States Parties which have accepted it, other States Parties still being bound by the provisions of the present Convention and any earlier amendments which they have accepted.

Article 51

1. The Secretary-General of the United Nations shall receive and circulate to all States the text of reservations made by States at the time of ratification or accession.
2. A reservation incompatible with the object and purpose of the present Convention shall not be permitted.
3. Reservations may be withdrawn at any time by notification to that effect addressed to the Secretary-General of the United Nations, who shall then inform all States. Such notification shall take effect on the date on which it is received by the Secretary-General

Article 52: A State Party may denounce the present Convention by written notification to the Secretary-General of the United Nations. Denunciation becomes effective one year after the date of receipt of the notification by the Secretary-General.

Article 53 The Secretary-General of the United Nations is designated as the depositary of the present Convention.

Article 54: The original of the present Convention, of which the Arabic, Chinese, English, French, Russian and Spanish texts are equally authentic, shall be deposited with the Secretary-General of the United Nations. In witness thereof the undersigned plenipotentiaries, being duly authorized thereto by their respective Governments, have signed the present Convention.

Contributors

From India

Prof. C.P.S. Chauhan is currently working as Professor of Education at Aligarh Muslim University, Aligarh. He has also earlier discharged successfully his duties as the *Chairman* of the Department of Education, *Dean* of the Faculty of Social Sciences, Member of the Academic and Executive councils, and Acting *Vice-Chancellor* in the same University. Previously, he has also worked as *National Fellow* at the National University of Educational Planning and Administration (NUEPA), New Delhi. He can be contacted at the Email ID cps_chauhan@yahoo.com.

Dr. Jignesh B. Patel is Asst. Professor, Smt. S.I. Patel Ipcowala College of Education, Petlad, Dist. Anand, Gujarat and Email is jig_har@yahoo.com.

Prof. K.P. Pandey, is the Formerly Vice Chancellor, Professor and Head, Department of Education, Mahatma Gandhi Kashi Vidyapith and Presently Director, SHEPA, Nibia, Bachchaon, Varanasi-2. His contact address is, E-6, Annapurna Enclave, Vidyapith, Varanai-2 and Email: director.shepa@rediffmail.com.

Prof. K.S. Misra is the Professor, Department of Education, University of Allahabad, Allahabad-211002.

Prof. P.N. Muthiah is the Dean CDC (Retd.) Madurai Kamaraj University, Tamil nadu. He can be contacted in the address, 7/414, Venkataraman Street, Nagamalai, Tamil Nadu–625019.

Dr. Magre Sunita Vithalrao is the Associate Professor, Department of Education, University of Mumbai and E mail ID is sunita, magre@gmail.com

Prof. R.G. Kothari is Professor and Dean, Faculty of Education and Psychology, Maharaja Sayajirao University of Baroda, Vadodara, Gujarat. He is the Former Vice chancellor of Veer Narmad South Gujarat University, Surat, Former head of the Department, CASE, Baroda and Email is-rgkothari@yahoo.com.

From Other Countries

Dr. Anthony Mugagga, Muwagga College of education and External Studies, Department of Foundations and Curriculum Studies, Makerere University. Mugagga has been a lecturer of Philosophy of Education and Teachers Professional Ethics since joining Makerere University in 1998. He has held a number of leadership positions in and outside the University.

Grace Kafulatira Mulima is working as Desk Officer for Secondary Schools, Ministry of Education, Science and Technology, Central West Education Division (CWED), Malawi. Her E mail ID is, gmulima@yahoo.co.uk.

Dr. Ngasbun Egar is working as Professor in Rahmawati Sukmaningrum, Siti Musarokah, IKIP PGRI Semarang (a Teacher Education Institute) in Indonesia. His E mail ID is, egar_ngasbun@yahoo.co.id.

Dr. Per Wickenberg is Professor in Sociology of Law at Lund University. SWEDEN. The Article mentioned here is related to his work in Swedish International training programme funded by Swedish government through SIDA. Swedish international Development Agency and operated through Lund university since 2003. He is one of the founders and mentors of the mentioned programme. His area of research is on education as an influencing and steering area with norm-creating processes in society, especially within the sphere of education relating to Child Rights Convention and Sustainable Development. Also, he had worked as a teacher in Swedish Comprehensive School for about 20 years.

Dr. Ulf Leo is working at the department of Sociology of Law at Lund University as a lecturer and a researcher. He has special interest in leadership and implementation of the democratic mission, CRC and Education for Sustainable development in schools. He had been working as a teacher in elementary schools for 10 years and as a school principal for 16 years.